SONIA IN POWER
UPA Government: 2004–2006

SONIA IN POWER
UPA Government: 2004–2006

C.P. BHAMBHRI

SHIPRA

ISBN: 81-7541-328-X

First Published in India in 2006

Sonia in Power – UPA Government: 2004–2006

Published by:
SHIPRA PUBLICATIONS
115-A, Vikas Marg, Shakarpur
Delhi-110092, INDIA
Phone: 91-11-55277210, 91-11-22500954
Fax: 91-11-22458662
E-mail: info@shiprapublications.com
www.shiprapublications.com

Preface

An intellectual engagement with current political developments may have a limited value because of its limited time frame, it does not mean that current political happenings does not deserve a careful study and analysis. This is the justification for the study of performance or lack of performance of the United Progressive Alliance government led by the Congress party. Sonia Gandhi-led Congress party has formed coalition government at the Centre by replacing and displacing the BJP-led National Democratic Alliance government of Atal Bihari Vajpayee. Has the UPA government at the Centre following different policies than its predecessor the BP-led UPA government? Can it be described as a break with the past dominantly Atal Bihari Vajpayee from 1998 to 2004? At one level, the formation of the UPA government has restored the secular fabric of society which had been completely destroyed by the practitioners of Hindu Rashtravad. At another level, the UPA government has followed economic and foreign policy of the BJP-led government. This study is focused on policies and programme followed by the UPA government while tackling the issue which have emerged during its years-in-office. The forces of study is one party politics, economic policies, foreign policy, centre-state relations and other allied issues faced by UPA-in-Government.

Thanks are due to the office staff of Distinguished Scholars of the Jawaharlal Nehru University for help in the completion of this study.

C.P. Bhambhri

Preface

Contents

1

Introduction

The Congress-led United Progressive Alliance government at the Centre was formed on May 22, 2004 and it was for the first time that the Congress party formed a coalition government at the Centre. The BJP-led National Democratic Alliance government at the Centre had exercised power for more than six years from 1998 to 2004 and its electoral defeat was welcomed by secular political forces in the country because BJP-in-power at the Centre had assaulted the secular fabric and democratic ethos of plural and diverse society of India. It has been suggested that the replacement and displacement of the BJP-led NDA government by the Congress-led UPA government at the Centre has liberated India from the forces of Hindutva and the votaries of Hindu Rashtra have been ejected from state power. It deserves to be clearly stated that an interpretation of electoral verdict of 2004 Lok Sabha elections cannot be dichotomized or even simplified by asserting that the voters during the elections showed their clear preference in favour of secularism and against the Hindu Rashtravadis. The Congress had mobilized the voters on the plank of 'vote for Hand which stands for *aam Admi*[1] and the BJP asked the voters to renew their confidence in the party/government which had created a 'Shining India'. Can it be stated that the Congress and the BJP were clearly identified by the voters on the basis of their ideology of secularism versus Hindutva, and other issues mentioned in the election manifestos of these two parties did not carry any conviction with the voters? It deserves to be clearly stated that electoral verdict cannot be interpreted on the basis of a single factor especially when victory and defeat of the two major contenders for power is extremely narrow. The Congress-led UPA government at the Centre has to follow and implement 'secular agenda for governance' because Congress is ideologically committed to 'secularism' and it has replaced the BJP-led government which is firmly committed to the ideology of Hindu Rashtravad. The only significance of the Lok Sabha elections of 2004 is that a party with an agenda of religion-based politics has vacated the office for a party which is practitioner of secular-based politics. A government-in-power can not be analysed and evaluated on the basis of just one agenda because multiple and diverse social groups look towards a government for the satisfaction of their specific demands. Not only this. A coalition government at the Centre has to accommodate diverse demands of different groups because partners in a coalition government represent the interests and demands of different social constituencies. The Congress-led UPA government at the Centre has to harmonise the conflicting interests of fourteen groups which are represented in the government along with the demands of the Communists parties which are 'outside supporters' of the government at the Centre. It was alleged that the Congress would not succeed in managing a coalition government at the Centre because it did not have any experience of working with diverse coalition groups at the Centre. The opponents of the UPA government, especially the BJP, were extremely skeptical about the survival of a coalition government led by the Congress but the Congress has belied the expectations of its critics and opponents and the UPA government has continued to remain in power at the Centre. The UPA government is working on the basis of a National Common Minimum Programme which has been agreed by all the coalition partners including the Communists, who are the 'outside supporters' of the government. It does not mean that the implementation of the Common Minimum Programme can be a smooth affair because inspite of agreements on the CMP, different coalition partners have different priorities of their own and different groups will like to push their agenda through the government. The upshot of above description is that coalition government at the Centre, whether led by the Congress or the BJP, is always at the tenterhooks because it has to accommodate diverse and competitive demands of its supporters in the government.

The UPA government has evolved a mechanism of Coordination Committee for dealing with the issues raised by the Communists who are its 'outside supporters'. It deserves to be clearly stated that the Congress and the Communists have never agreed to share power either at a formal or informal levels and it is for the first time in post-Independence India that Communists are 'supporting' the Congress-led UPA government. The Congress and the Communists represent different social constituencies and interests of different social classes and this is the reason that they have never cooperated with one another in the task of governance of the country. The Communists are supporting the Congress-led UPA government with a view to keep the forces of Hindutva out of governmental power. The Congress is a lesser political evil for the Communists because a full fledged party of the Hindutva has to be kept out of power with a view to defend the secular fabric of India. Hindutva is the greatest threat to the democratic Republic of India because its ideology of religion-based politics is a complete negation of the philosophy of secularism which is the foundational philosophical principle of Communists and for this purpose, they are extending support to the Congress at the Centre. Communist parties are extending support to the Congress to keep the BJP miles away from state power, it does not mean that the communists have abandoned their pro-poor ideological baggage in favour of pro-rich economic policies of the Congress party. The Communists have applied pressures on the Congress in every Coordination Committee Meeting with a view to keep it under check so that it does not violate the Common Minimum Programme which is the guiding framework of the UPA government. It id worthwhile to mention a few important differences which have emerged between the Congress and the Communists and both of them have tried to resolve contentious public policy issues on the basis of hard bargaining with a spirit of give and take. Communists and the Congress have been opposed to one anther on economic and foreign policy. The Communists have opposed economic liberalization and pro-American policies of the Congress and many a time, both of them have found themselves at loggerheads and a situation arose when the Communists 'decided to walk out' of the Coordination Committee meetings.

The Congress-led coalition has worked very smoothly, because except the Communists who have public policy differences with the Congress, other regional and sub-regional groups have cooperated with each other and the government has been able to project its United image. It does not mean that fourteen groups do not have inter-group or intra-groups tensions but the functioning of the government has not been adversely affected by inter-group conflicts. The State Assembly elections of 2005 in Bihar witnessed that Lalu Prasad Yadav of the Rashtriya Janta Dal and Ramvilas Paswan of the Lok Jan Shakti party were not able to work together at a common electoral platform inspite of the fact that both these parties are part of the UPA government at the Centre. Not only this. Sonia Gandhi also failed to reconcile the differences between these two groups during Bihar State Assembly elections of 2005. The same story was repeated in 2006 and in Tamil Nadu Vaiko decided to form an electoral alliance with Km. Jayalalithaa of the AIADMK against M. Karunanidhi's DMK inspite of the fact that Vaiko and the DMK are present in the UPA government at the Centre. The state level political contradictions do not get resolved inspite of the fact that some political opponents have decided to sit around the table as comrades-in-arm at the Centre.

If the above story of relationship between Communists and the Congress and the Congress and other regional partners of the UPA government leads us to conclude that coalition government at the Centre is an 'alliance of convenience', the problems which exist within the Congress also can not be wished away or put under the carpet. What is the relationship between Sonia Gandhi, the Congress party President, and ManMohan Singh, the Prime Minister of the Congress-led UPA government at the Centre? ManMohan is a nominee of Sonia for the office of Prime Minister of India. Sonia abandoned her claim to accept the office of Prime Minister inspite of the fact that her own party and every alliance partner represented in the UPA had shown a clear preference for Sonia's candidature as Prime Minister. It deserves to be clearly stated that Sonia has revived the Congress party and from 1998 to 2006, the Congress party has been led by Sonia who is an 'unchallenged' leader of the party. Sonia's political opponents like the BJP had to eat an humble pie because the voters have shown complete confidence by electing and re-electing Sonia for the Lok Sabha. The Lok Sabha elections of 2004 brought back Sonia-led Congress to power because her party could form a coalition government at the Centre. Sonia's pre-eminent position in the Congress has remained intact inspite of the fact that she has not accepted to be the Prime Minister of India. Sonia Gandhi decided to constitute a National Advisory Council under her Chairmanship and the constitution of such a NAC has given rise to a controversy that the UPA government has created 'dual centres of power' because in a parliamentary system, it is the Council of Ministers which is the real repository of 'executive powers' and Sonia's NAC is either redundant or 'extra-constitutional centre of power'. The fact of the matter is that Sonia shall continue to occupy a 'pre-eminent' position in the UPA government because of the 'pre-eminence' in the Congress party.

How does one evaluate the performance of UPA-in-Government irrespective of the fact that Sonia or ManMohan or both of them occupy equal or more than equal status in relation to one another? The Communist parties have a yardstick for the evaluation of the UPA government and they have maintained that it is a government with 'secular agenda' but its economic and foreign policies are flawed because they are pro-Big Business, Indian and foreign, and pro-America. The role of Communists is to apply 'correctives' and 'brakes' over pro-global capitalist policies of the government. Further, except the Communists, other allies of the Congress in the UPA government, have maintained smooth relationship with one another because every regional partner of the coalition government at the Centre does not have any clear cut ideological agenda of its own. Every group in coalition government is guided by the interest of its own social constituency.

It is not enough to maintain that the UPA government at the Centre is guided by secular ideology because its track record on socio-economic issues facing the country deserves to be clearly scrutinized. A few facts may be mentioned to highlight the essentials of socio-economic challenges faced by India in 2006. The Economic Survey of the Government of India (2005-06) has highlighted the reality of economy of the country. While the government has projected a rosy picture of 'economic growth', the Economic Survey on the basis of National Sample Survey Organization has mentioned that 'The Survey had estimated a reduction in the incidence of poverty from 36 percent in 1993-1994 to 26.1 percent during 1999-2000.'[2] If one-fourth of the population is still under the poverty line as defined by the government, the UPA government has to play an 'activist' role in attacking directly the issue of mass poverty. Not only this. Agrarian crisis is a reality and marginal farmers have taken recourse to 'suicide' because they cannot face economic distress suffered by them. How can rural poverty be tackled if investment in agricultural sector has been on the decline? The Economic Survey of the Government of India has itself referred to the basic cause of agrarian crisis.

CAPITAL FORMATIONAL IN INDIA AGRICULTURE

The decline in the share of the agricultural sector's capital formation in GDP from 2.2 percent in the late 1990s to 1.7 percent in 2004-05 is a matte of concern. This declining share was mainly due to the stagnation or fall in public investment in irrigation, particularly since the mid-1990s. However, there is indication of a reversal of this tend with public sector investment in agriculture reaching its highest level of Rs. 12,591 crore in 2004-05 since the early nineties. The share of public investment in gross investment increased by over 11 percentage point to reach 29.2 percent in 2004-05 relative to 1999-2000.

Gross Capital Formation in Agriculture**

Year	*Investment in Agriculture (Rs. Crore)*			*Share in Agricultural Gross Investment (percent)*		*Investment in Agri-culture as a percent of GDP at Constant Prices*
1990-19	14836	4395	10441	29.60	70.40	1.92
1995-96	15690	4849	10841	30.90	69.10	1.57
1996-97	16176	4668	11508	28.90	71.10	1.51
1997-98	15942	3979	11963	25.00	75.00	1.43
1998-99	14895	3870	11025	26.00	74.00	1.26
1999-00	17304	4221	13083	24.40	75.00	1.37
	New series (at 1990-00 prices)					
1999-00	43473	7754	35719	17.8	82.2	2.2
2000-01	38176	7018	31158	18.4	81.6	1.9
2001-02	46744	8529	38215	18.2	81.8	2.2
2002-03	45867	7849	38018	17.1	82.9	2.1
2003-04	47833	12809	35024	26.8	73.2	2.0
2004-05	43123	12591	30532	29.2	70.8	1.7

* Quick Estimates
* Source : CSO
** Economcy Survey 2005-06, pp. 169-70

Further, India is facing grave crisis of rising 'unemployment' and in a laobur surplus economy, the growth of unemployment gives rise to social conflicts and violence

The economic thinking in the UPA government is clearly anti-poor and the Economic Survey while dealing with a serious issue like growing unemployment focuses its attention on reform of 'labour laws' to eject the workers who are already employed.

"Some salient features of the trend of unemployment rates in the country are :

> The unemployment rate went up between 1993-94 to 2004. On the basis of current daily status (unemployed on an average in the reference week), during the reference period, unemployment rate for males increased from 5.6 percent to 9.0 percent in rural areas, and from 6.7 percent to 8.1 percent in urban areas.

Similarly, unemployment rate for females increased from 5.6 percent in 1993-94 to 9.3 percent in 2004 in rural areas and from 10.5 percent to 11.7 percent in urban areas.

Furthermore, unemployment rates on the basis of current daily status were much higher than those on the basis of usual status (unemployed on an average in the reference year) implying a high degree of intermittent unemployment. This could be mainly because of the absence of regular employment for many workers.

Urban unemployment rates (current daily status) were higher than rural unemployment rates for both makes and females in 1993-04. however, in 2004, rural unemployment rates for males was higher than that of urban males.

Unemployment rates varied sharply across States. States, where wages are higher than in neighbouring ones because of strong bargains or social security provision, such as high minimum wage; had high incident of unemployment, in general."

Unemployment Rates**

Status	*Rural*			*Urban*		
	Male	*Female*	*Total*	*Male*	*Female*	*Total*
Usual principal status	24	22	23	46	89	53
Current weekly status	47	45	46	57	90	64
Current daily status	90	93	91	81	117	88

** Economic Survey pp. 207-09

INDIAN LABOUR LAWS AND LABOUR MARKET

"Indian labour market is characterized by a sharp dichotomy. A large number of establishments in the unorganized sector remain outside any regulation, while the organized sector has been regulated fairly stringently. It can be reasonable argued that the organised sector has provided too much of job security for too long, while the unorganized sector has provided too little to too many.

Various studies indicate that Indian labour laws are highly protective of labour, and labour market are relatively inflexible. These laws apply only to the organized sector. Consequently, these laws have restricted labour mobility, have led to capital-intensive methods in the organized sector and adversely affected the sector's long-run demand for labour. Labour being a subject in the concurrent list, State-level labour regulations are also an important determinant of industrial performance. Evidence suggests that States, which have acted more pro-worker regulations, have lost out on industrial production in general.

Perhaps there are lessons to be learnt from China in the area of labour reforms. China, with a history of extreme employment security, has drastically reformed its labour relations and created a new labour market, in which workers are highly mobile. Although there have been mass layoffs and open unemployment, high rates of industrial growth especially in the coastal regions helped their redeployment. Inspite of hardship workers in China seems to have benefited from wage growth, additional job creation and new opportunities for self employment.[3]"

The UPA government at the Centre has become quite aware of the prevailing grave economic crisis in the country and its response has been in the form of National Rural Employment Guarantee Scheme. This is not only the response of the UPA government to resolve the crisis prevailing in the country. The Central Government has decided to 'modernise' paramilitary armed forces to tackle the so-called Naxal problem facing thirteen states of India. Naxalism is a consequence of the prevailing social discontent in the country and the UPA government does not have any strategy to eliminate the causes of social discontent and it has decided to take recourse to police oppression. India has been moving from crisis to crisis and the UPA government, whether Sonia-led or ManMohan-led, has not come forward with any policy package to tackle the prevailing social crisis in India.

The upshot of above description is that India has abandoned National Project for the Development of the whole country and every all-India and regional party represented at the Centre is implementing pro-rich and anti-poor public policies and Sonia Gandhi's Congress is the major carrier of the agenda of globalization, liberalization, deregulation and privatization. The poor masses of India are not in the reckoning in the economic and political agenda following by the pro-rich liberalizers and it is not surprising that the BJP and the Congress have continued to follow the same economic strategy while in power at the Centre. The UPA government has saved India from the forces of fanatic Hindutva and Narendra Modi could not dare to repeat his performance in Vadodra in 2006 because instead of his protector Atal Bihari Vajpayee, Manmohan Singh is the Prime Minister of India. The UPA has liberated the central government from the stranglehold of Hindu Communal forces, it has not risen to the occasion while dealing with the problems faced by *Wretched of the Earth* of India.

NOTES

1. Party claimed to stand for the cause of Common Man/Woman.
2. Economic Survey (2005-06) Government of India, Ministry of Finance, Delhi, p. 17.
3. Economy Survey, p. 209

2

Sonia's Congress and Manmohan's UPA Government

SONIA: MILES TO GO

Sonia Gandhi after her election as the Congress party president on May 28, 2005, stated that 'We should not rest on our laurels but be more active than earlier'. It deserves to be clearly stated that Sonia Gandhi's statement on the so-called 'laurels' achieved by the Congress party under her leadership from 1998 to 2005 is a highly exaggerated self-appraisal because the party still continues to be a pale reflection of its former self.

A few achievements of the Congress party under the leadership of Sonia Gandhi deserve to be stated before any evaluation is undertaken about the real strength and weaknesses of the party. It is not only that the Congress had lost the Lok Sabha elections of 1998, the party was completely directionless under the presidentship of Sita Ram Kesri. The first achievement of Sonia is that the Congress has been revived and the party is very much alive and kicking. Another important achievement of Sonia is the revival of the Congress in Jammu and Kashmir. It was an act of great political courage on her part to make her party a junior partner in the coalition government in the troubled state.

Further, Sonia Gandhi by her own electoral victories has humbled every political leader and group who had launched a political campaign on her foreign origin issue. Sonia, like Indira, won her elections from Karnataka and Uttar Pradesh and the voters of India snubbed her opponents who had thought that her 'foreign origin' would become a great political issue. Sharad Pawar and P.A. Sangma, who had walked out of the Congress party on the issue of the foreign origin of Sonia, have accepted her leadership by offering a lame excuse that Sonia declined to be Prime Minister when offered that post in 2004. The coalition partners of the Congress-led central government have accepted Sonia as chairperson of the United Progressive Alliance National Advisory Council on the National Common Minimum Programme.

The above narration establishes the fact that Sonia Gandhi has proved that she is a political asset to the Congress party. The other side of the story is that inspite of Sonia's efforts the Congress continues to be in a shambles in many parts of India and the party is finding it extremely difficult to regain political space which has been occupied by its opponents and competitors. The Communists have completely ejected the Congress from West Bengal and the same story has been repeated in Uttar Pradesh and Bihar. The present day Congress cannot be blamed for its decline in Tamil Nadu because the process had started during Indira Gandhi's phase of the Congress leadership and the Dravidian parties had successfully displaced the Congress in Tamil Nadu. Andhra Pradesh was always a Congress stronghold but a serious challenge to the Congress domination had emerged during Rajiv Gandhi's time when N.T. Rama Rao emerged in that state. The real test for the Sonia Gandhi-led Congress is in some of the major states of India where the party is struggling to show a reasonable and respectable political presence. Sonia Gandhi has tried Salman Khurshid, Jagdamba Prasad and projected Rahul Gandhi for reviving the almost dead Congress in Uttar Pradesh but she has not been able to move even an inch forward. The same story of a non-existent Congress party in Bihar was repeated in the state assembly elections of March 2005, when the party got only ten seats and the state party president lost his security deposit. The Congress party has the capacity to stand up to its main opponent, the BJP, in Madhya Pradesh, Rajasthan, Chhatisgarh and to some extent Jharkhand because these states have developed a two party system' of Congress versus the BJP.

The moot question is: Can the Sonia Gandhi-led Congress obtain 180 to 200 seats in the Lok Sabha elections? The Congress-led government at the Centre is surviving because coalition partners and especially the 'outside supporters' like the Communist parties and Mulayam Singh Yadav's Samajwadi party are committed to keeping the BJP out of power. The BJP is in a bad shape at present but it is very much in the reckoning. The Sonia-led Congress has only 145 scats in a Lok Sabha of 543 members and it cannot be a comfortable situation for any party which has to lead a coalition. Can Sonia bring the party out of its present vulnerability? – *Sahara Time, June 18, 2005*

WHITHER SONIA CONGRESS

Ms. Sonia Gandhi's stocktaking meeting of the performance of 14 Congress-led governments on 7 and 8 October, 2005, at Chandigarh shows her great concern for the health of the Congress party. No doubt, the Congress is the only all-India national party with presence in every region and sub-region of the country, although its 'decline' began with the erosion of its support base in many states. If the Congress party has to regain the glory of the Grand Old Party of India, its leadership has to make great efforts for strengthening the organisational machinery and win elections both at the level of state assemblies and the Lok Sabha.

The Congress party suffered its first political setback during the general elections of 1967 when it was defeated for the first time in a large number of states. The Congress party was in a bad shape from 1967 to 1971 not only because its 'traditional social constituencies' had shifted away their loyalty to other parties, but also because the Congress was involved in internal fraternal disputes leading to its 'split of 1969'. While Indira Gandhi succeeded in reviving the electoral fate of the Congress in the Lok Sabha elections of 1971 and the state assembly elections of 1972, the organisational structure of the mighty Grand Old Party of India suffered an irreparable loss because of the 'split' of 1969. But despite the 'split' Indira Gandhi could win electoral laurels because she succeeded in projecting the face of a new Congress party with a new radical programme of '*Garibi Hatao*'.

However, Rajiv Gandhi and P.V. Narasimha Rao were perceived by the Muslim minority, a powerful supporter of Nehru-Indira Congress, as 'betrayers' of the secular agenda of the party. Rajiv Gandhi and Narasimha Rao made Himalayan blunders while responding to the growing challenge of the forces of militant Hindutva who were engaged in mobilising a large section of fanatic Hindus around the programme of constructing a Ram temple at Ayodhya. If Rajiv Gandhi was held guilty by the Muslim minority community for his capitulation before the growing challenge of the BJP, the Rao government failed to protect the Babri mosque which was demolished by a fanatic Hindu mob. Subsequently, the Congress party was reduced to a pathetic condition and its real political and ideological opponent occupied power at the Centre from 1998 to 2004.

The politics of Hindutva succeeded not only because of its own 'appeal' but also because of the complete failure of the

Congress to defend its secular ideology and politics against Hindu communalism. If the BJP and the forces of militant Hindutva could succeed in displacing and replacing the opportunist Congress, a social process of caste-based politics, beginning with the 1980s, proved politically fatal for the socially-all-inclusive platform created by the Congress, especially in north India. The Congress failed to respond to the challenge of Hindutva because of its own ideological opportunism. The caste-based political mobilisation of purely casteist parties and leaders proved politically devastating to the Congress of the 1980s and '90s because it had no strategy to confront the 'caste versus caste' politics, especially in north India. The impact of the emergence of the forces of Hindutva and the 'caste versus caste' party platforms was directly felt by the Congress both at the state and Centre.

Ms. Sonia Gandhi met her party's CMs and the Dy. CM of J&K at Chandigarh with a clear understanding that an unambiguous political line has not only to be conveyed but also carried out by the CMs and the party organisation at every level in every state.

The greatest worry of the party president is not only to maintain its majorities and presence in the 14 Congress-ruled states, but also the fact that the Congress has miles to go to recover its political space in large states like UP, Bihar, MP, Rajasthan, and Gujarat. Besides, Maharashtra and Karnataka, like J&K, have coalition governments where Congress has to work along with other partners. Also the forthcoming Assembly elections in Bihar and the elections in Kerala, West Bengal and Assam in 2006 do not give any positive hope for the party.

The first step has been taken by Sonia Gandhi, as party president and UPA chairman, by projecting party and government as 'left-of-centre' with a powerful secular programme for *aam admi*. She along with her party, government and the National Advisory Council has extended and deepened the definition of 'the Rights of Man' by enacting laws for rural employment, for the rights of tribals on their forest resources, and also by a Right to Information Act which can act as a guarantor of implementation of new programmes for the rural poor and the tribals. It also goes to the credit of Ms. Gandhi that the Congress has upheld secular values and distanced itself from 'soft Hindutva' of Rajiv-Rao prime ministership.

It deserves to be clearly stated that the journey ahead for Sonia Congress is full of thorns, because of the logic of the coalition government at the Centre. Sonia's initiatives to revive the party in Bihar cannot succeed unless the party contests the forthcoming state assembly elections on its own. But such an option does not exist for Sonia because without Lalu Prasad of the RJD, the UPA government will collapse. Sonia's Congress in UP is caught in the same web of opposition and support to the Mulayam Singh government and such a situation cannot bring any political dividend to the party. In other words, the Congress party, if it wants to recapture power in states, is expected to play the role of an effective opposition against the state governments of the casteist Yadavas of UP and Bihar but it is not possible if the Congress-led UPA government has to survive at the Centre.

If the Congress is handicapped to confront its 'allies' at the Centre, who happen to be its opponents in the state, it can at least confront the BJP in Rajasthan, Madhya Pradesh, Gujarat, et al. The Congress as a left-of-centre party has bright prospects if it is seen to be implementing its pro-poor programme in the spirit of secular values. – *The Economic Times, October 15, 2005*

SONIA MUST INTERVENE

Chairperson of the UPA Sonia Gandhi has cautioned Prime Minister Manmohan Singh that in his enthusiasm for Free Trade Agreements between India and the ASEAN countries, the interests of domestic farmers must not be sacrificed.

Ms. Gandhi's policy intervention has generated a lot of political heat as Manmohan Singh, while addressing the Asian Development Bank's annual meeting at Hyderabad (May 5-6), aggressively advocated to pan-Asian FTA. Cautioning the Commerce Minsiter Kamal Nath about the fate of the farm sector in early March, she alerted the Minister, "We do need to face the reality and recognize that the debt crisis still exists, leading to suicides (by distressed farmers) even today."

She further said, "the Congress feels instead of opening up the agricultural and manufacturing sector through FTA, more effective domestic policy measures need to be adopted to protect and strengthen the growers and manufacturers in these sectors." Ms. Gandhi stressed the Government to implement the Swaminathan Committee report in its letter and spirit.

On April 15, Ms. Gandhi sent a letter to the Prime Minister, drawing his attention to the twin issues of FTA with ASEAN countries and farmers' distress. Already the M.S. Swaminathan National Commission on Farmers has stated that farmers' suicides "are not only persisting but also tending to increase and spread over wider areas."

In addition the commission's report stated (on April 14), "While farmers' families are crying for additional investment…the fact (is) that there has been a drop in Government investment." Ms. Gandhi allayed fears that domestic agricultural sector would be adversely affected by the proposed pact. When the correspondence between Ms. Gandhi and Mr. Singh became public in May 7, the Congress spokesman reacted saying, "There was nothing unusual on the part of the Congress chief writing to the Prime Minister on such issues… Ms. Gandhi was only conveying to Mr. Singh a perspective based on various representations she received on the FTA issue from many quarters."

The Congress party ahs evaded the reply because Ms. Gandhi did write the said letters as chairperson of the National Advisory Council. This letter has settled once for all the issue that the chairperson of NAC occupies the pre-eminent position in governance. And that the Council of Ministers headed by the Prime Minister has to work on the basis of "directions" from the NAC chairperson.

How can anyone accept Ms. Gandhi's letter on public policy to the Prime Minister as just a communication from the Congress president? The issue of relationship between the party president and Council of Ministers was settled long ago by Jawaharlal Nehru. He responded to Acharya J.B. Kripalani's interpretation of his special role "vis-à-vis the Government as Congress president under a parliamentary system of democracy", saying it was absolutely untenable.

The Cabinet is accountable to Parliament and the Prime Minister is the sole spokesperson on governmental affairs. The party president cannot give any policy directions to the Cabinet in a parliamentary democracy. At the most, the party can give suggestions to the Government; it cannot direct it to follow a particular public policy.

The Congress president is not at par with the Prime Minister. Neither Nehru nor Indira Gandhi accepted that the party president and the Prime Minister were 'equals'. The Congress from 1998 to 2006 has been a pocket borough of the party president, and the Prime Minister and other Congress Ministers in the UPA Government are working in the "reflected glory of Sonia".

Not only Manmohan Singh, all Ministers and functionaries of the Congress have to look up to Ms. Gandhi for guidance and leadership. Mr. Singh's policies are invariable subjected to Ms. Gandhi's approval or disapproval because she is the real center of power in the Congress-led UPA Government.

The UPA Government has functioned from May 2004 to 2006 on the basis of the extra-constitutional authority of Ms. Gandhi and the letters written in March-April between Mr. Singh and her on FTA and the agrarian crises betray the pattern of governance under her stewardship of the Congress. Mr. Singh's views or opinions on public policy issues are expandable and Ms. Gandhi's wishes are like a commandment for the Manmohan Singh government. *–The Pioneer, May 14, 2006*

MANMOHAN'S ACTIVE VOICE

Dr. Manmohan Singh's Press conference on September 4 was devoted to defending himself from criticism levelled by the Opposition against his prime ministership. Dr. Singh would have got the opportunity to clear some of the confusion created by the Opposition inside Parliament had it not disrupted parliamentary proceedings. The greatest attack on any person holding the highest office in a parliamentary system is to describe him as "proxy" or "shadow" of another powerful individual who is pulling the real strings of power from behind. This is an insult to both the Prime Minister and his political mentor, Ms. Sonia Gandhi, against whom such allegations are directed. At the news conference, Dr. Singh set the record straight by stating in front of the media that "there are no two power centres (in the country) and Ms. Gandhi as UPA chairperson has the right to take interest in governance..."

While such an assertion by the Prime Minister himself was essential to establish his credibility, the reality is that Ms. Gandhi and Dr. Singh are playing "complementary" and not "patron-client" roles. After all, the Congress has been revived solely by the efforts of Ms. Gandhi. She cannot sit over the victory in the 14th Lok Sabha election because the party still needs to make a lot of effort before it can be fully revived. The ghost of the BJP as the real opponent of the Congress haunts the party leadership and Ms. Gandhi needs to do a lot more to refurbish the organisation. The "division of labour" between Dr. Singh as the Prime Minister and Ms. Gandhi as the Congress president does not convey any message of either superiority or subordination of one by the other or that the two are not working together to revive the Congress to govern and also contain the Opposition led by the BJP.

If the Prime Minister's real status in the present scheme of things is seen in this broad political context, Yashwant Sinha's description of Dr. Singh as "shikhandi" is like repeating lies to make them appear true. It is essential to shift public discourse from peripheral and personalised matters to real issues of governance and offer a critique of the Government's policies for effective governance of the country.

India has a strong tradition where real prime ministers like Jawaharlal Nehru, Indira Gandhi, Rajiv Gandhi, P.V. Narasimha Rao and Atal Bihari Vajpayee were path-finders of the country's foreign policy for the protection and promotion of national interests in difficult and complex international situations. Foreign policy of any country is closely linked with domestic, economic and political aspirations of the country.

The Vajpayee Government from 1998 to 2004 had accepted the hegemony of the sole imperialist superpower, the United States, and rationalised it as a partner in global anti-terrorist war especially after 9/11. Will the Congress follow the footsteps of neo-colonial Vajpayee Government while dealing with the US? The Congress Manifesto and its Foreign Policy Statements have not come out with any clear-cut policy. Hence, the real worrisome issue is not the person of the Prime Minister, but the further "opening of domestic market" to foreign economic players who cannot operate unless India welcomes the governments of western investors with open hands.

Dr. Singh said, "No power can stop an idea whose time has come. It is the emergence of India as a global power whose time has come. We can realise this objective." Brave words. But it is the Left parties, supporting the UPA Government from outside, that have openly criticised Dr. Singh's economic blueprint. He made it clear that "economic reforms would be dictated by the commitments made in the Common Minimum Programme" and that "there will be no change in FDI policy.

The Left objected to the UPA Government's pronouncements because it would lead India towards becoming a camp follower of imperialist America. It is well known that West-linked dependent economy loses it autonomy in international affairs. The Left have alleged that the Government is taking "unilateral" decisions on

FDI, EXIM policy et al, and if this process continues "the coordination committee of the UPA and the Left would lose relevance". They asked for "consultations" on policies without any threat to break the coalition. The tone and tenor of Left critique is policy-directed and policy-oriented, unlike the BJP's whose approach towards the UPA Government is personality oriented like calling Dr. Singh "shikhandi" or Ms. Gandhi "Italian".

No one in the country, including the Left, is against forging economic ties with advanced industrialised countries. Absence of any domestic, economic and foreign policy framework of the UPA Government became obvious in its FDI policy and also in its "mechanical" dealings with Pakistani Foreign Minister Khursheed Mehmood Kasuri during his visit to India on September 4-5. The Prime Minister had stated that his Government would complete its full term. For the Government to stay in office for full five years, it should lead the country forward with new thinking on policy matters.

India and Pakistan are tied in knots on Kashmir and cross border terrorism and Kasuri-Natwar parleys on September 4-5 have not given even an iota of new thinking on the basis of which the deadlock between the two countries can be broken. If India has to reiterate that Kashmir is an integral part of our territory and Pakistan has to respect that "Pakistan originated terrorism", it is a flight of the imagination of Indians and negotiations and meetings between policy-makers of these two countries are not required because they would be an exercise in irrelevance.

Can India and Pakistan live in confrontationist frame in the 21st century or think of an alternative framework for resolving the Kashmir dispute bilaterally? Both the countries should take the bull by the horns by recognising that "Pakistan-sponsored terrorism and dispute between India and Pakistan on Kashmir" are the real issues and without resolving these two inter-connected disputes, the two will keep bleeding one another. "Enlightened" self-interests of India and Pakistan demand grasping forthrightly the dispute on Kashmir. It is an inheritance of the 20th century in which complications have arisen because of motivated foreign interlocutors with their own axes to grind.

The Indo-Pak dialogue process should be taken out of the hands of tried, tired and retired bureaucrats masquerading as foreign policy-makers. Bureaucrats are meant to prepare position papers; it is at the highest political level that real solutions have to be sought. India has to reinvent Nehru-Indira political leadership to deal with contentious domestic and foreign policy issues. Dr. Manmohan Singh along with Ms. Sonia Gandhi and other real all-India forward looking leaders should evolve a national consensus on Kashmir.

The UPA Government should be faulted and supported on the basis of its public policies relevant to the 21st century India. Vision for the 21st century has to be provided by political leaders who understand the pulse of the people and not by self-proclaimed bureaucrats-turned-foreign policy-makers.

– The Pioneer, September 09, 2004

A PRESCRIPTION FOR THE DOCTOR

The diplomatic endeavours of Prime Minister Manmohan Singh have shown some xpositive results during his visit to France and the US between September 12 and 16. It seems the UPA Government has come a long way since its woolly-headed, confused and ambivalent foreign policy, which was quite evident during its first year.

The Government's journey from ambiguity to clarity in its foreign policy became clear when Manmohan Singh visited New York with the ostensible purpose of attending the Kumbh Mela of the 60th anniversary of the United Nations General Assembly. The Prime Minister converted this phoney ritual into a serious diplomatic meeting with important political leaders, especially of the United States, Pakistan and China.

It is natural for us to take great interest in the parleys between Manmohan Singh and President Pervez Musharraf. However, it is the message of US President George Bush from the General Assembly that deserves scrutiny, as its contents will have great bearing on the making of India's foreign policy. President Bush repeated his goal to establish 'democracies at global level' and 'target global terrorism with global efforts'.

It seems the UPA Government – following the line adopted by the NDA regime – has accepted President Bush as the global headmaster. Instead of this, Mr. Bush's claim to 'Global Democracy Initiative' should have been exposed as a means to intervene in the internal affairs of countries like Afghanistan, Iraq and Central Asia. After all, the US is establishing 'democracy' in Afghanistan and Iraq by militarily occupying these countries. Is it acceptable to India's foreign policymakers?

Both Manmohan Singh and Congress president Sonia Gandhi are mere 'pretenders' to the Jawaharlal Nehru-Indira Gandhi legacy of foreign policy. After all, the Congress under Nehru and Mrs. Gandhi would have served notice to the 'champions of democracy' to desist from interfering in the internal affairs of a developing country. Hence, the country's diplomats have to be on guard from interventionist foreign policy of the US on the pretext of establishing democracies and fights against global terrorism. President Bush has conveyed a message to every country from the platform of the General Assembly that unilateral interventionism is the US's foreign policy doctrine, and India cannot be an exception to it.

Being handicapped by India's unresolved 'disputes' with Pakistan and China, our leaders have failed to challenge the aggressive and interventionist policies of the self-appointed promoter of global democracy. Herein lies the significance of Manmohan Singh's talks with leaders of Pakistan and China in New York. The normalisation of India-Pakistan and India-China relationship is a pre-requisite for the country's autonomous foreign policy.

The Manmohan-Musharraf joint statement in New York is a step forward in improving the relationship between India and Pakistan. The two countries have reiterated their commitment "to ensure a peaceful settlement of all pending issues including Jammu & Kashmir to the satisfaction of both sides".

This is a great step forward in resolving the Kashmir issue by bringing it on the negotiating table. Earlier, India regarded it as an internal matter, while Pakistan proclaimed that Kashmir was at the core of any settlement with India. It is a sign of maturity that the two neighbours have agreed to resolve the issue through negotiations.

The two South Asian leaders said that peaceful solution of the Kashmir issue would be sought "in a sincere spirit and peaceful manner". This is the greatest CBM between India and Pakistan, whose estranged relationship has led not only to wars, but also nuclear misadventures in the subcontinent. Pakistan suggested India to withdraw its Army from Baramulla and Kupwara, and Manmohan Singh reiterated that President Musharraf should take steps to check cross-border terrorism.

The Prime Minister reiterated that 'territorial reorganisation' of Jammu & Kashmir was not on the agenda, but a situation could be created in which 'borders' between India-Pakistan and Kashmir could be made 'irrelevant'. President Musharraf also stressed that the existing Line of Control was not acceptable, and negotiations needed to proceed further to resolve the dispute. The very fact that President Musharraf himself read the joint statement and Manmohan Singh clearly stated that he was 'very satisfied with the outcome', shows a meeting of minds.

The two leaders reaffirmed their commitment to the decisions taken at their meeting in New Delhi, and agreed to expedite their implementation. They welcomed the progress made within the framework of the composite dialogue – including promotion of trade and economic relations, people-to-people contact and further CBMs.

Anybody with an understanding of the degree of distrust between India and Pakistan would not have expected more than the joint statement. A greater vigil is needed to control the elements whose interest lie in keeping unrest in the subcontinent.

Both India and Pakistan have powerful military establishments that feel threatened by any movement towards peace, as it disturbs its apple cart of pecuniary gains from war preparations. Also, the Western merchants of death find lucrative business opportunities to sell arms to New Delhi and Islamabad.

It is equally essential to mention the significance of discussions between Manmohan Singh and Chinese President Hu Jintao on September 14. India and China agreed to find a 'reasonable solution' to the boundary question with 'greater urgency', and it does not need to be re-emphasised that this is precisely what India and Pakistan should be doing on the Kashmir issue. Mr. Jintao and Manmohan Singh stated that 'guiding principles and political parameters' would form the basis of solutions to the dispute.

Pragmatism has to be the guiding factor in resolving all outstanding issues between India, Pakistan and China. The wounds inflicted by a history of hostilities and wars has to be ignored, keeping in mind the imperatives of imperialist-led unipolar global system in the first decade of the 21st century.

US imperialism cannot be wished away by foreign policymakers of India, Pakistan and China. The logic of a unipolar world order dictates that either India and Pakistan resolve their problems at the bilateral level, or the sole superpower will impose solutions with the military might at its command. US Secretary of State Condoleezza Rice made such an attempt in New York with a view to influence Manmohan Singh.

India, China and Pakistan should intervene on the nuclear dispute between Iran and the US. The Bush Administration cannot be trusted on its declaration that Iran possesses nuclear weapons, especially after it used the same propaganda for launching war against Saddam Hussein's Iraq. Since President Bush has already made the agenda of targeting Iran — just as he had in the case of Iraq — India, Pakistan and China should collectively tell Iran to follow every 'condition' of maintaining nuclear weapons, if any. Besides, the Americans should be advised to support the IAEA to deal with Tehran on the nuclear issue.

The message from New York is clear: India, Pakistan and China cannot ignore the new hotspot of US-Iranian confrontation on nuclear weapons. – *The Pioneer, September 20, 2005*

DO WE HAVE A PRIME MINISTER?

Parliamentary democracy in England or Canada or Australia has in reality become a prime ministerial government; the office of the PM has evolved from the status of primus inter pares or first among equals to the present position of the leadership of the Cabinet and elected House of Parliament. The council of ministers is collectively responsible to the elected House of Parliament, but in reality the writ of the PM runs over all the members of his Cabinet. Not only this. The PM can ask for the resignation or even the dismissal of a dissident member of his council of ministers because appointment of a minister is his sole prerogative. The PM can act as an unquestioned leader of his council of ministers if he enjoys the unquestioned political authority over his own party.

Unfortunately, Dr. Manmohan Singh is a PM nominated by Sonia Gandhi, who is the real and unquestioned leader of the Congress Party which is leading the UPA government at the Centre. Dr Singh is not even a light weight leader of the Congress; the real repository of power is Sonia Gandhi who is the president of the Congress and the chairman of the National Advisory Council. Not only this, every coalition partner of the UPA looks towards her as the final arbiter of disputes or differences between the Congress Party and its coalition partners. The Communist parties, supporting the Congress-led UPA government from outside, look towards Sonia for their coordination with the Dr Singh-led government.

It is noteworthy that Pranab Mukerjee, or P. Chidambaram or Arjun Singh, or Kamal Nath of the Congress Party care for the opinions and wishes of the PM because Sonia Gandhi, the supreme leader of the Congress, is supporting Dr. Singh in his present position. The Congress CMs too look towards Sonia Gandhi and not Dr Singh, for guidance, advice, instructions and orders. It is Sonia Gandhi who decides to hold meetings of Congress CMs and they have to explain their record of activities to her and not the nominated PM. A telling example is provided by the manner in which Natwar Singh, the former external affairs minister, was made to 'quit' the Cabinet because Sonia Gandhi had got annoyed with her own favourite minister in the Volcker Affair. Natwar Singh was shown the door not by Dr. Singh but by Sonia.

The upshot of the above description is that the PM has no authority or freedom to exercise his real prerogative of either appointing a minister or in asking for his resignation. The Congress party representatives in Dr. Singh's Cabinet can continue at the 'pleasure' of Sonia and not on the basis of choice or goodwill of the PM. The essential point to be noted here is that Dr Singh is shinning in the reflected glory of Sonia. He is in office because of his 'loyalty' to Sonia.

Jawaharlal Nehru or Indira Gandhi or Rajiv Gandhi or Narasimha Rao or Atal Bihari Vajpayee were not only PMs in their own right, they controlled the party organisation. Complete support of a party is a precondition for becoming a PM in a parliamentary democracy. It is not without reason that Jawaharlal Nehru threatened to resign from the CWC if Purushottam Das Tandon continued as party president. The clash and conflict between these two personalities was resolved in favour of the PM and the party president was made to quit his elected office.

Indira Gandhi decided to 'split' the Congress party in 1969 when the party president Nijalingappa had ganged up against her on the choice of the party nominee for the post of President of India. Indira Gandhi again 'split' the party in 1978 because a powerful section within the party was 'hostile' to her. In fact, every Congress PM, except Dr. Singh, had been either the unquestioned and unchallenged choice of the party or managed and manipulated party support in his/her favour.

A PM has to 'control' his party for his authority to be fully accepted by every minister in his Cabinet. Indira Gandhi fought against her opponents within the party because her authority as PM would have been completely diluted, even eroded, if she had allowed parallel or 'dual' centres of power. It is not without reason that V. P. Singh or Chandra Shekhar or H. D. Deve Gowda or I K Gujaral could remain PMs only for a very short period because none of them had either firm support of a party or a coalition of parties. Mr. Vajpayee could remain PM from 1998 to 2004 because he was fully supported not only by the BJP but also other coalition partners. In other words, a PM is effective only on the basis of his own political strength within the party of which he is the leader.

Dr. Singh is not the leader of the Congress or of the UPA and hence he cannot lead the council of ministers. It has been observed that every pubic controversy involving the UPA government is resolved by the active intervention of Sonia Gandhi and not the PM. He does not have any role in the party's internal affairs because Sonia has the real power. The functioning of the government is also affected by such an unnatural 'dual control system' because every party or group in the UPA looks towards Sonia for the final word. The Left parties had walked out and boycotted the coordination committee meetings in the middle of 2005 because they had developed serious differences with the UPA government on economic policies of liberalisation, globalisation and privatisation and it was Sonia Gandhi's intervention which bought back the Left to the co-ordination committee meetings. Sonia Gandhi's National Advisory Council carries more weight in decision making than Dr Singh and it had become clear on the issue of National Rural Employment Guarantee Scheme and the Right to Information Act 2005.

It deserves to be reiterated that the office of the PM in the UPA government has been completely devalued. It is not only that Dr Singh owes his job to Sonia, all Congress ministers look towards Sonia for their continuation in office. Sonia has power without responsibility and Dr Singh is shouldering responsibilities without real power. – *The Economic Times, January 21, 2006*

OFFICIALLY THE WEAKEST?

Parliamentary democracy revolves round the personality and leadership qualities of the Prime Minister, who is nearly always the sole spokesperson of the country's foreign and domestic policies. Manmohan Singh's press conference on February 1 was therefore a significant aid to understanding the policies of the UPA Government.

The Prime Minister chose to address the media at a time of sharp divisions within the country not only on the issue of foreign policy, but also on questions being raised regarding his own leadership qualities. It is not surprising that the country is debating the issue of Mr. Singh's political authority, thanks to the circumstances that made him the Prime Minister in May 2004. The Congress had elected Ms. Sonia Gandhi to lead the Government at the Centre after the electoral debacle of the BJP-led NDA in the 2004 Lok Sabha election. Ms. Sonia Gandhi, however, 'nominated' Manmohan Singh to lead the coalition Government at the Centre.

Manmohan Singh has been the Prime Minister for 20 months and his press conference was an appropriate forum to clarify the issues that are in people's minds. The crux of the matter is the relationship between Manmohan Singh and Congress president Sonia Gandhi. After all, the UPA Government is led by the Congress, which is fully controlled by her.

Is the Prime Minister leading the Government without any authority? Manmohan Singh dismissed L.K. Advani's allegation of being the "weakest Prime Minister" by observing: "If I am a weak Prime Minister then how strong was Mr. Advani when he went to Jinnah's mausoleum and had to resign as party president because the RSS didn't like it?" It was easy for Manmohan Singh to dismiss Mr. Advani's charges because the BJP-led NDA Government was dictated to by the RSS.

The BJP is the political front of the Sangh parivar. K.S. Sudarshan, the RSS sarganghchalak, not only guided the BJP Government, but also ensured that both Atal Bihari Vajpayee and Mr. Advani were reduced to insignificance after the 2004 Lok Sabha election. It was, therefore, quite easy for Manmohan Singh to tackle the BJP at his press conference. If Ms. Sonia Gandhi is perceived as an 'extra-constitutional centre of power', the Vajpayee-led Government too was subservient to the RSS. Also the Manmohan Singh Government is far more stable than the regimes of V.P. Singh, Chandra Shekhar, H.D. Deve Gowda and Inder Kumar Gujral.

The Congress has always provided prime ministers who have governed the country without any other power centre, thanks to their control over party apparatus. In the current scenario, however, Manmohan Singh is the head of the Government while Ms. Sonia Gandhi is the leader of the party. Little wonder, Manmohan Singh observed in the press conference: "She (Sonia Gandhi) is a source of strength for me. I'll probably be less effective in many of the tasks she has to perform as UPA chairperson and Congress president."

Ms. Sonia Gandhi is aware of the Congress's culture of backstabbing. The party leaders have perfected the art of duplicity and, to quote Rajiv Gandhi, "They are power brokers." P.V. Narasimha Rao, during his prime ministership, provided enough opportunities to Ms. Sonia Gandhi to come to the conclusion that traditional Congress leaders did not have the virtue of loyalty or even political integrity.

During the Rao regime, Arjun Singh and N.D. Tiwari walked out of the Congress to float a new party, the Congress (Tiwari). If party leaders could walk out of the Congress at the behest of Ms. Sonia Gandhi and betray Narasimha Rao, they would not hesitate to do the opposite for profit. Manmohan Singh is not like a traditional khadiwala politician. Not surprisingly, Ms. Sonia Gandhi trusted him over others in May 2004.

A storm broke out soon after the Prime Minister's press conference when a television channel showed a series of letters written by the PMO and the Cabinet Secretariat over the past 20 months, pleading the ministers to keep the Prime Minister in the loop about various policy decisions taken by their respective departments. It can be argued that the UPA allies are not following the principle of collective responsibility. Every party or group considers itself as an 'equal partner of the Congress'.

The UPA came into existence to keep the BJP out of power. Except this binding principle, the UPA partners have nothing in common either among themselves or with the Congress. The lack of coordination in the Government, therefore, could easily be attributed to the lack of commonality within the UPA.

On the issue of the PMO letter, BJP president Rajnath Singh observed: "We feel sorry for the Prime Minister's helplessness. It would not be off the mark to say that Manmohan Singh is indeed the weakest Prime Minister our country has ever had." It seems Rajnath Singh has forgotten RSS's interference during Atal Bihari Vajpayee's regime. In fact, Rajnath Singh has succeeded L.K. Advani as BJP president because of the Sangh's disapproval of the latter.

As far as the role of the Leftist parties is concerned, Manmohan Singh said, "I do not think they (the Left parties) will do so (stall policy-making). In the long run, some pressure does perform a useful function in a democracy. We will complete five years and with regard to pressure from Left, it is not unexpected." It is not only Manmohan Singh but every Prime Minister of a coalition Government who has to work under 'constraints'.

Parliament holds the Prime Minister responsible for the acts of the Government. Ms. Sonia Gandhi and her party cannot pretend on the floor of the House that the Government's authority is not exercised by the Prime Minister. Manmohan Singh is in the seat of the most powerful office of the Government and this role provides him with enough room to exercise discretionary powers. Manmohan Singh is not just primus inter pares in his Council of Ministers; he is also not in the category of other Congress prime ministers like Jawaharlal Nehru, Indira Gandhi, Rajiv Gandhi and Narasimha Rao. Also, he does not belong to the category of stop-gap prime ministers like Chandra Shekhar, H.D. Deve Gowda and Inder Kumar Gujral.

If Mammohan Singh is constrained by Ms. Sonia Gandhi's role in politics and Government, he is only emulating Atal Bihari Vajpayee. After all, Mr. Vajpayee too was held in check by the RSS and other outfits of the Sangh parivar.

– *The Pioneer, February 7, 2006*

CONGRESS SEARCH FOR DIRECTION

The forthcoming Assembly elections in Maharashtra, Haryana and Arunachal Pradesh, the completion of 100 days of the Congress led-United Progressive Alliance Government at the Centre, and the All-India Congress Committee session held in Delhi on August 21, 2004, provide an opportunity to analyse and understand the working of Congress party organisation and the actual performance of the UPA Government. These are all inter-related issues because the Congress organisation and the coalition Government are on test and any failure or weakness within the party will provide opportunity and political space to its main political rival, the BJP.

It deserves to be mentioned that both the Congress and the BJP, the main contenders for all-India political space, are very much in the reckoning for political power on their own at the Centre. This is because the electoral verdict of the 14th Lok Sabha elections has neither completely weakened the BJP nor has it given a pre-eminent position to the Congress. The BJP-led NDA Government lost because its major coalition partners like the TDP, the AIADMK and the INLD suffered electoral setbacks. The

Congress allies like the DMK or the RJD et al achieved electoral victories and that made it possible for the Congress to form a coalition Government at the Centre.

The Congress is still in a bad shape as compared to its glorious past and the BJP is looking for an opportunity to displace it from power. The Congress has to tackle this new political situation by clearly articulating its ideology and by reviving its extremely sick grassroots organisation. Ms. Sonia Gandhi, the sole architect of the Congress's revival, brought to the attention of party leaderships on August 21, 2004, at the AICC session, that the core issue before the party is "Government-organisation relations". She clearly stated: "It generally happens that in the wake of a party's victory in election and the establishment of Government, the organisation takes a back seat."

Ms. Gandhi unambiguously told factional warhorses of the party: "This has also been a reason behind our electoral defeat in some states where the Government had eclipsed the organisation. This should not be repeated in future." Ms. Gandhi's call for "revival and rejuvenation of the party organisation" seems to be a will-o'-the-wisp because the organisation's office bearers, including the PCC presidents, are themselves reluctant to serve the organisation and instead prefer to wallow in the luxury of their ministerial chairs. The Congress has lost the culture of dedicated organisation workers because ministerial berths are too profitable to be sacrificed at the altar of faceless party organisation.

It is not without reason that important ministers of the Manmohan Singh Government like Natwar Singh, Shivraj Patil, Arjun Singh et al, are given ministerial berths without being members of the Lok Sabha. Shivraj Patil, the Home Minister, was defeated in the elections. The BJP-led NDA, too, had ministers from the Rajya Sabha because they could not be elected to the Lok Sabha. Ms. Gandhi thus gets the credit for reminding every Congress leader about the need for renewal of the party organisation.

A committed party organisation is necessary but not a sufficient condition for the survival and success of the party in a democracy where alternative ideologies and policies compete against one another. Ms. Gandhi's second theme at the AICC session was to bring into sharp focus her party's differences from its main competitor, the BJP. The Congress resolution said that "the political fraud resorted to by the BJP in trying to camouflage its narrow, communal beliefs and attitudes, inspired and directed by the RSS, behind a facade of a variety of pseudo-political issues almost derailed the country from its secular foundations". This anti-BJP resolution of the Congress may remain a paper document because the party's commitment to secular politics does not go deep down the line within the party organisation.

Also, the Congress has recognised and reiterated its belief that "India has entered the era of coalition Government". If this is so, coalition partners have also to be committed to the ideologies of secularism as expounded by the Congress. The UPA Government is known more for its internal differences among its partners than a united front of anti-communal parties and groups. The mudslinging between Lalu Prasad Yadav and Ram Vilas Paswan has not brought any credit to the Singh Government in its first 100 days. If one part of the story is the deadlock in Parliament because of the BJP's "negative tactics", the other is the Congress chief ministers of Punjab and Manipur who have shown that neither the Congress nor the UPA Government has any semblance of unity.

Is it the "coalition dharma" to witness Cabinet ministers charging one another in pubic as to who is more dishonest? Can any party be taken seriously in which its own chief ministers act like "regional barons"? The Congress should also learn the lesson that its allies cannot be taken for granted, especially the Left which stands for programme and policies. The UPA ministers have forgotten that in a coalition Government, policy announcements like the hike in FDI in insurance, telecommunication and civil aviation require the consent of all partners in the Government.

The Congress should learn to practice coalition dharma and "coordination" with allies and partners, which is the foundational principle of coalition politics. Further, the performance of the UPA Government would also be noticed in the forthcoming Assembly elections in Maharashtra, Haryana and Arunachal Pradesh. Maharashtra is ruled by a coalition of the Congress and the NCP, and both these parties are sharing power at the Centre. Therefore, it is natural that the BJP-Shiv Sena alliance will raise issues about the functioning of not only the State Government but also the Central Government. Similarly, in Haryana, Om Prakash Chautala will hammer the point about Captain Amarinder Singh's decision in Punjab to abrogate all water sharing agreements with neighbouring states.

A unilateral action by a Congress Chief Minister without caring for neighbours projects a pan-Indian party like the Congress in very poor light. Ms. Gandhi called upon the Congress governments in the states to ensure that "organisational workers" are not alienated, but the signals from Punjab and Manipur have proved that the all-India Congress party's writ does not run over its own chief ministers. It is also true that in any competitive political system, a political party has to project its own achievements as well as the failures of the Opposition. The Congress and the BJP are ideologically poles apart, their competition is unlike other sectarian, regional chauvist casteist parties and both of them are suffering from internal party factionalism.

It is a fact that in its behaviour, the BJP has not been any different from the Congress, though it still has a solid organisation to support it during the elections. Ms. Gandhi is making Herculean efforts to rejuvenate the Congress's sick organisation and provide direction to the party that has become "directionless" because of loaves and fishes of office. She must remember that Rajiv Gandhi was not only attacked by "power brokers in the Congress", he was also destroyed by the same power brokers as well as professional factionalists. The euphoria of forming a Government at the Centre is attracting Congressmen to Ms. Gandhi and she has to guard herself against such forces within the party.

The upshot of above description is that the Congress is involved in a struggle to come to grips with the new political situation and one hopes that Ms. Gandhi may be able to inject some vitality into this slow, dying party.

–The Pioneer, August 28, 2004

POLITICS OF CONTINUITY

The Maharashtra elections attracted national attention because political stakes of the major contenders for power — Congress-NCP and BJP-Shiv Sena — were high; these were, after all, the first high voltage contest after the Lok Sabha elections of April-May 2004. In this context it is important to understand the real all-India significance of the victory of the Congress-NCP combine and the defeat of BJP-Shiv Sena combine. Did the BJP reinvent itself after its defeat in the Lok Sabha elections to face the Congress challenge in Maharashtra? Further, Maharashtra occupies a very special position among the states as Mumbai is the nerve centre of the Indian economy.

The State has always attracted migrant population from every north Indian State. The composition of migrant population in Maharashtra was reason enough to attract leaders like

Ms. Mayawati of the BSP, Mulayam Singh Yadav of the SP, Lalu Prasad Yadav of the RJD and Ram Vilas Paswan of the LJP to contest the elections with a view to earn the status of pan-regional party.

However, the real fight was between the Congress-NCP and the BJP-Shiv Sena combines, because victory here would have meant strengthening their all-India status. Ms. Gandhi's Congress and Sharad Pawar's NCP are partners at the Centre and victory in Maharashtra will certainly help them not only in enhancing their political credibility but also would help the Manmohan Singh-led UPA Government feel secure. The BJP-Shiva Sena combine contested the elections not only for the purpose of establishing pre-eminent political position in Maharashtra but also to recover political space which it had lost with the NDA's defeat in the 14th Lok Sabha elections.

It is inherent in the logic of pure casteist politics that parties, groups and leaders proliferate on the basis of their limited support from their castes or sub-castes, and caste appeals of casteist leaders is limited to specific region. Pan-Indian or across the region parties cannot succeed on the basis of caste politics, because Yadavs of Bihar or UP may be Yadavs but they are different from one another. And any effort by Ms. Mayawati or Mulayam Singh Yadav or Lalu Prasad Yadav or Mr. Paswan to become pan-regional casteist leaders is inherently flawed.

Ms. Mayawati was honest when, during the Maharashtra elections, she said that her main aim was to steal the Dalit votes from the Congress so that none of the two major alliances gets a clear majority. And in that fluid post-election scenario, her role as king maker to the highest bidder would become crucial.

However, the most important signal from Maharashtra is that the electoral results of 2004 were a continuation of the 1990s, and politics has stabilised to revolve around four major parties: The Congress, NCP, BJP and Shiv Sena. Every other contender is either marginal or, at best, a "spoiler". Congress-NCP had not contested the 1999 elections as alliance partners, but they joined hands to form the State Government to keep the BJP-Shiv Sena alliance at bay. The so-called Independents extended support to the Congress-NCP Government, but for a price in the form of lucrative positions. But today such an eventuality has not arisen, as the "spoilers" or casteist parties or independents have been marginalised.

Why has Maharashtra politics been polarised between the secular and communal chauvinist forces? And why has such polarised politics stabilised in the last 15 years? Public political culture of a country or a region provides an important key to unlock the processes of understanding of any stabilisation of political trends and tendencies.

Tamil politics of 2004 is a continuation of the political culture created in the 1920s by Rama Swamy Naicker, whose anti-Brahminism and pro-non-Brahmin Dravidians caught the imagination of the political and the literati classes. Since then, every group or leader has to identify with the DMK or the AIADMK or any nomenclature linked with the Dravidian identity. Bengal politics cannot be understood without linking it with the public political culture created by Partition of 1905-1911, an event which electrified Bengal's politics. Gun culture and mass mobilisation around Swadeshi and the boycott of foreign goods brought the culture of "street politics" to Bengal. The Congress's decline in Bengal began with the appropriation of "mass street politics" by the communists, who are reaping its political benefits.

Likewise, public political culture of Maharashtra which has impacted its politics deeply deserves to be understood to explain the emergence of different secular, modernists and socially regressive and communal trends which get concretised during elections. The 20th century Maharashtra witnessed the contest of ideologies of the Congress, the communists, the socialists, the Savarkarites and the different approaches adopted by Gopal Krishna Gokhale and Balgangadhar Tilak towards achieving independence from the Raj.

It was not without reason that Mahatma Gandhi, on his arrival into the Indian political scene, described Gokhale as his "political guru". Further, Maharashtra also witnessed a kind of "cultural and social" renaissance which transformed the levels of consciousness of Maharashtra's Dalits and women. From Phule to Ambedkar is a very powerful period in Maharashtra's social story, and the levels of Dalit consciousness are not comparable with Uttar Pradesh or Bihar. The Marathi Press and the Marathi literati have been catalysts of change in society. Democratic electoral politics is integrally linked with socio-cultural forces operating in the State.

Today Maharashtrian society has shown many contradictory trends as reflected by the Congress, NCP, Shiv Sena and BJP. The Maharashtrian society has a very progressive, forward looking and modernist strata. However, it also has extremely chauvinistic, localist and communal tendencies. It has supporters for "progress" and also for social regression. Bal Thackarey emerged in the late 1960s as an authentic chauvinist and localist who played on the sentiments and insecurities of the lower middle class Marathi. Also emerged Datta Samanta in the late 1960s as a great trade union adventurists who successfully marginalised other "secular working class struggles" by making trade unionism a wrecker of industrialisation.

The late-1950s and early-1960s witnessed the emergence of the powerful Samyukta Maharashtra Samiti to protect the Marathi identity. Maharashtrian violence and emotive irrationality was at its peak during the struggle for Bombay. In the 1990s, the Shiv Sena successfully manipulated the issues concerning Maharashtrian identity by playing the politics of "the other", or "the outsider". The 1990s also brought into focus the Hindu-Muslim divide that has been always present in the State. The destruction of Babri Masjid on December 6, 1992, the post-demolition communal frenzy and the serial bomb blasts in 1993 in Mumbai underlined that the Maharashtra Hindu had not forgotten his lessons in communalism in the 20th century.

Further, cultural identities like local chauvinism or communalism do not hang in the air; they are embedded in society and its economy. Maharashtra's economy has seen several positive and negative trends — for instance, from the modern industrial bourgeoisie to the mafia. Maharashtra is a great social laboratory where politics of progress is closely shadowed by politics of social regression and communalism. – *The Pioneer, October 20, 2004*

IN THE DNA OF UPA

The gradual revival of the Grand Old Party has created political ripples among the opposition, whether aligned with the Congress-led UPA or those represented by the BJP-led NDA. The DMK, which is very well represented in the Government, has opposed the recent hike in petrol, diesel and cooking gas prices. The BJP's decision to launch an agitation against the rising cost of living is understandable because the Congress-led UPA Government and the BJP are involved in ideological and political struggle against each other. The Left, though it is supporting the coalition Government from outside, has publicly criticised many of the economic policies of the UPA Government.

It is not incumbent on parties supporting the Government from outside to endorse the policies with which they disagree, because they have decided not to be part of the "formal" and "institutional" arrangements of governmental decision making. It is a very unique situation in which the "partners" in a coalition government have consciously joined ranks with the Opposition. The Manmohan Singh Government is going through the same process that was first witnessed during the Vajpayee-led NDA coalition – when the Opposition space was occupied not only by parties which were outside the NDA Government but also by some of the parties represented in the Council of Ministers from 1998 to 2004.

It is an important political phenomenon that a party leading the coalition Government at the Centre receives brickbats from its own partners. This is because, irrespective of whether a Council of Ministers consists of one party or a coalition of parties, it is expected to be collectively responsible for every decision made by the Government. A coalition partner can walk out of the Government if it has differences with a policy decision, but it cannot have its cake and eat it too – as shown by the DMK's opposition to the UPA Government's decision increasing the oil prices.

There must be very compelling reasons for the Left, as "outside supporters", and the DMK, as an "insider", to preserve and maintain their opposition space against the Congress. The Left parties have explained their "dual" public posture on the basis of their "ideology". It has extended its support to the UPA Government with a view to keeping the communal forces, represented by the BJP, out of power. This does not mean that the Left agrees with the Congress totally. On the contrary, the Left parties are fundamentally opposed to the Congress's new economic policies based on globalisation, privatisation and opening of the Indian market to foreign investors. The communists cannot easily accept the Congress's policies on privatisation of public sector undertakings because the interests of the working classes, represented by the Left, cannot be mortgaged to the whims and fancies of the market forces. The Left parties are opposed to foreign investment, especially in the strategic sector. It is interesting to watch the development of relations between the Manmohan Singh Government and the Left because the latter's "dual" and "dichotomous" approach of "support to secularism", and firm opposition to "economic policies" of the Congress, are bound to come under strain sooner or later. Such prospects will increase when the Congress and communists face each other in the forthcoming Assembly elections in West Bengal and Kerala. It will prove difficult to convince the voters in Bengal and Kerala that the Congress and communists are two political "opposites" in a State, while they can work together at the Centre.

The Congress and communist voters in Bengal and Kerala see each other as political enemies, and elections in these two states are contested on the basis of Congress versus communists and not as Congress-communists allies. Further, the decline of Ms. Mamata Banerjee's political stock in West Bengal has again brought the Congress and the communists in direct confrontation. Likewise, every other regional or sub-regional party and group has complicated relationship with the Congress. The Congress has an all-India presence and its revival creates serious problems for other regional groups, which have gained political strength at the cost of the Congress; for instance, the TDP in Andhra Pradesh.

The DMK and the AIADMK have emerged in Tamil Nadu after vanquishing the once mighty Congress. The Congress was ejected in Bihar and Uttar Pradesh by parties representing the interests of the "backward caste peasantry" and Dalits. It deserves to be noted that every Prime Minister except Atal Bihari Vajpayee has been an erstwhile Congress leader. But it is not true in the case of regional and sub-regional parties which took birth in opposition to the Congress such as the Akali Dal, National Conference, BSP, Rashtriya Lok Dal, etc.

The NCP of Sharad Pawar walked out of the Congress and it is a marriage of convenience that keeps Mr. Pawar with the Congress in Maharashtra. The NCP has always demanded its pound of flesh from the Congress, as witnessed during Government formation in the State. Lalu Prasad Yadav of the RJD maintains an alliance with the Congress in Bihar and at the Centre, but the real test is coming soon because the Congress will have to decide on its political options in the forthcoming Assembly elections in the State. Also, the Congress is supporting the Mulayam Singh Yadav Government in Uttar Pradesh while the two parties are at loggerheads because the Congress is struggling to regain lost ground in the State.

The Congress and it allies at the Centre have an uneasy political relationship because in every major State, the Congress and the regional and sub-regional parties are in confrontation with each other. The Congress had lost its all-India political space to the regional and sub-regional parties, and these parties are contesting the Congress's efforts to revive itself at their cost. The real implication of this situation is that the coalition governments at the Centre, whether led by the Congress or the BJP, are just conglomerates and a kind of sum-total of disparate groups which just wish to be a part of the ruling coalition.

It would be incorrect to describe either the NDA or the UPA as coalition because the constituent groups have nothing in common. They are together because of political convenience. It is inherent in the logic of such disparate and spurious coalitions that parties in government will not surrender the opposition space to the Congress; else, their very raison d'etre will get eroded. It does not disturb their conscience to support or launch an opposition against government policies in spite of the fact that they are part of the decision-making process.

The Congress is facing genuine opposition from its traditional opponents like the Akali Dal and DMK as well as its ideological opponents like the BJP and Shiv Sena. The Left parties have historically been involved in a basic struggle against the Congress. India is witnessing an ideological battle between secularism and communalism. But the UPA coalition consists of secular Congress and non-ideological floating groups which are in Government as well as in the Opposition at the same time. This presents an engaging caricature of the great Indian coalition experiment.

–The Pioneer, November 17, 2004

MAKE INDIA A STRONG AND EGALITARIAN NATION

Avery powerful, ideologically committed social constituency exists in India which suffers from the hallucinations of "national greatness". It is reflected in the ruling elites' claim for permanent membership for India in the UN Security Council and to be counted as a Nuclear Weapons state. Indian jingoism has attracted the attention of American imperialists, and this has been unambiguously stated officially when the US Ambassador to India, David C. Mulford, said: "It is the policy of the United States to help India become a major world power in the 21st Century." This is what US Secretary of State, Condoleezza Rice, conveyed to Prime Minister Manmohan Singh during her recent visit to India – marking an exciting turning point to years of hard work to transform US-India bilateral relationship into a strategic partnership.

The issue deserves to be analysed properly, because it has serious repercussions on Indian society, polity and democracy. The moot question is: Should India strive to be a normal democratic, secular, pluralist and welfarist nation-state or abandon these essential national goals in favour of a highly militarised and nuclearised power with a capacity to influence and dictate the behaviour of other smaller countries especially its neighbours? Should India be counted a welfare, pluralist and secular democracy with reasonable strategic strength to safeguard its liberal national goals, or, should it move towards the rule of "military-industrial" centres of power linked with and strengthened by "military-industrial imperialist" America?

India at the beginning of 21st Century is witnessing the "clash of jingoist, militarist nationalism versus normal democratic, egalitarian peaceful nationalism". India's project to "become a major world power with the full support of American imperialism is a non-starter because of constraints imposed by domestic and external factors. A few facts may be mentioned to substantiate the argument that the project is doomed to fail:

First, India and the South Asian region has failed to achieve the mutually beneficial arrangement of "regional economic integration" because India, Pakistan, Bangladesh and currently Nepal are unable to resolve their disputes. The telling example of political disharmony in the region has been provided by the decision to postpone the 13th SAARC Summit of 2005, as India has expressed its inability to attend the summit. The Indian government is not in tune with the prevailing political regimes of Bangladesh and Nepal. India and Bangladesh cannot have a common meeting ground if their mutual perceptions are based on negativism.

Second, Nepal's current monarchical dispensation does not have any support from India's democratic, social constituency, and the bilateral relationship is "deadlocked" because Nepal and India are divided on the issue of democracy in Nepal.

Third, it is believed by many South Asians that SAARC is held at ransom by Indo-Pak political conflicts.

India cannot dream of "gigantism" till it is bound by its bilateral disputes with its neighbours. Incidentally, a reference to China seems relevant to understand the predicaments of India becoming a "world actor". During Mao's phase, China used force to integrate Tibet with the mainland and also fought a war with India. The China of the 21st Century has peacefully resolved its bilateral boundary dispute with Russia, and has abandoned its aggressive attitude towards India. China has set its own house in order by proclaiming "one country, two systems" while peacefully negotiating with Hong Kong and Taiwan.

It is the Americans and some South-East and East Asian countries like Japan which fear the emergence of China as a future superpower. China has the potential to play the role of a "major world power", because, unlike India, its immediate neighbours have a "friendly" attitude towards it. Similarly, America, Canada and Mexico are fully integrated, and American imperialists are not chained by "local troubles with neighbours".

India has to attract its neighbour countries as friends before it jumps on the world stage. India and Pakistan are involved in a cut-throat competition on defence and security preparedness against each other. The recent US offer of sale of F-16s to India and Pakistan will trigger an arms race in the region. The two countries are building their "war machines" without resolving their bilateral disputes. And one common accelerator of "war competition" between these two countries is imperialist America.

During her recent visit to India, Ms. Rice conveyed that President Bush shares "a vision for a decisively broader strategic relationship with India, to help the country achieve its goals as one of the world's great multi-ethnic democracies. This vision embraces cooperation on a global strategy for peace, defence, energy and economic growth." America is searching for markets for Lockheed-Martin (manufacturer of F-16) and other American based "merchants of death" for profits. But have Indians decided their own national goals?

The founding fathers of the Indian republic clearly spelt a "vision" for a peaceful, normal Indian nation state" committed to peaceful co-existence with its neighbours and the world. During the Cold War phase of world politics, Indian leadership openly castigated America for creating a situation that triggered an "arm's race" in South Asia. But, unfortunately, the present Indian leadership is looking towards America for acquiring military might. It is clear that somewhere down the road Indians have lost their way. Instead of working for creating a peaceful South Asian region, the country has jumped into the race for military power. Defence preparedness and economic development are always involved in antagonistic and irresolvable contradictions, while the policy of peaceful co-existence has great economic and social dividends for developing countries like India and the South Asian region.

India's priority of becoming a "major world power" with the active support of America is completely misplaced national jingoism and chauvinism. It will have disastrous consequences for the future development of a normal, peaceful democratic state of India. It is not suggested that India should not take care of its legitimate security requirements. The argument is that a section of the so-called patriotic and nationalist Indians are projecting a "grandeur vision of national power". Democratic political groups should oppose this project. The first priority for India is to settle its disputes with its neighbours to reduce its own growing defence burden.

In conclusion, it may be stated that national effort should be directed towards building a peaceful and harmonious South Asian region where cooperative effort can be made to overcome the miserable living conditions of the population. The choice before global power dreamers in India is clear: Either India should become America, that is, democracy at home and imperialist abroad and fight wars, or become a true democracy.

– *The Pioneer, March 5, 2005*

THE RELEVANCE OF INDIRA GANDHI

More than any other leader from recent history, the relevance of Indira Gandhi lingers through even two decades after her death. It is not only apt to remember her on her death anniversary that falls on October 31 but also think about how would have she reacted to the present day's world had she got a chance to live longer.

The essence of Indira Gandhi's personality and leadership lies in her immense capacities to convert every big challenge into an opportunity. She was a great leader who showed immense courage during periods of crisis in India both at the domestic and external levels and country suffered and gained immensely because of her courageous stands on external threat to national security and integrity of the country. Indira had all the makings of a ruthless dictator and a leader committed to the defence of national interests under adverse international conditions and situations. World has changed ever since she passed away.

A few facts may be mentioned to highlight the specifics of the present global scenario under which Indian policy makers have to find their answers. First, the fall of Berlin Wall in 1989 and the collapse of the erstwhile East European Socialist state systems in the 1990s brought an end not only to the bipolar cold war phase of international relations, it led to the emergence of American-led and America-controlled unipolar global order.

The old Balance of Power among the nation-states came to an end and it was replaced by one hyperpower directed Global Order. George Bush, Sr. characterised the beginning of the 1990s as a New International Order and he showed a trailer of this new unipolar world by launching an aggressive war against President Saddam Hussein of Iraq and his son George Bush, Jr. repeated his father's aggressive policies by repeating an attack on Saddam Hussein in 2003. This is the New World of the first decade of the Twenty First Century. Second, the sole global policeman has declared its right to declare a pre-emptive war against any country which is perceived as a threat to the American security. Third, military options and military interventions in the name of anti-terrorism have been practiced by the Americans against Afghanistan, Iraq and now Iran and Syria are on the hit list of the Americans.

The concept of national sovereignty and territorial integrity of the nation-states is not acceptable to the sole hegemonic power of the Twenty First Century and its claims to the sole prerogative of interfering in the international affairs of any and every country either with a view to fighting against terrorism or to restoring democracy and democratic regimes in various countries around the world. The invading and occupying American military forces are establishing democracies in Afghanistan and Iraq because the Americans are committed to the creation of a democratic world order. In central Asia, every breakaway region or state or country from the erstwhile Union of Soviet Socialist Republics, has to get testimonial from the Americans on democratic elections in their countries.

How would Indira have faced this unipolar imperialist militarist power of the 21st century? How did she face a hostile America during the Bangladesh crisis of 1971? The then American President Richard Nixon and the US Secretary of State Henry Kissinger were pathologically anti-Indira Gandhi. Nixon-Kissinger team supported Yahya Khan of Pakistan's atrocities against defenceless Bangladeshis because their personal hatred for non-aligned Indira Gandhi was ruling over their heads and values.

Bangladesh emerged as a separate and independent country with full Indian support in spite of completely anti-India and hostile America. A Third World developing country could stand against mighty United States, while dealing with the deep crisis faced by East Bengal, is a testimony to the personal courage of Indira Gandhi who could stand against any external challenge in defence of national interests of her country.

The Vajpayee government had no reason or justification to indulge in nuclear adventurism in 1998 but the worst action of any government claiming to be a nuclear weapon state was to write to Bill Clinton that 'India indulged in nuclear explosion to face threats emerging from China and Pakistan'. Clinton performed a yeoman service by making public this confidential letter of the Vajpayee government and Indian emperors were found naked without clothes.

Not only this, Indira Gandhi would never have recognised 'Israel' because she was committed to the democratic cause of Palestinian nation. Israel has been a policeman of the Americans in the Arab world and Indira aligned with the Arabs who have faced repeated wars of aggression by Israel supported by the Americans. The Twenty First Century India led by the Congress and the BJP have built bridges of deep friendship with Israel at the behest of the Americans who are the real patrons, protectors and promoters of aggressive Israel. Indira would have always bargained and negotiated with the sole super power of the world on terms and conditions decided by Indira in the national interest of her country.

She was never a believer of an unchanging global order and she would never have voted against Iran at the Vienna meeting of the International Atomic Energy Agency because she would have looked to her neighbours for India's burgeoning energy needs than remote Americans. Indira would have gone alongwith Russia and China not only on the issue of Nuclear Iran but also with a view to creating a 'trilateral' world to act as a countervailing force to the American dominated unilateral imperialism.

– Sahara Time, November 5, 2005

PARTY OF GATE-CRASHERS

Public statements and actual political actions of our leaders provide some inkling of their belief system and ideological persuasion. Congress president and chairperson of the National Advisory Council Sonia Gandhi is the real power centre in the UPA Government. It is, therefore, worthwhile to analyse and evaluate her impact on the working of the UPA Government.

As the euphoria over Ms. Gandhi's decision not to accept the office of Prime Minister in May 2004 gets over, it is time we evaluated her role in politics by analysing 18 months of the UPA regime. A distinct feature of Ms. Sonia Gandhi's politics is her fascination with non-government organisations (NGOs). She has concretised her preference for feedback from NGOs by constituting a National Advisory Council (NAC). The Government is expected to respond to the views and opinions of the NAC because of the Congress president's receptiveness to idea of non-Government activists.

The National Rural Employment Guarantee (NREG) scheme and the Right to Information Act, 2005, have received a stamp of approval by the UPA Government because of Ms. Sonia Gandhi's support to the idea of the NAC. It is well-known that neither the NREG scheme nor the RTI Act had smooth sailing, thanks to the opposition of powerful ministers and bureaucrats within the Government.

Noises were made against the NREG on the specious plea of expected financial leakages, which are only to be expected in the course of implementing such schemes. It was argued that the experience of the Government with programmes like food security and food-for-work has been bitter because, at the delivery level, the intended beneficiaries of such welfare schemes do not receive any substantial advantages.

The Finance Ministry resisted the scheme on the plea of constraints of resources for such a large-scale operation in rural India. The dust has settled and the Government, willingly or unwillingly, has agreed to operationalise the NREG scheme in 2005.

The Right to Information Act was a tough nut to crack. Bureaucracy, with clandestine prodding by politicians, put stiff resistance to the opening of Government files to citizens. The two thrive in secrecy of the Government's functioning, and the "national interest" argument is advanced to maintain the secrecy in governance. The NAC threw its full weight behind the Right to Information Act, which finally received the President's assent on June 15. It deserves to be stated that the UPA's common minimum programme had mentioned that the RTI Act would be made more "progressive, participatory and meaningful". Yet, the NAC performed yeoman service in ensuring that the amended RTI Act was put in the statute book of India. If the NREG scheme and the RTI Act have seen the light of day, the Constitution (104th) Amendment Bill has also been approved by Parliament, as the UPA Government has supported it.

The Supreme Court judgement had created the need for constitutional amendment if the Scheduled Castes, Scheduled Tribes and Backward Castes were to be admitted on the basis of quota in "private unaided educational institutions". The first Constitutional Amendment of December 22 has been undertaken by the UPA Government. It has been declared a "landmark legislation for SCs/STs and OBCs in private educational institutions". Human Resource Development Minister Arjun Singh has declared this action as a great step towards social justice for the non-privileged sections of society.

Will it be correct to maintain that the UPA Government has provided a new welfare-oriented ideological agenda for the Congress? Is it a 'new Congress' with 'Left-of-Centre' ideology; or, are its cosmetic actions concealing its pro-rich reality? How does Ms. Sonia Gandhi reconcile her Government's pro-rich reformist economic policy with her claims of fresh thinking on public policies?

The essence of the Congress's social ideology is reflected in both its pro-private enterprise and pro-American foreign policy. Its social essence cannot be understood by focusing attention on Ms. Sonia Gandhi's preferences for NGOs. The Congress-led Andhra Pradesh Government and the Congress-NCP regime in Maharashtra are both guilty of criminal negligence of debt-ridden farmers. Can we call ourselves a democracy if poor farmers have to commit suicide to be heard, and the Government has failed to come to their aid?

Maharashtra Chief Minister Vilasrao Deshmukh woke up this year when more than 1,000 cotton-growing farmers in Vidarbha committed suicide because of the debt they had taken from private moneylenders. It is clear that the Maharashtra Government's credit agencies have failed to rescue them from the clutches of private moneylenders.

Union Agriculture Minister Sharad Pawar admitted on December 21 that "agriculture is in deep trouble." Besides, he has observed that "declining public investment in agriculture, low productivity levels, unabated degradation of natural resources, low growth in inputs use, lack of buoyancy in farm prices, failure to carry out essential reforms to provide remunerative prices to farmers and to conserve water and soil, and a rundown extension support system" are responsible for crisis in agriculture.

The story of agrarian crisis and the non-responsive attitude of the UPA regime does not end here. The Manmohan Singh Government is supported by the backward caste middle peasantry, which cannot allow the implementation of much-needed land reforms essential for the revival of agrarian economy. It was 'Operation Barga' that rejuvenated the West Bengal countryside. Former member of the Planning Commission N. K. Singh states: "Bihar never proceeded to any meaningful implementation due to inadequate political will and the enormous clout of the rich landed class."

He further adds, "Its (land reforms) implementation, including conferring tenancy rights to tillers, ownership rights to share croppers, and implementation of land ceilings was and is disappointing." How could RJD president Lalu Prasad Yadav have allowed any restructuring of agrarian economy when it would not have got him any votes?

The tragedy of Bihar is a legacy of past Congress governments. The party does not have any agenda for Bihar's revival and therefore it has been marginalised. It has failed to disturb the social status quo in that State for fear of disturbing its own Government at the Centre. The agrarian crisis has directly impacted on the crisis in urban India because of largescale migration of rural population to cities for livelihood. India has no future without transforming the rural countryside.

The BJP does not have any blueprint for agrarian revival. Its social base has been confined to small and medium towns and cities. The Congress, in contrast, has a presence in the vast countryside, and the party is aware of the causes of growing rural unrest. Maoism in Andhra Pradesh is a phenomenon that is a product of callous neglect of rural areas in that State. The Maoists are sustained by rural unrest and the weaponsiation of police is not an answer to this social and agrarian problem.

The Congress has always witnessed generational changes in its leadership — from Jawaharlal Nehru to Ms. Sonia Gandhi. While Ms. Sonia Gandhi has age on her side, she is disadvantaged by her incapacity to create new social constituencies for the party. UP and Bihar have reflected this failure, where she has failed to revive the Congress by winning over new social groups. Her Congress party is old wine in new bottle.

– *The Pioneer, December 27, 2005*

MORE AND MORE OF THE SAME

The Congress held its plenary session in Hyderabad from January 21 to 23 not only to take stock of its performance both at the Centre and different states, but also identify a future leader for the party. One of the secrets of the longevity of the Congress has been its capacity to renew its organisational and political leadership to cope with new challenges facing the country.

It is part of the Gandhian tradition to hand over power to young and capable leaders. In fact, Jawaharlal Nehru came to prominence at a young age and Mahatma Gandhi declared: "Jawaharlal, not Patel or Rajaji, would be my heir and he would speak my language when I am gone". It is not incidental that it was younger Nehru and not older Patel who became the first Prime Minister of India.

It deserves to be understood that a young and dynamic leadership is necessary to provide energy and vitality to a political party to keep it flourishing in a democratic political order. The AICC session in Hyderabad had to think about the forthcoming state elections, especially in West Bengal, Kerala and Tripura. Besides, the AICC session was held after about 20 months of Congress-led UPA governance at the Centre and the party had to convey a political message to its workers so that they could go to the voters with confidence.

It is for the first time in the history of post-Independence India that the Congress has formed a coalition government at the Centre. The party's experience and problem with its coalition partners, therefore, needed to be addressed. While it is customary for the party to discuss its government's economic and foreign policies, the Hyderabad session also delivered two significant message to UPA allies: One, they are equally responsible for the success of the coalition; two, the Congress will not hesitate to expand the area of influence into the states controlled by its allies. Yet, the party did not forget that its main opponent was the BJP.

The purpose of the AICC deliberation has been to convey a message that the UPA has been formed to keep the BJP out of power; and if partners in the government are involved in mutual criticism and mud-slinging, the only beneficiary will be the BJP. At the same time, it appreciated the UPA government's new people-oriented schemes like National Rural Employment Guarantee Scheme, the Right to Information Act and the active involvement of Panchayati Raj institutes in grassroots governance It should not be forgotten that the Congress had contested the 2004 Lok Sabha election in the name of the "common man". The AICC session was only an endorsement of the government's pro-poor policies like the NREG scheme. In the process, the party forgot about the plight of the debt-ridden farmers committing suicides in Congress-ruled states like Andhra Pradesh and Maharashtra.

What is the pro-poor government doing when the poor are committing suicide?

Political parties do not hold their meetings with the purpose of "self-criticism or celebrations" alone. These also examine their future courses of action and development. The Congress, like any other party, has to show its concern for the future. It cannot rest on its laurels. Today, the party is not in a good shape. It has vacated its all-India space because it has failed to renew itself by representing the needs and aspirations of diverse groups. The Congress party's situation can be understood by its weak presence in Lok Sabha, where it has only 145 members out of the total strength of 543. It has to win over many new social constituents if it wants to maintain a respectable presence in Indian politics.

It is not an exaggeration to state that Sonia Gandhi is the undisputed leader of the Congress. Besides, It seems to be in the fitness of the Congress tradition to induct either Rahul Gandhi or Priyanka Gandhi to strengthen the party. Indira Gandhi had inducted her son, Sanjay Gandhi, in the party. And after his death, she did not hesitate to persuade Rajiv Gandhi to occupy the central position in the Congress. Today when Sonia Gandhi wants to induct her children to the party, she is only following in the footsteps of her mother-in-law. Also, the rank and file of the Congress is mentally conditioned to look towards the Nehru-Gandhi family for leadership.

Sharad Pawar walked out of the Congress because he felt that there was no democracy at the top. He did so not only because of Sonia Gandhi, but also her natural successors—Rahul and Priyanka. Pawar, being an insider, knew the reality of the Congress culture and realised that there was no space for him to assert himself within the party.

No one, therefore, was surprised when Gurudas Kamat, the Mumbai Congress chief, in November 2005, called for Rahul Gandhi being given a central position in the party. Similarly, several Congress leaders from Uttar Pradesh demanded on January 21: "All of us in UP want him (Rahul) to come to the Congress Working Committee." On the first day of the Hyderabad session itself, the 2,000-odd delegates clamoured for Rahul Gandhi to be seated at the dais with CWC members. Banners and slogans were also raised in his support.

Priyaranjan Dasmunsi, after attacking the Communists and the BJP, observed: "The chariot which Rajiv Gandhi wanted to steer in order to take the country into the 21st century must be steered by Rahul now." This chorus continued throughout the AICC session. At the end, Rahul Gandhi responded positively to the requests on January 23 when he sought time to "learn and understand the party and the people" before taking up such an important role.

Further, Rahul Gandhi appealed to the youth by stating: "Of all the political parties today, we have the largest number of young leaders." He expressed his commitment to the building of a modern India and observed that "the party got weakened when it failed to address the expectations (of the people) and lost the spirit to raise its voice".

What is the Congress' message from Hyderabad? The party wants to make a success of the coalition government at the Centre. Besides, it wishes other coalition partners of the UPA government should follow coalition dharma. The party wants to expand its social base and it has realise that the party has miles to go in extending its social reach.

And for that purpose, the party has to focuss its attention on youth. Rahul Gandhi, unlike his father, has rightly got the desire to fist learn the tricks of politics before entering it

The upshot is that the Congress is involved in strengthening itself for the arduous future tasks. The chorus for Rahul Gandhi's induction seems to be its preparation for the future.

– *The Pioneer, January 28, 2006*

NEED TO PRACTICE SECULARISM IN LETTER AND SPIRIT

Public intellectuals commonly described as secular intelligentsia have to take up cudgels against social forces and public policies which either weaken or even destroy the secular fabric of multicultural Indian democracy. A few facts may be mentioned to substantiate the argument that the letter and spirit of Indian secularism has been violated and completely nullified by some of the events in recent times.

It was not unexpected of Rajnath Singh, the BJP President, who on assuming his office, reiterated his commitment to strengthen the forces of "cultural nationalism" which, in reality, means the strengthening of fanatic anti-minority Hidutva. His commitment to "cultural nationalism" or fanatic Hindutva is just an old wine in a new bottle because the Sangh Parivar and its political frontal organisation i.e. the BJP had never abandoned its ideological commitment for the establishment of Hindu Rashtra in place of secular, democratic and cultural pluralistic and diverse Republic of India.

The secular intelligentsia of India can never take a holiday from its role and duty to oppose the anti-secular forces in the country. The lesson from history is that anti-democratic and socially fanatic movements have succeeded in their mission because the liberal intelligentsia equated their struggle against racism or fascism by just winning electoral victories over such negative social forces.

A struggle in support of secular parties and politics during the elections is a necessary but not a sufficient condition to weaken, even destroy anti-democratic forces because ideological battles have to be consistently fought at intellectual and political levels. This is the reason why the Congress' model of secularism has to be opposed. A few decisions of the UPA government or its states, especially in Andhra Pradesh, have the potential of making society communal.

First, the Rajasekhara Reddy government in Andhra Pradesh provided 5 per cent reservations for Muslims and the courts have quashed this action. The issue raised by the government's action and the judicial verdict is neither legal nor constitutional. The policy of reservations in public institutions is a political decision and the yardstick of evaluating any political choice is always normative.

A religion-based preferential treatment by the government in the name of "reservations in public institutions" is bound to create religion-based social distance among the religious communities. If the BJP is dividing Indian society on the basis of Hindus versus the "others", the Congress' policies of religion-based reservations in public services are also divisive religiously and culturally.

Second, university education for secularism is a key input in strengthening the secularisation of society because scientific temper among the recipients of higher education is an essential recipe for breaking their inherited religious boundaries. A storm in tea cup has been crated by the Allahabad High Court judgment that Aligarh Muslim University is a "non-minority" institution and in such an institution religion-based reservation for admission is not permitted by the law of the land.

The Allahabad High Court ruling should have a sobering effect on the government and the citizens because a purely Muslim educational institution where students and teachers are only

Muslims is a breeding ground for sectarian Muslim identity. The Centre promptly maintained that the AMU Act will be amended to "get past the High Court ruling" and instead of non-minority Muslim community university so that Muslim students receive an assured system of admissions". AMU will be "of, by and for Muslims only", it said.

Union HRD Minister Arjun Singh advanced a spurious argument that the AMU's status is a "commitment made by Indira Gandhi and the UPA government is committed to it". When she got the AMU Act amended in 1981, the Allahabad High Court declared it ultra vires. This amendment was Indira Gandhi's bid to curry favour with the Muslim elite in return for Muslim vote. Her opportunistic politics of 1980 Lok Sabha elections resurfaced this year. For the Congress with just 145 Lok Sabha seats in a precarious political and electoral position and its electoral strategists are following in Indira Gandhi's footsteps while forgetting the reality of politics of 2006.

The Congress cannot meet the challenge to Indian secularism in 2006 by playing crypto-secular card of reservations for the Muslim elite. The Hindutva of the Sangh Parivar is a reality and the Hindu Rashtravadis are engaged in destroying every secular institution of the country. But the Congress is completely incapable of answering Hindu communalism with real secularism. Rajiv Gandhi failed to rise to the occasion and socially destructive Ram Temple movement of the Hindutva forces was legitimized when the Congress government allowed Shila Puja at the disputed site in Ayodhya.

Why is the Congress like French bourbons unable to learn any lessons from its past blunders like the Shila Puja? Indian secularism, its theory and praxis, has always been problematic because the Indian model of "parity of religions" for every religion practiced by the Indian state has always led to a situation of the weakening of secularism. The Indian model of secularism of equal protection and promotion of every sect or sub-sect or religion is logically flawed because the Indian state in reality ends up in offering concessions to every religious community as in the case of the AMU Act.

Secularism based on complete neutrality of the state in religious matters has to be practiced if the BJP's Hindu majoritarian politics and the Congress' politics of accommodation of every religions group have to be ejected from public life. The upshot of this is that the crisis of secular politics as witnessed in the fist decade of the Twenty First century should make Indians rethink about the model of secularism, i.e., "religious parity versus religious neutrality".

India has not been able to strengthen secular forces because "confederation of religions" has been a preferred Gandhian model which had failed even to stop India's Partition. The "complete separation of state and religion" is the only viable model in which no secular party can be accused of being pseudo-secular or crypto-secular and secular policies for the poor, irrespective of their religion, replace religion-based preferences and reservations.

–Tribune, March 19, 2006

DISCORDANT ORCHESTRA

A motley crowd of the Congress-led UPA Government has been bumbling like the extremely temporary regimes of V.P. Singh, Charan Singh, Chandra Shekhar, H.D. Deva Gowda and Inder Kumar Gujral in the 1990s. The sole achievement of the Manmohan Singh regime is that it has continued to remain in power for about two years.

The existing confusion was revealed in the manner the Congress and the Government handled the office-of-profit controversy and now the issue of reservation in premier educational institutions. In fact, Congress president Sonia Gandhi became the victim of the incompetence of her party leaders when she had to quit the Lok Sabha on the issue of office-of-profit.

The Congress think tank failed to foresee the impending crisis when Parliament was busy debating Ms. Jaya Bachchan's fate. Her exit was followed by a spate of resignations from Ms. Sonia Gandhi, Karan Singh, Ms. Kapila Vatsyayan, among a few others.

It deserves to be stated that the UPA Government has shown political and legal bankruptcy while handling the office-of-profit issue. The dust was yet to settle down when HRD Minister Arjun Singh announced that the Government had decided to reserve 27 per cent seats for OBCs in educational institutions to fulfill the sprit of the 93rd constitutional amendment of Article 15(5).

The announcement came as a bombshell because the Election Commission was engaged the ongoing process of Assembly elections Tamil Nadu, Pondicherry, West Bengal, Kerala and Assam. The commission immediately served a notice to the government demanding an explanation for such a public policy pronouncement, especially when the Electoral Code of Conduct had been in operation.

Arjun Singh tried to outmanoeuvre the Election Commission when he said that it was just a proposal sent by his Ministry to the Cabinet. How could such a controversial decision be made when the idea is at preliminary stage?

No wonder the Election Commission did not accept Arjun Singh's alibi and asked him to reply on the violation of the Code of Conduct by April 18. Congress spokesperson Abhishek Singhvi observed on April 12: "The Cabinet has not taken any decision on the issue of quota for the OBC." Then why did the HRD Minister jump the queue?

The Cabinet may evolve some criterion to implement the 93rd amendment. In fact, it may not be based on the blanket category of caste-based reservations alone. At the same time, it should be understood that the Congress is managing a coalition of 14 political parties, with the outside support of the Communists. Thus the Council of Ministers has to arrive at a "consensus" on the issue of reservation as coalition partners represent varied and, at times, opposite social constituencies in the country.

One-upmanship seems to have become a fundamental trait in the UPA Government and every minister is a law unto himself. Arjun Singh has either taken the Cabinet decision for granted, or he has cleverly pre-empted any modification of proposals sent by his Ministry to the Council of Ministers for deliberation. The issue is not the manner in which the UPA has handled, or mishandled, the issue. The kernel of the problem is the duality, or even multiplicity, of the centre of authority in the UPA Government.

Manmohan Singh is operating under the reflected glory of Ms. Sonia Gandhi who is undoubtedly the most acceptable leader of the Congress. However, it needs to be clarified that the UPA is a coalition of different parties and the Congress is just "first-among-equals". Moreover, Ms. Gandhi's authority is just limited to 146 party MPs. Worse, the Prime Minister is widely regarded as a leader without mass support.

The UPA had displaced the NDA Government. The secular experiment was expected to be a grand success. It was believed that its performance would desist the voters from supporting the Hindu rashtravadis in future. However, the UPA's record has been uninspiring. A coalition Government at the Centre should have minimum coherence of purpose; and if the Congress is plagued with conflicting individual ambitions of its members, its coalition partners have no reason to accept the leadership of the grand old party.

Today, the UPA is surviving because the BJP is a house in disarray and the idea of Third Front has few takers. A coalition should have minimum coherence, which is absent in the case of the UPA Government. How can this regime govern if its ministers keep themselves engaged in pursuing their petty political agenda?

Yatras of Hindu rashtravadis and petty politics of UPA ministers can provide much entertainment, but it will be without any serious governance. *–Pioneer, April 19, 2006*

CONGRESS ON TIGHT RED LEASH

Prakash Karat, General Secretary of the CPI(M), and Jyoti Basu have demanded that the UPA-led Coordination Committee meeting should be held after the State Assembly Elections in Assam, West Bengal, Kerala, Tamil Nadu and Pondicherry because the government is 'deviating' from common minimum Programme.

Karat during Kerala elections on April 24, 2006 stated that, "After the elections, we are going to examine which Common Minimum Programme the Manmohan Singh Government is going to implement – the one of the UPA, or the one dictated by George Bush. We would like the Government we support to implement the former." Karat observed that "India had thrown to the wind the basic tenets of non-aligned movement" and this is the compelling reason for holding the Coordination Committee meeting after the elections of May 2006.

Prime Minister Manmohan Singh while campaigning in Kerala stated on April 19, 2006 "we are implementing the CMP of the UPA of which CPM is a very important and valuable partner. We have absolute commitment to the CMP in its entirely and it guides the future direction of all our politics".

The real contentious issue that divide the UPA government and the Communist parties is the Pro-American foreign policy pursued by the Central Government. The Communist Parties had organized anti-Bush demonstrations in March 2, 2006 and it was alleged that India should not support an anti-Iraq and anti-Iran policies of the American aggressors. The Left parties have also organized public meetings against the Central Government on its support to the Americans on dispute with Iran on nuclear issues.

The Communists are also opposed to the India-US agreement on nuclear cooperation for civilian purposes.

Why are the Communists supporting the government with which they have basic differences both on domestic and foreign policies? Is common secular agenda of the UPA government and the Communists enough to sustain such a political arraignment at the centre? The Communists parties have a minimalist commonality with the Congress and this is the reason that these two political formations are finding it difficult to cooperation with one another at the level of Central Government. A common struggle against religion-based politics as practiced by the BJP can be a necessary but not a sufficient condition to sustain any kind of 'alliance' between historically well-known opponents like the Congress and Communists. Communists are not only committed anti-religion based politics of the forces of Hindutva, they are also fundamentally opposed to the economic and foreign policies of the Congress party. The Common Minimum Programme was agreed in May 2004 and every Coordination Committee meeting ended up in a patch work and they have temporarily agreed to work together on the plant of defence of secular agenda for Indian politics.

Sonia Gandhi, the real centre of power in the Congress party, during election campaign in Kerala stated on April 18, 2006 that "The United Democratic Front alone can ensure social harmony and development" because "only the UDF has a positive agenda for the state". Communists and Congress are not only electoral opponents, these two political formations represent two different social polls in Indian politics and this is the reason that Chandra Babu Naidu of the TDP. Jayalalithaa of AIADMK, Mulayam Singh of the Samajwadi Party at al have been asking the Communists to follow their traditional politics of forming an anti-BJP and anti-Congress alliance at the Centre. Prakash Karat, in People Democracy, the official organ of the party, has stated that the Third Alternative will emerge on the basis of "joint action" by parties "believing in secularism, pro-people economic policies and anti-imperialism." This according to Prakash Karat "will lead to the emergence of a common platform and ultimately a third alternative". The main purpose of attack by the left parties against the Congress and demand for a meting of the Coordination Committee after the state Assembly elections on May 8, 2006 is to effectively "intervene" in the economic and foreign policies of the UPA government, and also apply "Correctives"; whenever possible, in the directions of policies followed by the Central Government. It does not mean that the Communists have closed their political options by supporting the UPA Government because it has an "open alternative options" of aligning with strong regional parties against the BJP and the Congress. The Communist Parties are working on "Two options" i.e. continue to support the Congress-led UPA government in common struggle against the BJP and also keep their doors and windows open for anti-Congress and anti-BJP political alliance. The primary purpose of the communists at the present is to weaken and defeat the forces of Hindustva represented by the Sangh Parivar and in this political enterprise either ally with the Congress or opt out of the Congress and form a third political alliance to continue struggle against BJP and the Congress. It is a well-known fat that the Congress and the BJP, the only two claimants for all Indian political space, seen to be in an extremely vulnerable political position and possibilities of revival of the Congress and the BJP as formidable all India political force are quite remote. The Congress and the BJP are witnessing a phase of political exhaustion and both these so called all India parties need allies to form any government at the center. And the Congress with just 146 Lok Sabha Members is not in any position to form any government without allies. Are Communist parties awaiting for political developments, which may necessitate the formation of anti-BJP and anti-Congress third alternative alliance of parties. The main strategy of Communist parties is to keep "pressure" on the Manmohan Singh Government by remaining "outside the UPA government". The Communists are overtly or covertly working to create a Third Alternative Alliance and withdraw the support from the Congress-led UPA Government. This is the explanation for the Communist parties demand for the holding of Coordination committee meeting after the State Assembly elections of May 8, 2006 because they want to exert maximum pressure on the UPA Government to follow the CMP in letter and spirit. It is also very clear that the Communists are not closing any "option" and the present "marriage of convenience" between the Congress and the Communists may end any time and lead to political divorce. *–Sahara Time, May 6, 2006*

3

Supporting Parties, Left and Politics

PARTY OF POOPERS: POLITICAL ADVENTURISTS

Aprocess of multiple electoral contests is taking place both in the Lok Sabha and Assembly elections. This phenomenon of free-for-all polls was again demonstrated in Maharashtra on October 13, in which about 2,678 candidates jumped into the electoral battle for 288 Assembly seats. This unending proliferation of contestants in elections is primarily because of the desire of political footloose adventurists to try their luck in the extremely profitable market of electoral politics. A few facts may be mentioned to understand the reality of the growing number of contestants in elections.

First, the decline of the once dominant Congress has created political space for caste, community or language-based social groups to float their own platforms with a purpose to share power with other parties. Several Dalit parties like the Republican Party of India or the BSP of Mayawati or Ram Vilas Paswan's shifting Dalit shops or backward caste and sub-caste parties of Yadavas, Koeris, Kurmis, Thavars or Jats have taken birth to make their limited presence felt. Many of these sectarian caste or community political groups can never win a majority on their own. After all, Mulayam, Lalu, Mayawati or Paswan represent a specific, limited social constituency, and on the basis of limited support for their group, they contest elections, knowing their pretensions to represent entire society are hollow.

In spite of tall claims, every caste or community-based sectional party gets a limited number of seats in the elections although it nominates a large number of contestants under the party symbol. The impact of growing number of parties and small political shops is felt not only on the performance of the Congress, but also on the total result of elections. The Maharashtra elections substantiate the argument that sectional political shops create a situation which logically leads to an "uncertain electoral verdict". The Congress and NCP contested on 157 and 124 seats as partners, and the BJP-Shiv Sena on mere 111 and 163 seats respectively.

Neither of the two coalitions partners are contesting 272 out of 288 seats, which the BSP, a purely UP-based political shop, is doing. Thus the first "spoilers" in the elections are sectarian political shops which contest the largest number of seats only to secure a "limited presence" in elections with a view to making a dent in the social base of major contestants so that no single party or pre-election coalition is able to get a majority. The only purpose of parties like Mulayam's or Mayawati's in Maharashtra is to facilitate the emergence of an "uncertain electoral verdict" by cornering limited votes so that the major contenders are on the horns of a political dilemma about Government formation.

Second, if small and individual leader-based parties are in the business of the lucrative democratic market, a large number of so-called "unattached", "independent" or party "rebel" candidates become visible during the elections and try to win elections on the basis of their personal popularity. Parliamentary democracy functions on the basis of an organised party system with a view to providing a Government and an Opposition. How can any electoral verdict of the voters carry democratic legitimacy where fly-by-night individual candidates are in the playground of elections with a view to damage organised parties? Maharashtra proves that parties like the BSP, Samajwadi or unaccountable "individual" candidates are contesting elections with a clear purpose of making things difficult for the two major parties.

Third, even factional leaders of a party make many so-called independent candidates contest against a party-nominated candidate with a view to hurt the factional strength of the opponent especially after elections. Thus parties and intra-party factional leaders are all involved in elections and the game of electoral politics has become a "lottery" for the winners regardless of their size.

What are the implications for democracy? First, electoral battles do not tell anything about governance after elections. Second, in absence of a clear electoral verdict, the middle men and money-changers jump into the battle of Government formation because every party – major or minor – is engaged in the business of constructing a majority.

It is absurd to maintain that India has entered the era of coalition governments because in reality, India has entered the phase of fragmentation of parties and the encirclement of major parties by growing political adventurists. Political elephants have been reduced to the status of pygmies with the emergence of large number of political shops which have impacted on the electoral process. Can something be done to cleanse democracy of political time-servers and adventurists? – *Sunday Pioneer, October 17, 2004*

TOWARDS AN ALTERNATIVE

George Fernandes, Jaya Jaitley, Subramanian Swamy and Chandra Shekhar met on October 12, 2004, and announced the formation of a group that will act as a 'forum for political deliberations'. The scanty statement issued by these four leaders on October 12, 2004, conceals much more than the public posture depicted. Further, the formation of this 'group of four' should not be dismissed as politically inconsequential or a meaningless activity to gain cheap publicity. George Fernandes is not only a convenor of the weakened National Democratic Alliance, he has been a great champion of 'anti-Congressism' in politics. The greatest advantage of democracy is that public leaders can never hide their real politics.

Chandra Shekhar has not only been a former Prime Minister, he battled Indira Gandhi from within the Congress party as a 'Young Turk' and openly supported Jai Prakash Narayan's anti-Congress and anti-Indira Gandhi Movement in 1974-75.

While George Fernandes or Chandra Shekhar may not have a strong and solid political party organisation behind them, but they definitely occupy an important position in Indian politics and carry great rapport with the fragmented Lohia-JP socialists. Hence the real significance of the coming together of George Fernandes and Chandra Shekhar along with Jaitley and Swamy is to create an anti-Congress political front that will persevere to replace and displace the Manmohan Singh-led United Progressive Alliance government at the Centre.

A few facts may be mentioned to substantiate the argument that the opponents of the UPA government have started working on the creation of political alternative to displace the weak and shaky UPA government.

First, the most important premise underlying the formation of the alternative to the Congress-led government is that the solid bloc of 62 MPs of the Communist parties in the Lok Sabha will withdraw its "outside support" to the government because the Congress and the Communists can never agree on the economic policies of the liberalisers like Manmohan or Chidambaram or Maran and others. Moreover, the Communists have been quite comfortable with anti-Congress governments led by V.P. Singh or Chandra Shekhar or H.D. Deve Gowda or Inder Kumar Gujral and have always played crucial roles in creating anti-Congress Alternative governments at the Centre or the states.

Second, the UPA government cannot be replaced inspite of the fact that the Communists and the Congress marriage of 'inconvenience' is not expected to last long but George Fernandes and Chandra Shekhar have excellent relationships with very formidable socialist leaders like Mulayam Singh Yadav of UP and Lalu Prasad Yadav of Bihar and other socialists in the country to fall back upon for anti-Congress Alternative. It does not require great effort to organise a united group of formidable socialists who are as firmly committed to anti-Congressism as the Communists of India.

The upshot of above description is that the process of forming an Alternative to replace the Congress-led UPA government is on because the Congress with 145 Lok Sabha MPs in a House of 543 members is quite vulnerable because democracy is a game of numbers.

The DMK of Karunanidhi had supported the Vajpayee-led NDA government from 1999 to 2004, and a few months before the April/May 2004 Lok Sabha elections left the NDA, and Jayalalitha of AIADMK came forward to support the BJP. Every regional party has been aligned with one or the other non-Congress or anti-Congress Prime Ministers or coalition governments at the Centre. Chandrababu Naidu of Andhra or one of the DMK's or the Indian National Lok Dal of Om Prakash Chautala or Akali Dal of Parkash Singh Badal or National Conference of Farooq Abdullah et al are willing candidates for any anti-Congress front with a view to form the government at the Centre.

The only nut to crack is Lalu Prasad Yadav and Mulayam Singh Yadav because they have become formidable leaders in Bihar and UP where they have successfully decimated the Congress. While erstwhile socialists are committed to anti-Congressism, these two leaders do not face competition from the dwarfed Congress. George Fernandes and Chandra Shekhar carry great conviction with UP and Bihar leaders of Samajwadi Party and

Rashtriya Janata Dal and it is hoped that with some bargaining both these leaders can be brought into the anti-Congress Alternative political front. – *Sahara Time, November 13, 2004*

CHASING A CHIMERA?

Mulayam Singh Yadav is a diehard Lohia socialist and a compulsive Congress hater. But unlike his political guru, he added the BJP to his list of political opponents. The motive was to float an anti-Congress, anti-BJP Third Front alternative. On January 3, he elaborated that he will form a Third Front at the Centre because the people had rejected the NDA in May 2004 and "now the mood is to reject the UPA". "Therefore, the Third Front is the need of the hour," he said.

Mr. Yadav also maintained that the CPI(M) had not rejected this suggestion. The People's Democracy, CPI(M)'s official mouthpiece, in its editorial on January 6, clearly stated: "Any front that confines itself to political manoeuvring and electoral bargaining does not meet the CPI(M)'s desired objective. For it, a Third Front forged on the basis of people's struggles is the instrument that – while steadfastly defending the interests of the people and the nation – will contribute to a progressive shift in Indian politics."

The real meaning of CPI(M)'s approach to Third Front is that a distance must be maintained between its own politics of people's movements, leading to non-Congress and non-BJP political alternative, and Mr. Yadav's opportunist and conspiratorial politics. It is not just Mr. Yadav, even the CPI(M) has indicted other opportunist parties and leaders for whom the logic of power is a driving force and principles are subservient to the fruits of ministerial and governmental positions.

Then, what is Mulayam Singh Yadav's politics? First, in a Mandalised and casteised society in UP, he is always busy manipulating caste identities to win. Second, he has no hesitation in patronising criminals who are useful allies in winning elections. Third, his party, the Samajwadi Party, is his "pocket borough". Though a so-called believer of socialist democracy, he does not practice internal democracy. He was re-elected party president on January 6. There was none to stand against him. Fourth, Mr. Yadav is ruthless against his opponents. BSP leader Ms. Mayawati has been his special target for political vendetta.

Finally, Mr. Yadav claims to be a practitioner of secular politics. However, this did not prevent him from breaking away from other parties and supporting the BJP-led NDA candidate for the office of the President of India. Mr. Yadav's democratic credentials are doubtful as he is reported to have patronised the Sri Ram Sena of the landlords to take on the Maoists. Ironically, the chief architect of the Third Front does not believe or practice any ideology except that of grabbing power at any cost.

Mr. Yadav is not alone in this game of opportunistic politics. TDP leader Chandrababu Naidu was the national convenor of anti-BJP and anti-Congress Third Front Government at the Centre from 1996 to 1998. But Mr. Naidu's conscience gave away when he supported the BJP-led NDA Government from 1998 to 2004. Both the DMK and AIADMK have practiced politics of shifting alliances from 1996 to 2004. Every erstwhile supporter of Third Front politics has practiced unprincipled and opportunistic politics. Hence, the CPI(M) has clearly stated that it "was not available for mere electoral front."

It is not only Third Front alliance politics, but every coalition government at the Centre — from V.P. Singh to Chandra Shekhar and H.D. Deve Gowda to I.K. Gujaral (or even the two Vajpayee-led Governments from 1998 to 2004) — has been engaged in fire-fighting among the so-called allies. Every coalition government has been a marriage of convenience and every Prime Minister of such shaky alliances was engaged in saving such marriage. Hence, not only does the idea of Third Front alliance politics needs to be completely rejected, even the idea of coalition Government at the Centre should be swallowed with tonnes of salt.

The phenomenon of one Central coalition replacing another has strengthened the idea that India has entered the era of coalition politics. Also the defenders of coalition politics vouch that instead of one-party system, coalition governments are real representatives of regional and sub-regional aspirations of our continent-size democracy. The only binding factor among the coalition partners, whether within the Government or "outside supporters", is the maximisation of political benefits for their small parties or groups with a view to win an election by extending governmental patronage to their caste or communal or regional social constituencies.

A few facts may be mentioned to substantiate the argument that displacement of the once dominant Congress has not done any wonders for India under shaky and unstable coalition governments at the Centre: First, the role of "outside supporters" of the above-mentioned six prime ministers has been extremely harmful for the governance of India because by remaining "formally" outside the government, these supporters have enjoyed political power without any responsibility. Every outside supporter got advantages from the obliging Prime Minister. Do the votaries of coalition government at the Centre approve of politics of unaccountability in a democracy?

Second, every coalition partner, whether numerically large or tiny, followed its own pet politics on issues dear to its heart. Was the Ram temple an agenda of the BJP or of its other 23 partners like the TDP or the BJD? The Sonia Congress is compelled and coerced by the TRS to create a separate Telengana state or face political opposition. Coalition governments have faced coercion and threats from partners with a view to just remain in power — ten months by V.P. Singh, six months by Chandra Shekhar, ten months by Deve Gowda and six months by I.K. Gujaral.

Third, the Council of Ministers of the six coalition governments at the Centre consisted of some ministers who were always busy in the game of belittling the office of the Prime Minister. The Prime Minister of every coalition government at the Centre was involved in fire-fighting to maintain a modicum of stability in a situation which is inherently "unstable", because nothing binds the coalition partners except the fruits of power.

Fourth, every coalition Government at the Centre has experienced not only bitter feuds among its coalition partners, but also witnessed a kind of anarchy among the ruling coalition partners. Ms. Mamata Banerjee of the Trinamul Congress, as an NDA ally, and Sharad Pawar or Lalu Prasad Yadav or Ram Vilas Paswan as allies of the UPA Government, have behaved as "individuals" and as law unto themselves instead of as members of a united council of ministers. Can Manmohan Singh ask Mr. Yadav and Mr. Paswan to stop their war of words or quit the Government?

Finally, votaries of coalition governments have also maintained that a new India has emerged because of the birth of powerful regional parties, groups and political bosses. If the birth of regionalism in Indian politics is a great virtue, it should have been reflected during the Vajpayee-led NDA Government which consisted of 24 allies and partners.

Did the great regionalists in the Vajpayee Government go to sleep when the NDA Government did nothing to protect the hapless Muslims in Gujarat? The explanation for the continuation or collapse of coalition governments at the Centre lies in complete de-ideologisation of regionalists who have abandoned every principle concerning the destiny of the Indian nation.

Principles have been replaced by politics of opportunism, and coalition governments provide a "mask" to every political group to gain legitimacy as partners. India has not entered a virtuous era of coalition politics; nor have the regionalists brought in any new political culture for the governance of the country as a whole. The upshot of above description is that opportunistic ideas on Third Front alternative politics, along with opportunistic coalitions, have greatly harmed the growth of democracy in India.

– *The Pioneer, January 12, 2005*

COALITION AND CONFUSION

The phenomenon of one coalition replacing the other at the Centre has strengthened the idea that India has decisively entered the era of coalition governments at the Centre. Not only this. It is also claimed by the defenders of the system of coalition governments that instead of a one party dominance system, coalition governments are the real representatives of regional and sub-regional aspirations of a country like India.

It deserves to be clearly stated that coalition governments at the Centre led by V.P. Singh or Chandra Shekhar or H.D. Deve Gowda or Inder Kumar Gujaral or Atal Bihari Vajpayee or Manmohan Singh need a very critical analysis because all these Prime Ministers have presided over political marriages of pure convenience. The only binding factor among the coalition partners, whether within the government or as "outside supporters", is maximisation of political benefits for their small parties or groups with a view to win an election by extending governmental patronage to their caste or communal or regional social constituencies.

A few facts may be mentioned to substantiate the argument that replacement and displacement of the dominant Congress has not brought about any wonders for India under shaky and unstable coalition governments at the Centre.

First, the role of 'outside supporters' to the above mentioned 'six prime ministers' has been extremely harmful for the governance of India because by remaining 'formally' outside the government, these supporters have enjoyed political power without any responsibility. If L.K. Advani, an outside supporter of the V.P. Singh government, succeeded in bringing his protégé Jagmohan as governor of J&K, Vajpayee always kept his doors open for a demanding Chandrababu Naidu – be it for special funds, grants and schemes for Andhra Pradesh.

The privileges of power were fully enjoyed by the 'outside supporters' of shaky coalition governments and their recommendations were accepted and acted upon by the 'six Prime Ministers'. Do the great votaries of coalition governments at the Centre approve of such politics of unaccountability in a democracy?

Second, every coalition partner at the Centre, whether numerically large or tiny, followed its own pet politics on issues which were dear to its heart. Atal Bihari Vajpayee, the Prime Minister of India declared that the 'construction of a Ram Temple was based on the national sentiment' of Indians. Was the Ram Temple an agenda of the BJP or of its other 23 partners like the TDP of Andhra Pradesh or Naveen Patnaik of the Biju Janata Dal of Orissa? Is the creation of a new and separate Telengana state in the existing Andhra Pradesh a Congress party agenda or of a 'localist' political outfit of Telengana?

Thirdly, the council of ministers of the 'six' coalition governments at the Centre consisted of some Central ministers who were always busy in the game of belittling the office of the Prime Minister. Morarji Desai's Janata Party rule of 1977-79 gave enough warning that coalition governments cannot have any cohesion within the council of ministers because the leaders of various groups made the life of the Prime Minister quite miserable. V.P. Singh was caught in an extremely difficult situation when his home minister Mufti Mohammad Sayeed and J&K chief minister Farooq Abdullah wanted to follow different approaches to deal with the 'kidnapping' of the daughter of Mufti.

Fourthly, every coalition government at the Centre has experienced not only bitter feuds among the coalition partners, they have also witnessed a kind of anarchy among the partners of the ruling coalition. Mamata Banerjee of the Trinamul Congress as an ally of the Vajpayee coalition, and Sharad Pawar or Lalu Prasad or Ram Vilas Paswan belonging to the UPA government have behaved as 'individuals' and a law unto themselves instead of members of a united council of ministers.

Finally, the votaries of great coalition governments have also maintained that a new India has emerged because of the birth of powerful regional parties, groups and political bosses. If the birth of regionalism in Indian politics is a great virtue, it should have been reflected during the Vajpayee-led NDA government consisting of 24 allies and partners.

– Sahara Time, January 22, 2005

POINT OF DEPARTURE

The BJP and the CPI(M) held their conferences in Delhi recently. However, for the BJP, the after effects of its conference, instead of being positive, proved extremely disastrous when RSS sarsanghchalak K.S. Sudarshan remarked that Atal Bihari Vajpayee and L.K. Advani should quit and make way for the younger generation of leaders. On the contrary, the CPI(M) conference ended on a good note and elected Prakash Karat as party general secretary replacing Harkishan Singh Surjeet. The communists conducted themselves in the best traditions of "inner party democracy".

The BJP, which is always searching for an occasion to celebrate so as to get noticed by the media, held its National Council Meeting on April 5-6 with an ostensible purpose of celebrating its silver jubilee. The CPI(M)'s 18th party congress on April 5, held after every three years, was an occasion for stocktaking of its progress and for spelling out its future programme.

The political messages from these two conferences are very clear. The BJP talked about the polarisation of the Hindutva forces and the all-India Congress party. Party president L.K. Advani said the BJP "is the party of hope" and that the central task for the BJP is "consolidation plus expansion". The party hoped that by the year end (2005) when the party holds its maha adhiveshan in Mumbai, the BJP would be in a position to say it did a good job. Targeting the Congress, the BJP described Manmohan Singh as the weakest Prime Minister of India, as the real repository of power is Congress president Sonia Gandhi.

But the BJP forgets that the boot fits it well because it is only a political extension of the RSS. It is not without reason that BJP chief ministers of Rajasthan, Madhya Pradesh, Gujarat and Chhattisgarh had gone to Nagpur on April 9 to seek instructions from the RSS chief. It should not be forgotten that Mr. Vajpayee, as Prime Minister, always paid "obeisance" to the sarsanghchalak because he, as a swayamsevak, has to accept the supremacy of the

RSS chief and not the Constitution of India. Incidentally, all these meetings between the RSS, the real centre of power, and the elected representatives of the BJP – be it PM, CM, MP or MLA – have to be held in "secrecy and confidentially".

The BJP did not spell out any new political idea. It is still convinced that its brand of anti-Muslim and anti-Christian Hindutva is a winning card. The party shies away when questions like why its Ram Temple agenda did not find any takers even in Uttar Pradesh? Ms. Uma Bharati kept herself away from the conference. Dissidence within the BJP was conspicuous.

The BJP leadership got a tsunamic jolt when RSS chief stated on April 10 that "Vajpayee did not perform well as Prime Minister" and that he could not stop his "family" from interfering in the government business, in addition to his statements mentioned above. He also stated that Vajpayee "...was not among the country's best PM". To add salt to injury, Giriraj Kishore of the VHP stated on April 11 that Mr. Vajpayee merely talked of "aar-paar ki ladai" (fight to the finish) with Pakistan. The assault from its own Parivar has done much damage to the BJP.

In contrast, the CPI(M)'s message was clear. It said Indian politics is not polarised and that the country has a multi-party system and that the CPI(M) will try to form an anti-BJP and anti-Congress Third Alternative. Further, the CPI(M) leadership clarified its reasons for support to the Congress-led UPA Government. The concerns for the CPI(M) are the policies and programmes of different political parties.

Outgoing party general secretary Surjeet said, "While we extend support to the UPA Government to meet exigencies of the current situation, let me make it clear that we will not give up on our basic agenda. We will act as sentinels of the people. We will make independent assessments and decide our course of action." The message was that the CPI(M) will do everything to keep the BJP out of power, and support the UPA Government only to defend the pluralistic character of the Constitution. Jyoti Basu stated that "the people expect the UPA Government to fulfill the commitment to the aam admi".

The CPI(M) devoted its attention to evolve strategies for expansion in North Indian states like Uttar Pradesh and Bihar where it has a negligible presence. Similarly, in the southern states of Andhra Pradesh, Tamil Nadu and Karnataka, the party has to strengthen itself to expand its political reach beyond West Bengal, Kerala and Tripura. The CPI(M) is conscious that it cannot lead a third alternative without expanding its mass base. The party clearly highlighted the serious agrarian crisis prevailing in India and blamed the NDA Government for neglecting rural development. The landless Dalits and poor farming communities continue to suffer. The CPI(M) reiterated its commitment to "land reforms".

Prakash Karat on April 11 said, "Many have commented that our party is having a generational change. Our strength is not centred on personalities. The CPI(M) has a strong collective leadership." He reiterated that the party's efforts will be concentrated on creating a Third Alternative with secular-democratic parties. "It is a difficult task because all region-based parties have been practitioners of political opportunism, personalism and authoritarianism. How can the practitioners of the worst kind of casteist politics be described as democratic?"

Summing up, the BJP and the CPI(M) have sent out sharply different messages. The BJP leadership is completely confused and factionalised and it is expecting miracles. Why is it that the majority of Hindu voters do not support the BJP's brand of Hindutva and the Sangh parivar? The BJP's tired leadership has failed to throw new light on its ideological and political limitations. In contrast, the CPI(M) has clearly and unambiguously clarified its ideology, political line and electoral concerns. Its 18th congress was not a "celebration like the BJP" but was devoted to listen to the voices of its party workers.

Delhi witnessed a study in contrast: Whereas the BJP meeting was devoted to "form", the CPI(M) congress was devoted to "substance". Mr. Advani's declaration that the BJP is a "party of hope" fell flat. But the CPI(M)'s sincere effort involved serious political stock-taking. The BJP leadership is sulking and the CPI(M) is marching on with hope. Will the CPI(M) be able to crack the hard nut of primitive casteism in politics? The third alternative depends on the CPI(M)'s ability to create a large social constituency of popular classes which can transcend narrow casteism and communalism. —*The Pioneer, April 19, 2005*

POLITICS OF TIRED FRONT

A sizeable section of the political class has always been engaged in creating a Third Front political alternative which is anti-Congress and anti-BJP. Notable among them are the Left parties. Indeed, V.P. Singh, Chandra Shekhar, H.D. Deve Gowda and I.K. Gujaral could become prime ministers because the Left was able to keep the Congress and the BJP out of power. Incidentally, these freak governments at the Centre survived with the 'outside' support of either the BJP or the Congress. And whenever these parties withdrew support, the governments fell.

In 2005, the Left changed its policy and announced that it would not forge an alliance with a party that did not subscribe to its ideology. This decision was a result of its experience with Third Front allies. The Left found out that its so-called Third Front allies were political opportunists. This shift in policy has compelled other anti-Congress and anti-BJP parties to reconsider their strategies for the formation of a Third Front alternative in the future. The Left has sent a clear message that it will not be party to opportunistic and shifting Third Front alliances just to keep the Congress or the BJP out of power.

Samajwadi Party chief Mulayam Singh Yadav stated on June 5 that "it was time the Left gave a lead to provide an alternative combine at the national level". He said that an alternative Third Front should be available to the voters and that such an alliance would consist of regional parties.

Sharad Pawar of the NCP, in its convention on June 10 at Surat, announced his party's opposition to the disinvestment policy of the UPA Government. He is a part of the Congress-led Government, but his political ambition to emerge as a leader of future 'alternative' depends on his acceptability to the Left. This is why he is opposing the disinvestment policy of the UPA Government.

L.K. Advani's comments on Mohammed Ali Jinnah and the subsequent political crisis within the BJP and the Sangh parivar have activated some of the allies of the BJP-led NDA because developments within the BJP and the Sangh Parivar have a direct bearing on the political future of the NDA. George Fernandes and Nitish Kumar of the Janata Dal (United) made public statements in support of Vajpayee-Advani leadership because any continuing crisis within the BJP would have a direct impact on the future of JD(U)'s leadership.

Chandrababu Naidu of the TDP had announced that his party could not get the support of Muslim voters because of its association with the BJP-led NDA Government at the Centre. He is now distancing himself from the BJP. Mr. Naidu said on June 9 that he, like Mr. Advani, wanted a debate on Jinnah. In his opinion, Mr. Advani had done nothing wrong by making statements on Jinnah during his visit to Pakistan. The NDA consists of only those parties which can never be with the Congress in their states. This is the logic of anti-Congress or anti-BJP alliances because these two national parties are in competition not only against one another, but also against regional parties.

Secular versus communal politics is the agenda of the Congress, the BJP and the Left. For every other regional party, ideological issues like secularism are simply political tactics.

What this means is that both Mulayam Singh Yadav and Sharad Pawar are looking for an 'alternative' to replace the Congress as the leader of the UPA and establish a non-Congress, non-BJP Third Front to replace the shaky Manmohan Singh Government. Incidentally, a Third Front government, if it gets formed, too will be unstable and temporary.

What is the explanation behind the formation of alliances at the Centre and why are these alliances farcical and temporary? The compulsion of forming alliances at the Centre is that the electoral verdict is completely fragmented. Neither the all-India parties nor the multiple regional parties are getting enough seats to form a stable government.

The UPA consists of major, minor and insignificant parties with a view to creating a workable majority in the Lok Sabha. The publicly-stated goal of the Congress and other groups in the UPA is to keep the "communal" BJP out of power. But past record of regional parties is not at all encouraging because a majority of such parties have never hesitated to form alliances with the BJP.

Not only this. If, on the one hand, some regionalists have felt comfortable in the company of the BJP, others, which are secular pretenders, have extended clandestine support to the party. For instance, Mulayam Singh Yadav in UP is a great champion of non-Congress and non-BJP third alternative, but he is keeping intact his line of communication with the BJP. Further, the socialists and other varieties of Jayaprakash Narayan-inspired Janata Dals have never hesitated in forming alliances with the BJP. Mr. Fernandes is the best example of a socialist sitting comfortably with a communal BJP.

At the national level, anti-Congressism is more important than anti-BJPism because every regional party from Arunachal Pradesh to Jammu & Kashmir has to reckon with the Congress and not the

BJP on its home turf. The Akali Dal in Punjab, the National Conference in Jammu & Kashmir, the Janata Dal (Secular) in Karnataka, the TDP in Andhra Pradesh, the DMK and ADMK in Tamil Nadu, the AGP in Assam are all contenders for power and everyone of them has to confront the Congress in the State.

This is why anti-Congressism has greater appeal to the regional parties. The Communists are supporting the Congress-led UPA Government for the first time because they are ideologically committed against the BJP's politics of Hindutva. The BJP of 2005 is not the Jana Sangh of 1952. BJP-in-Government from 1998 to 2004 has alerted the Communists that Hindutva is a force to reckon with. The party has polarised politics of Himachal Pradesh, Rajasthan, Madhya Pradesh, Jharkhand, Chhattisgarh and Gujarat.

The BJP's growing political influence cannot be contained without involving the Congress in a struggle for anti-communal politics at the national level. The Congress has made subtle concessions to the Hindu sentiment, but it has consistently fought against the Jana Sangh/BJP, and the Communists, as committed anti-communalists, need a national level ally. The Congress is the only available option.

The Congress and the Communists are simultaneously competing and cooperating with each other because of the logic of the growing strength of the BJP in 2005. The Congress and the Communists can be comrade-in-arms on an ideological platform of anti-communalism; the rest of the regional and sub-regional parties have flexible ideologies. Politics of opportunistic alliances is the guiding principle of the regional forces. Every regionalist has tasted the fruits of political power at the Centre and this is the only compelling reason for them to make alliances at the Centre.

The regional and national parties do not have any common cementing factor. This is the reason why the DMK and the AIADMK feel comfortable with both the Congress and the BJP at the Centre depending on their need of the hour. For instance, M. Karunanidhi's DMK has been a comrade-in-arms of both Atal Bihari Vajpayee's NDA and Manmohan Singh/Ms. Sonia Gandhi's UPA.

The upshot of all this is that politics of alliances, coalitions and fronts is based on pure opportunism and self-advancement. Thus all the political alternatives in the 1990s and the 2000s have been farcical political marriages of convenience.

– *The Pioneer, June 16, 2005*

HAMMER AND TONGS: LEFT MEANS BUSINESS

The Manmohan Singh led-UPA Government celebrated one year of its rule with great fanfare mid-May. And hardly a month after their self-congratulatory functions, the Congress has received a stern message from the Communists who have said they would abstain from the UPA-Left front Coordination Committee meetings indefinitely.

The proposed boycott of Coordination Committee meetings by Communists has rattled Ms. Sonia Gandhi and Manmohan Singh who immediately began negotiations with the Left Front leaders to be assured of the latter's active support to the UPA coalition. Prakash Karat, the general secretary of CPI(M), announced on June 26 that the boycott of the Coordinating Committee Meeting was because of serious policy differences.

In a letter to the Prime Minister, the Left Front stated, "Right now we want to give a serious message to the coalition leadership that we cannot be taken for granted on economic policies, especially disinvestment." The announcement by the Government that "it will go ahead with disinvestment in Bharat Heavy Electricals Limited and other public sector undertakings" was the last straw which completely alienated the Communists from the UPA.

The Left Front is concerned that Manmohan Singh, P. Chidambram, Montek Singh Ahluwalia and other reformers in the Congress, by policies of disinvestment of the navratnas, are laying the foundation for "gradual privatisation" and the Left cannot accept this "creeping privatisation" of profit making public sector units. Not only this; the Communists have let known their unhappiness with the UPA Government on price hike of petroleum and its dilly dallying on National Employment Guarantee scheme which has yet to receive parliamentary sanction.

All this led Prakash Karat to state that disinvestment of BHEL was "the first serious violation of the common minimum programme." He concluded his stern statement saying the Left "will continue to extend support to the Government but we do not want to give an impression that there is coordination because there is none." The crux of the matter is that the political understanding between the UPA Government and the Communists has reached a yield point.

It is wrong to conclude that the Communists are distancing themselves from the Congress because in the forthcoming 2006 State Assembly elections in West Bengal and Kerala, the two have to contest against each other. This interpretation shows an ignorance of Communist economic philosophy which is fundamentally different from 'Manmohanomics'. Decisions of globalisation, liberalisation and privatisation have directly hit the poor workers and peasants who happen to be the main constituency of the Communists. At no cost can a political group be indifferent to the concerns of those who play the main role in bringing it to power one election after another.

How can anti-poor and anti-labour class policies of this Government be accepted by a political group representing the poor of India? Unlike the Congress and other bourgeois parties, the Communists cannot act as the gatekeepers of capitalists. The Prime Minister in the National Development Council meeting on June 27-28 admitted that the country was facing serious agrarian crises. The Communists cannot rest assured merely with verbal rhetoric unlike the Prime Minister, seeing that the plight of the rural poor is still not being redressed.

It is not only starvation deaths or the suicides committed by small and marginal indebted farmers which are a testimony to the deep agrarian crisis, it is complete callousness and inaction of the Congress-led UPA Government towards these suffering classes that the Communists cannot accept. It is an overall disenchantment with the Congress on basic economic policies that has brought about the current impasse.

It must be clearly stated that the Communists follow principled national and international policies and their ideological commitment to fight against the forces of Hindutva is the only rationale behind their "outside" support to the Congress-led UPA Government. Religion-based politics is diametrically opposite to the communist ideology of dialectical materialism and secularism.

The opposition of the Communists to religion-based politics is based on their firm commitment to secular and social values. The outside support by Communists to the Congress-led UPA was basically at keeping the forces of Hindutva out of power. Communists are now faced with a predicament. They must support the Congress to keep BJP out of the corridors of power. But at the same time they cannot be taken granted. This time they mean business. – *Sunday Pioneer, July 3, 2005*

RED SUNRISE, SAFFRON SUNSET

It is correct public perception that the BJP and the Communists are ideological puritans who have an elaborate organisational structure to carry forward their ideological and political goals. The BJP is a party of Hindus, by Hindus and for Hindus, while the social constituency of the Left consists of the working classes. The major ideological goal of the BJP is to establish a Hindu rashtra, while the Communists are committed to the liberation of the oppressed.

The BJP and the Left parties are goal-oriented formations that draw support from different social constituencies. No wonder, the two parties are fundamentally different from one another. It is, therefore, essential to analyse their differences in the context of their role in Indian society.

The BJP and the Communists have been well-known for their organisational discipline and capability to resolve their internal differences. The Left parties have 'split' on the basis of their ideological differences alone – the CPI(M) was created because of ideological differences within the CPI. Post-Independence history testifies that the Communists have never fought among themselves for power, and their 'cadre' is ideologically committed and stands united.

Any cadre-based party can have individual deviant cases, and Indian Communists cannot be an exception. The Communists have shown their organisational strength while dealing with internal 'individualistic' tendencies of its politically-ambitious individual cadre, but there is no evidence of washing of dirty linen in public by party dissidents.

The BJP and the Jana Sangh were always known for their ideological and organisational discipline, and the RSS too prided in attracting committed swayamsevaks. In his classic, Political Parties, Maurice Duverger has maintained that "modern political parties" of the 20th century are different from those of the 19th century because modern parties are based on an elaborate party organisational structure of their own.

Robert Merton, an American sociologist, has pointed out that modern parties are led by "party machine and party bosses". In India, the Sangh Parivar and its political face, the BJP, along with the Communists, fulfill the criterion of their "distinct organisational machine", as suggested by Duverger and Merton.

The claims of the Right-wing organisations – that they have dedicated cadre' – have been sustained by their early post-

Independence history. After all, the Jana Sangh/RSS could show the door to Mauli Chandra Sharma and Balraj Madhok when they allegedly crossed the Lakshman Rekha of disciplinary boundaries. Of late, this image of committed cadre seems to have shattered, as BJP chief ministers have been engaged in resolving internal factional disputes in public.

The BJP State governments in Uttar Pradesh, Madhya Pradesh, Chhattisgarh, and Jharkhand have been shifted midstream because of factional revolts within the party. The latest in the list of factional fighting is Ms. Uma Bharati, who has written a letter to RSS chief K.S. Sudarshan criticising the role of the Sangh in the factional tussle within the Madhya Pradesh BJP. Worse, Ms. Bharati has challenged the BJP and the RSS by publicly staking her claim to chief ministership of the State on October 15.

When Jyoti Basu decided to step down as West Bengal Chief Minister, his successor, Buddhadeb Bhattacharjee, stepped into his shoes without any fuss or public controversy. Can the BJP claim such a dedicated and disciplined cadre? The answer to this question is a big 'no'.

It took the BJP, a late entrant to the corridors of power—just a few years in governance—to expose its tall claims of being a committed party. While the Bangaru Laxman case questioned the integrity of BJP leaders as far as corrupt practices were concerned, the spate of indiscipline – from M.L. Khurana to Ms. Uma Bharati – showed that 'absolute power corrupts absolutely'.

Growing indiscipline in the BJP-in-power, unlike the Communists-in-power, proves that theoretical claims of moral superiority by the BJP (or the Communists) should be tested only when they are in power. It is the logic of power that should determine the validity of claims of integrity and discipline. Undoubtedly, it is the BJP's entry in the corridors of power that has ripped open the claims of its dedicated cadre.

The other claim of the two parties – that they are ideologically different – also needs to be examined. The Left has always promoted its essential ideological programme, whether in power or outside. Recently, it walked out of the joint meeting of the UPA coordination committee on the issue of 'disinvestment' of BHEL and other profit-making public sector enterprises. The Left and the Congress have fundamental differences on the country's economic policy.

The Communists are supporting the UPA Government to save the secular fabric of the country; yet they have not abandoned their commitments towards the oppressed classes. Later, they rejoined the coordination committee meetings only after getting a letter from Congress president Sonia Gandhi and Prime Minister Manmohan Singh that reassured them against reckless disinvestment of PSUs.

The Left's 'outside' support to the Manmohan Singh Government did not prevent it from announcing a nationwide strike on September 29 against the Centre's anti-people economic policies. The Communists are following a 'two-legged' policy of support to the UPA Government against the BJP, and also oppose its anti-working class economic policies. They are promoting their ideology, whether in Government or in Opposition.

The BJP, too, has not abandoned its anti-minority policies, whether in power or outside. It has not compromised with its ideological agenda of Hindutva during its regime at the Centre between 1998 and 2004. The Vajpayee-led NDA Government successfully implemented its cultural, educational and political agenda. Though the BJP has always claimed that communal riots take place only during the Congress's regime, it proved hollow when Narendra Modi's Gujarat saw riots in 2002, and the Vajpayee Government remained a mute spectator.

After the formation of the Congress-led UPA Government, a few organisational outfits of the Sangh Parivar criticised the Vajpayee-Advani leadership for failing the Hindu cause during the NDA regime. Is this allegation valid? It does not seem to be so, as the BJP has never abandoned its core Hindutva ideology. In fact, the party showed its firm commitment to the Hindu cause during its regime at the Centre.

The BJP and the Communists have been consistent in their commitment to their basic ideology. The only difference between the two cadre-based parties is at the organisational level: While the BJP workers got corrupted by the logic of power, their Communist counterparts could maintain their integrity in the same or similar context. This is the difference between the BJP and the Communists. – *The Pioneer, October 18, 2005*

SQUABBLING SECULARISTS

Lalu Prasad Yadav has always claimed that only he, as the Chief Minister of Bihar, not only stopped the BJP Rath Yatra for the construction of Ram Temple at Ayodhya in the beginning of 1990s, but he also arrested L.K. Advani who was leading this 'socially divisive Yatra' from Somnath to Ayodhya. Lalu Yadav received voter's support for full fifteen years to rule over Bihar with a clear mandate to checkmate communal forces represented by the Sangh Parivar. Lalu Yadav's journey as a secular Messiah of Bihar came to an end in February 2005 because the voters of Bihar gave a fractured verdict in favour of the RJD-led coalition, JD(U) and BJP, and Ram Vilas Paswan's Lok Jan Shakti party. The voters of Bihar did not give clear verdict in favour of any contender for power, however, the verdict was in favour of the fractured secular forces represented by the RJD, LIP, JD(U), Congress, CPI(M), CPI, and CPI(ML).

A coalition government of secular forces could have been formed if Lalu Yadav, Ram Vilas Paswan and Nitish Kumar, all erstwhile comrades-in-arm in struggle for secularism, could come to a minimum common understanding on an anti-communal platform. An analysis of February, 2005 state assembly elections clearly establishes the point that the voters had voted for secular majority, in spite of their fractured political loyalties. The State Assembly was dissolved by the President on the recommendation of the State Governor on May 23, 2005 because these quarrelsome 'secularists' failed to uphold their tall ideological claims.

The story of fractured and competing secular forces of February 2005 is repeating itself in the State Assembly elections of Bihar in October-November 2005. It is a repeat performance by the political class and a 'triangular electoral contest has taken place for the second time for the State Assembly elections and the political class has not been able to come to any agreement or understanding to evolve a United Front of the secular forces in past eight months or so. A few facts about the disunited and quarrelsome secular groups may be mentioned with a view to understand the tragedy of the forces of secular politics in Bihar.

First, the Left Front which consists of CPI(M), CPI, Forward Bloc and the RSP is caught in the fractional politics of Bihar because all these four Leftist parties work together in the Lok Sabha or West Bengal but they cannot work together in Bihar. It has the distinction of not only dividing only the non-Left secular political formations, but even the Left Allies are not able to contest together in Bihar elections. Second, the RJD and LJP of Bihar are allies of the Congress-led UPA coalition government at the centre, but Lalu Yadav and Ram Vilas Paswan, outside Delhi have become political opponents who are involved in a mutual destructive and suicidal politics in Bihar. Indian secularists are strange bedfellows as revealed by the fragmentation of Left Alliance and the LJP and the RJD in Bihar because the Left Front, the RJD and the LJP can sit together in anti-BJP secular alliance at the Centre, but they cannot take this journey on secular train from Delhi to Patna.

It has been said about democrats of the Western Countries that they are freedom loving in their own country and enemies of freedom in the Third World. It can be said about the Left Alliance, the RJD and the LJP that they are 'secularist' and 'anti-BJP' in Delhi and they forget anti-communal struggle in Patna.

Third, the Congress party is a minor secular force in Bihar politics but it is the only all-India secular formation at the national level. The Congress has also an added advantage of leading the UPA government at the Centre in which all secular forces are fully represented. Why did Congress fail to resolve the personal egos of secularists like Lalu and Paswan and act as a catalyst for the formation of United Secular Front in Bihar? The Congress failed because it was not perceived as an honest broker and a neutral umpire between Paswan and Lalu because Lalu with 28 MPs and Paswan with 4 MPs are 'unequal' at the central coalition arrangement. It is clear that Lalu's RJD gets hurt by Paswan's LJP during the Bihar State Assembly elections because Paswan is competing against Lalu on a similar platform of support from Backward multiple castes and sub-castes and Muslim community voters. The voters of Bihar have given a clear verdict in favour of secularism. Yet this could not become effective because of rivalry among messiah of secularism like Lalu and Paswan. Secularists, indeed, betray cohesion despite the risks involved.

– Sahara Time, November 26, 2005

AN INHERENTLY WEAK COALITION

The UPA government at the Centre has completed 18 months in office. Its journey has, however, not exactly been smooth. The UPA is much more than a coalition of 14 parties, groups and individuals, though. Apart from managing its disparate constituents, it also has to do business with Mulayam Singh Yadav's Samajwadi Party and the Communists on whose outside support it depends heavily for its survival.

It is obvious, therefore, that such a coalition would have a rather rough ride. Manmohan Singh, in an interview to Rajat Gupta of McKinsey, had stated: "We are a coalition government and that limits our options in some ways.... Privatisation happens to be one such area." He went to say, "I must confess to you that in the prevailing milieu, the thinking in our coalition is that for enterprises that are doing well under competitive conditions, we must have a special justification to prove to our coalition colleagues that there is need for privatisation." But has the PM given us the whole truth about his predicament?

Each of the 14 parties, groups, which constitute the coalition, evidently want to use their presence in the government to promote their own interests, which often enough have little or no correspondence. The blame for all the government's acts of omission and commission, as a consequence, has become the Congress's headache.

That is the story from inside the coalition. The government's dealings with its 'outsider' supporters, mainly the Left parties, have turned out to be no better. The Left and the UPA have in place a 'panel' to jointly oversee the implementation of the Common Minimum Programme (CMP), which was forged on a supposed consensus between the various outfits that constitute the alliance and its outside supporters. The actual working of this panel, however, has not only been smooth, but appears to have brushed consensual functioning against its grain. Recently, there was a deadlock in the coordination panel after the Communists walked out of it because of serious differences with the government on disinvestment and privatisation of profit-making PSEs.

The essential reason for such paralysing acrimony is not far to be found. Congress, the principal player in the UPA, and the Communists have fundamentally different ideological approaches and social constituencies. Thankfully, though, the Left 'boycott' of the coordination panel has ended, and it is back to business as usual. The routine of coordination committee meetings, between the government and the Left parties, has been restored. Nevertheless, the gulf between the two on crucial economic issues, as also the orientation of foreign and defence policies, has remained as unbridgeable as ever.

To figure out the origins of the UPA government's current predicament, it is important that one examine the various coalition experiments that India has seen. The country has been witness to some successful coalition governments, especially in states. A coalition can survive well only if parties that constitute it form a pre-election alliance on the basis of a well defined common minimum programme. It's precisely this that is responsible for the enduring success of coalitions in West Bengal and Kerala.

Other more recent instances of similarly successful coalitions have been the Nationalist Congress Party-Congress government in Maharashtra, which rode to power and has retained its grip on it, by basing its unity on a cogent and programmatic opposition to the BJP-Shiv Sena alliance. Nitish Kumar of the Janata Dal (United) and the BJP routed Lalu Yadav in Bihar by evolving consensus on an agenda of governance that it has projected as an alternative to Lalu's populist misrule.

The one common lesson that all these coalition experiments offer is that partners in a political alliance must have ideological convergence on some key and fundamental issues if they are to remain united in power. The UPA government, unfortunately, fails to fulfil even the most basic pre-condition of a durable coalition; it is not a product of any pre-poll alliance of parties and groups. It is more akin to the freak phenomenon that various so-called United Front coalition governments of the '90s epitomised. All those governments were products of accidents of India's political history, and their political transitoriness is best captured by their rather short-lived tenures. The UPA government, by the look of it, is destined to either follow its freakish predecessors in having a rather short life, or, live longer by lurching precariously from one crisis to another.

That a Congress-led government is cooperating with the Communists for the first time in the history of post-Independence India must, nonetheless, be underscored here. That it is largely because they want to keep their common enemy, the Hindutva-peddling BJP, out of power should, however, be equally emphasised. The Left parties of India are unambiguously committed to fight the vicious and dangerous politics of the forces represented by Hindutva, and this has been a compelling enough reason for them to come together with the Congress. It does not, however, mean that the Communists are ready to sacrifice their fundamentals while supporting an anti-BJP government. The Congress and the Communists know all too well that the issue that unites them is as important as the ideological fundamentals which divide them, and which have kept them apart for more than 55 years.

The real weakness of the UPA government, in such circumstances, lies in the incapacity of the Congress to truly fulfil its role as leader of the coalition. That it has 144 MPs in a house (Lok Sabha) of 543 members has not helped matters.

The crisis-ridden UPA government's weakness certainly stems from the fact that it is a conglomeration of disparate groups. And the Congress's inability to demand its right of leadership from its partners, because of its precariously small numerical presence in Lok Sabha, has further complicated matters. Manmohan Singh is handicapped, not so much by the diverse clamour of his partners and supporters, but because the Congress, no thanks to its below par electoral performance in 2004, is not in the driver's seat.

– *The Economic Times, December 24, 2005*

FRIENDS AT THE CENTRE, FOES IN THE STATES: ASSEMBLY ELECTIONS 2006

The Assembly elections in Assam, Tamil Nadu, Kerala, Pondicherry and West Bengal have been formally announced by the Election Commission of India on March 2, 2006 and the Code of Conduct for elections to be followed by all political contenders has been enforced to keep the ruling parties under proper check. It is essential to refer to the necessity of a Code of Conduct because the holding of free, fair and fearless elections has become a Herculean task and it was reflected when the West Bengal Left front Government strongly protested against the election commission's decision to hold elections for 294 Assembly seats in 'five phases' on April 17, 22, 27, and May 3 and 8, A general impression exists among the political opponents of the Left Front that the Communist-led government has sophisticated methods of rigging elections with the support of a partisan bureaucracy and active communist party cadres. The Election Commission has decided to hold elections for 140 seats in Keralas in three phases on April 22, 29 and May 3 and the Assam Assembly with 126 seats will witness elections on April 3 and 10. The sole exception to these staggered schedules is Tamil Nadu where elections will be held on May 8 for 234 seats.

The Left parties are quite upset with such discriminatory treatment by the Election Commission between Tamil Nadu which will witness elections on only one day and West Bengal will remain engaged in elections in five phases form April 17 to May 8, 2006. The upshot is that political controversies have already begun. Further, these State Assembly elections are not only important for every political player and competition but more so for the Communists and the Congress because these two secular formations will be 'confronting' one another in spite of the fact that the Communists are supporting from the 'outside' the Congress-led UPA Government at the Centre. The Congress as the real and only all-India party and has always been involved in bitter political and electoral struggles against the Communists especially in Kerala and west Bengal and the formation of the UPA government at the Centre cannot bring to an end this traditional political rivalry at the time of elections for either the State Assemblies or the Lok Sabha. Mamata Banerjee of the Trinamool Congress has formed an 'alliance of small groups' to oppose the CPM-led alliance and the Congress has declined to join Mamata Banerjee's alliance because the BJP, a real ideological opponent of the secular Congress is associated with Mamata's Alliance. Thus a 'triangular' content in West Bengal is necessitated by the Congress' ideological anti-BJP position and Mamata refusal to part company with the BJP.

Kerala is politically polarised between the Congress-led United Democratic front and Communist-led Left Democratic Front and the voter in this state has always opted for one or the other front. A new development in Kerla is the emergence of a 'splinter' group named the Democratic Indira Congress led by K. Karunakaran. an erstwhile united Congress party leader. The Kerala political society, unlike West Bengal, is infected by communal politics at the fringes but the RSS/BJP and a small section of Muslim fundamentalists have never been able to make any dent in the 'vote bank' of the two Fronts.

In Assam, the State Assembly elections are contested on highly 'emotive issues' of the presence of a sizeable Bengali population and also Bangladeshis who find it quite easy to enter Assam because of the 'porous' border between two neighbouring state. The Assam Congress party which is now in power is primarily opposed by the Asom Gana Parishad (AGP) which champions the cause of anti-Bengalis and the pro-Assamese Indigenous population. The polit-buro of the CPM at its meeting on March 12 decided to form a non-Congress and non-BJP alliance with the AGP. The BJP and RSS have some presence in Assam with the present State Assembly having eight BJP MLAs out of the total strength of 126 members. The presence of the BJP/RSS in Assam has led to communalisation of the difficult problem of Bangladesh migrants, but inspite of this.

Assamese society has not accepted communal BJP as an alternative to the Congress or the AGP.

If Kerala, West Bengal and Assam are involved in electoral politics of multiple alliances in Tamil Nadu the political space is divided between the DMK and the AIADMK and small splinter groups following either of these Dravidian political formations. The most interesting feature of these elections is that the UPA Alliance partners are engaged in electoral battles against one another in the State and MDMK's Vaiko has walked out of the DMK Front to join the AIAMMK-led plat-from. The MDMK walking out of the DMK-led alliance on the eve of the elections has created a ridiculous situation. Partners of the UPA Government at the Centre are contesting against their own comrades-in-arms in the states. How can Vaiko sit with Jayalalaithaa who will target the Central Government as the real villain of the piece for neglecting the interests of Tamil Nadu? This story of comrades-in-arms opposing one another is the hard reality of State Assembly election in Kerala, West Bengal, Tamil Nadu and Assam.

An important larger question facing Indian politics is about the very 'rationale' of a coalition Government at the Centre because nothing seems to be binding the partners of the UPA Central Government. The divisions among 'partners' are more important than unifying factors holding the UPA Government together at the Centre. The Communist parties are the main contenders for power against the Congress and they are already involved in a bitter struggle against the UPA Government's Pro-American foreign policy. While the protests witnessed during Bush's visit to India or against a Danish newspaper's publication of a cartoon of Prophet Mohammed have come to an end, the electoral battles will be fought by the Communists against the Congress on its pro-USA policies also on its vote on the Iran nuclear issue at the IAEA. The Congress party has not only to defend its two important state Governments in Kerala and Assam, it is also bound to challenge the Communists in West Bengal and the AGP and its allies in Assam.

Kerala. West Bengal, Assam and Tamil Nadu are politically very conscious states and voters in these states have high level of 'commitment' to one or the other party. This leads to a very volatile situation during elections. The issue of the legal process of identification of Bangladeshis in Assam has created sharp divisions between the congress and the AGP and other splinter local groups and elections have always led to 'polarisation' of voters on purely local, regional in Assam cannot be an exception to this rule.

The State Assembly elections of 2006 have a national significance because the Congress party is engaged in a life and death struggle not only to save its two state Governments in Assam and Kerala but also to put up a credible performance in Tamil Nadu, Pondichery and West Bengal. The focus will be on the electoral performance of the Congress because any weakening in its position in the major southern and eastern states will directly impact its standing as the leader of the UPA Government at the Centre. The BJP has a minor role in these states and any electoral victory for this party is just a 'political bonus' but the Congress is in the reckoning and the electoral verdicts in these states will have a direct impact on its political standing and credibility in the whole country. This is the real significance of the State Assembly election of 2006. – *Sahara Times, March 25, 2006*

CAUTION: LEFT HAND DRIVE

A very significant feature of the five Assembly elections was that pre-election alliances were formed in West Bengal for 294 seats, Kerala for 140 seats, Tamil Nadu for 234 seats, Pondicherry for 30 and Assam for 126 seats.

Some elaboration of pre-election alliance politics in these states is required to understand the relationship between the all-India parties like the Congress and the BJP with the regional and sub-regional political formations. A distinctive feature of West Bengal and Kerala politics, repeated in 2006, was that the Left-led Front and the Opposition were competing against one another for the last almost three decades.

The Communist parties have dug deep roots in these two states and their competitors like the Congress and the Trinamool Congress of Ms. Mamata Benerjee, have to form alliances to contest. The Communist-led alliance has almost become "irreplaceable" in West Bengal but in Kerala, the Congress versus the Communist alliance has successfully competed against one another. Now, the Left-led grouping has replaced the Congress alliance in Kerala.

In Tamil Nadu, the Democratic Front led by M. Karunanidhi has displaced the ADMK-led front of Ms. J. Jayalalithaa. The Congress had tied itself with Mr. Karunanidhi and the DMK-led Front's electoral victory is quite beneficial to the Congress-led UPA Government at the Centre. After all, the DMK is a part of the UPA Government at the Centre. Their association will create a new spirit of harmony between the Centre and the State Government.

An important feature of verdict 2006 was that the voters renewed their faith in the Left Front Government in West Bengal but preferred alternatives in Kerala and Tamil Nadu. Results in Assam derive to be very carefully analysed because it is a "socially disturbed" State and politics is not only volatile but also violence ridden.

The Congress in Assam has maintained a decisive lead over its regional competitor like the AGP, as also communal forces represented by the BJP and a sectarian Muslim organisation under the banner of Assam Untied Democratic Front led by State Jamait Ulema-e-Hind president Maulana Behadruddin Ajmal. The growth of the BJP in Assam is extremely worrisome because with its pro-Hindu and anti-Muslim agenda, it can play havoc with its fragmented fabric. Sensitive problem of Bangladeshis deserves careful handling.

The BJP has openly stated that Muslim Bangladeshis should be "deported" and Hindu Bangladeshis should be "protected" as refugees. This can play havoc in Assam because the issue of Bangladeshis is complex.

If Hindu communalism is attempted to take deep roots in Assam, as shown by this electoral verdict, the Shahi Imam of Jama Masjid Syed Ahmed Bukhari campaigned against the Congress in Assam on the plank that the voters should "ensure the defeat of the so-called secular parties, which have always exploited the minority". Are minorities losing confidence in the capacity of secular parties to safeguard their legitimate interests?

In south, the electrical space is polarised between two fronts, the regional and national. The Congress in Kerala, Tamil Nadu and Pondicherry ahs arrived at a working relationship with regional political formations. But in north, particularly Assam, the party is unable to form a strong coalition with sub-regional parties. The AGP has emerged in opposition to the Congress on the specific issues of the presence of "foreigners" and AASU and AGP have projected Congress as a protector of "outsiders".

Hence, the Congress and AGP/AASU do not have any meeting ground while in the south, the party has been able to form workable coalition because its opponents are not raising "emotive" political issues.

The Congress and BJP must either compete against the regional parties or form alliances with them for Assembly elections. The five verdicts clearly state that the voters have maintained a proper balance between the national and State-level parties. Ms. Sonia

Gandhi's contesting as a candidate in Rae Bareli added the national dimension and the democratic verdict of the elections 2006 is not on "State versus national". Rather, it is in support of the states and national politics and the same time. This is where its importance lies.–*Pioneer, May 16, 2006*

A MEANINGFUL VERDICT

Though Prime Minister Manmohan Singh ahs hailed the verdict of elections as a victory of secular forces and Untied Progressive Alliance, the end of struggle for power is going to be confined at best to the five States that went to polls. And the story at the Centre may turn out to be quite different. Not sooner than the results were announced, the Left that significantly gained in the polls stalled the move to hike petrol, diesel, kerosene and LPG prices.

Yet in West Bengal, Kerala, Tamil Nadu, Pondicherry the victorious and the vanquished have accepted the verdict of the electorate of May 11, 2006. A very important feature of April/ May 2006 polls is the pre-election alliances were formed in West Bengal for 294 seats, Kerala for 140 seats, Tamil Nadu for 234 seats Pondicherry for 30 and Assam for 126 seats.

A distinctive feature of West Bengal and Kerala politics, which ahs been repeated in 2006, is that the Left-led front and opposition-led front, have been in competition against once another for the last about three decades. The Communist parties have dug deep roots in these two states and their competitors like the Congress or the Trinamool Congress of Mamata Banerjee have to form alliances to face the Communists. The Communist led Alliance has almost become 'irreplaceable' in West Bengal but in Kerala the Congress versus the Communist alliance has successfully competed against one another and in 2006, Communist alliance has replaced and defeated the Congress Alliance in Kerala. The story of West Bengal elections is quite interesting because Mamata Banerjee of the Trinamool Congress was projected as real competitor against the Communists but in 2006 elections it is not only that Mamata Banerjee has lost her appeal, her party has not crossed even the figure of 40 seats in an Assembly of 240 seats. West Bengal has voted for ideologically oriented Left Front and Mamata has been found ideologically bankrupt and this is the reason for her political eclipse.

The United Democratic Front led by Mr. Karunanidhi has replaced and displaced the AIADMK led front in Tamil Nadu and J.Jayalalitha has been made to vacate her seat in power as Chief Minister. The Congress party had tied herself with M. Karunanidhi in Tamil Nadu State Assembly elections of 2006 and the DMK-Led Front's electoral victory is quite beneficial to the Congress-led UPA government at the Centre because DMK is a part of this coalition government. The DMK led government in Tamil Nadu and DMK's association with the UPA government at the Centre may well create a new spirit of harmony between the Centre and the State government and it will bring to an end acrimony between Jayalalithaa led government and the Centre.

A very important feature of the electoral verdict is that the voters have renewed their faith in the Left-Front government in West Bengal, but, the voters have preferred alternative governments in Kerala and Tamil Nadu where the incumbent parties and Chief Ministers have been replaced by their opponents and competitors. Electoral verdict in Assam deserves to be very carefully alanysed because it is a 'socially disturbed' state and politics in this state is not only volatile but also violence ridden. The Congress party in Assam has maintained a decisive lead over its regional competitor like the Assam Gana Parisha, but the communal forces represented by the BJP and a sectarian Muslim organisation under the banner of Assam Untied Democratic Front (AUDF) led by State Jamait Ulema-e-Hind President Maulana Bahadurddin Ajmal have succeeded in creating a political space for themselves. The growth of BJP in Assam is quite important because with its pro-Hindu and anti-Muslim agenda, it can find ideal playground play in Assam given its fragmented social fabric of Assam. Assamese society needs a healing touch and very sensitive problem of Bangladeshis in Assam deserves to be tackled with great care. The BJP has openly stated that Muslim Bangladeshis should be 'deported' and Hindu Bangladeshis should be 'protected' as refugees. This line of reasoning can play havoc in Assam because issue of the presence of Bangladeshis is quite complex. If Hindu communalism is attempting to take deep roots in Assam, as shown by this electoral verdict, the Shahi Imam of Jama Masjid Syed Ahmed Bukhari campaigned against Congress party in Assam on the plank that the voters should 'ensure the defeat of the so-called secular parties, which have always exploited the minority'.

Congress in Kerala, Tamil Nadu and Pondicherry has arrived at a working relationship with regional political formations and unlike the southern states, Congress is not able to form a formidable coalition with sub-regional parties in Assam. The Assam Gana Parishad has emerged in opposition to the Congress on the specific issue of the presence of 'foreigners' in Assam and AASU and AGP have projected Congress as a protector of outsiders like Bangladeshis in Assam. Hence, Congress and the AGP/AASU do not have any meeting ground in Assam, while in the Southern states, Congress has been able to form workable coalition because its opponents are not raising any highly 'emotive' political issue, Jayalaitha of the AIADMK had launched a campaign against the DMK and its launched a campaign against the DMK and its alliance partner the Congress, on the issue of step-motherly treatment by the Central government and it cannot be an emotion issue.

The verdict of the five Assembly elections is clear that the voters have maintained a proper balance between the all-India parties and also specific state-based parties during the elections. The voters in the five Assembly elections have not given a clear verdict in favour of state-level parties and they have not ignored the presence of all-India parties in their states. Sonia Gandhi's presence in these elections as a candidate in Rae Bareily has clearly added national dimensions during the elections and democratic verdict is not like state versus all-India, it is in support of states and national politics. Both call for strong leaderships despite the coalitions winning or loosing. The undercurrents of this can well be sensed in Ajit Jogi's demand for Sonia Gandhi taking over as Prime Minister. It is important that each party, and more so the Congress resolves its internal crisis and contradictions to come up to the people's expectations.–*Sahara Time, May 20, 2006*

4

Bharatiya Janata Party, Hindutva and Allied Parties

WHAT IS THE BJP'S POLITICAL FUTURE?

The BJP's electoral defeat in the Lok Sabha elections in April-May 2004 and in the Maharashtra assembly polls of October 2004 has stirred a hornet's nest. The party of fanatic Hindutva is now completely preoccupied with trying to formulate future strategies of political revival. In short, it's worrying itself over how it would stage a comeback at the Centre. The BJP has undertaken an internal cleansing process by holding chintan baithaks. And the organisational reshuffle that it conducted recently, with old warhorse L.K. Advani being brought in once again as party president, is with the express purpose of rejuvenating its political machine. The question, however, is, has the BJP introspected enough and properly ascertained the reasons behind its electoral defeats? Would a simple leadership change be enough to restore its electoral health?

It is essential to state here that the BJP is not like any other centrist or regional party, and any meaningful understanding of its future prospects is possible only by locating the salient features of this 'party with a difference'. The BJP, the Sangh parivar's political mask, is involved in electoral politics with a clear goal of establishing what it calls Hindu Rashtra. Every activity of the sangh fraternity, including the BJP, is directed towards capturing state power and the transformation of civil society with the sole purpose of refashioning India into a Hindu nation. And BJP-led governments, both at the Centre and in states, have used governmental authority to effect the Hinduisation of civil society.

The greatest achievement of BJP governments has been to convey a clear message to minority communities that they have to accept the definition and practices of Hindutva as laid down by the parivar and its governments. It is not without reason that Atal Bihari Vajpayee, as prime minister, had declared that the construction of Ram Temple, an integral part of the parivar's agenda, was a 'national sentiment', because in its scheme of things the Indian nation can't be anything else but Hindu. It is not surprising that Advani, in his coronation ceremony as party president on October 27, 2004, declared that Ram temple will be constructed. He also stated that this goal of Hindutva would have been achieved if the BJP had been re-elected.

Vajpayee, as prime minister, desired a national debate on religious conversions, a pet theme with fanatic Hindus, to confront the Christian missionaries. It is erroneous to maintain, therefore, that the BJP becomes moderate while in power and a militant fanatic force while mobilising voters for elections. The shadow-boxing among the various fraternal constituents of the Sangh is for the mass media's consumption. An electoral defeat for the BJP is just a temporary set-back, because every member of the parivar, the BJP included, inside or outside the government, are always engaged in strengthening the roots of their ideology of Hindutva in every institution of civil society. Democratic elections are a 'necessary evil' for the Sangh, because the Constitution, though not to its liking, is a fundamental law of the land. Governance, therefore, is not the be-all and end-all as far as the parivar is concerned. Its final aim is Hinduisation of civil society.

The Sangh parivar is a whole and while some of its parts manage shisu mandirs, others work towards the Hinduisation of tribals. There are yet others, pracharaks like Narendra Modi, who have been assigned the responsibility to man the levers of governmental power. Hence it would be quite misleading to maintain that Vajpayees or Advanis or Modis are 'moderate' while in government and turn their coats when in Opposition. It is no accident that Vajpayee and Advani, as leaders of the central government, attended the pubic coronation of Narendra Modi after he had been re-elected as chief minister of Gujarat. The message is loud and clear: the Supreme Court's indictment of the Modi government "as Neros" during the post-Godhra riots in Gujarat in 2002 has no significance for Vajpayee, the prime minister of the Sangh parivar.

Hindutva stands for a 'polarised India, and every swayamsevak, whether prime minister or chief minister, has to work for it. That is the real face of the BJP and its prospects for electoral victories are bright if social cleavages are widened and sharpened by the parivar. – *The Economic Times, November 2, 2004*

KEEP RELIGION PRIVATE

The arrest of the Shankaracharya of Kanchi Kamakoti Peetham, Sri Jayendra Saraswati, on charges of abetting the murder of Sankararaman, the manager of Sri Vardarajaswamy Temple, by the Tamil Nadu Government, has invited the ire of a large number of devotees, both in India and abroad. The arrest of such a revered person is extraordinary and a very sad event for millions of believers. The decision of the State Government to implement the law of the land has created a storm in the political class because its fallout will be felt by every major political party, leader and group.

One of the questions being raised is, how could a democratic, secular and constitutional republic dare to hurt the religious feelings of its Hindu believers by arresting the Shankaracharya under the ordinary laws of the land meant for ordinary criminals? The action of a secular state in implementing its legal rights and, in the process, affecting the religious sentiments of the believers, is bound to create a political earthquake.

Every political party under the Representation of Peoples' Act is expected to perform its duty to defend the law of the land without caring about adverse political consequences. However, this has not happened in the present case. The political class is divided; the public postures of its representatives are either in defence of the rule of law or against it, as in the current case. What is the significance of such a polarised opinion among the major political parties? The Prime Minister has stated that the Central Government is not "involved" in this decision of the State Government and he has clearly implied that the law will take its own course even when dealing with the Shankaracharya. The Left parties, RJD and DMK shares the same view. Some have played a clever game by either keeping quiet or by pretending to be neutral.

The BJP and every other organisation linked with the RSS also represent formidable public opinion in the country. What has been the reaction of the "holy joint family" of the Sangh Parivar? The arrest of Shankaracharya has once again showed that the forces of Hindutva have an "uneasy" relationship with Indian democracy: First, the RSS has always maintained that all its affiliates are "cultural" organisations baring the BJP, which is a political party. While opponents of the Hindu parivar have never accepted the "non-political" and "cultural" claims of the RSS, the Shankaracharya's arrest has brought all important outfits of the Sangh, including the BJP, on the streets in united opposition against the action of the constitutionally elected State Government.

Second, the BJP, as a political party, stands exposed because it is expected to defend the rule of law and not oppose the legal and normal activities of any State Government. Just after the news of the arrest, former Prime Minister Atal Bihari Vajpayee and a senior member of the Lower House stated that the manner in which the seer was arrested has hurt the sentiments of the people of the country. Mr. Vajpayee, who is under oath to defend the Constitution, is not expected to criticise the legal rights of a State Government.

Third, many Ministers, MPs and MLAs, especially of the "Hindu family", are involved in mobilising protests and demonstrations against the seer's arrest, in defence of the "hurt feelings of the Hindus" and not in defence of the rule of law.

Fourth, NDA convener George Fernandes stated that "it is unfortunate" and he (Shankaracharya) "did not deserve that kind of treatment". Where does the NDA stand regarding "treatment" meted to law-breakers? This clearly establishes that the BJP and the Sangh give more importance to Hindu religious priests and symbols rather than the rule of law.

Promoting the cause of religious "priest" in public life is very harmful to the secularisation process of Indian society, where public life has to be separated completely from the private beliefs of religious preachers and practitioners. Do critics of Shankaracharya's arrest accept the notion that there are different categories among citizens who break the law?

The BJP is caught on the horns of a dilemma. It is bound under the Constitution to stand by the law and not by the religious affiliation and special status of a citizen alleged to be a law-breaker. The country is on trial because it must act as guardian and defender of the law of the land and also face hostility by the legally constituted political parties which are completely disunited on this "First Principle" of a democratic Constitution. This is because a few parties are projecting the doctrine of religion-based hierarchy of citizens, as opposed to the law of the land.

– Sunday Pioneer, November 21, 2004

PRIESTS AND POLITICS

The Shankaracharya of the Kanchi Kamakoti Peetham, Sri Jayendra Saraswati has been 'arrested' on charges of 'abetting' the murder of Sankararaman, manager of the Sri Varaderajaswamy' Temple. The arrest has created a big storm in the political class because the political fallout of such an event will be felt by every major political party, leader and group. The political class and political parties are completely "divided" amongst themselves and their public postures are either in defence of the rule of law as applied to the Shankaracharya or some of them have publicly condemned and criticised such an action of the state government.

What is the significance of such a polarised opinion among the major political parties of India which have to act as defenders of the processes of the law of the land. The Prime Minister has stated that the central government is not 'involved' in this decision of the state government and he has clearly implied that the 'law will take its own course even when dealing with the Shankaracharya. The Communist parties, the Rashtriya Janata Dal of Lalu Prasad and the DMK have also supported the doctrine that the 'law of the land should take its own course.' A few political leaders belonging to the mushrooming regional, sub-regional and casteist parties have played a 'clever' game by either keeping quiet or pretending to be neutral.

What has been the reaction of the Holy Joint Family of the Sangh Parivar? A few facts may be mentioned to substantiate the argument that the arrest of the Shankaracharya has once again revealed that the forces of Hindutva have an 'uneasy' relationship with Indian democracy which is a 'necessary evil' for the Parivar. First, the RSS has always maintained that all its affiliates are 'cultural' organisations and the BJP alone is a political party. While the opponents of the Hindu Parivar have never accepted the 'non-political' 'cultural' claims of the RSS, the Shankaracharya's arrest has brought out all important outfits on the action of the constitutionally elected state government. Second, the BJP, as a political party in a democracy, stands exposed because it is expected to defend the rule of law and not to oppose the legal and normal activity of any state government in arresting a person including the mighty Holy Shankaracharya. Just after the news of the Shankaracharya's arrest, Atal Bihari Vajpayee stated that 'the manner in which the religious guru has been arrested has hurt the country'. Vajpayee who has taken the oath of defending the

Constitution and the rule of law is not at all expected to criticise the legal right of a state government on the plea that the arrest has 'hurt national feelings.' Third, many ministers, MPs and MIAs, especially of the Hindu Family are involved in organising protests and demonstrations against the Shankaracharya's arrest. In a democracy, every political party and leader has a right to organise demonstrations and protests but in a specific situation of the arrest of the Shankaracharya, the protests are being held by political leaders in defence of 'hurt feelings of the Hindus' and not in defence of the rule of law. Fourth, the BJP-led NDA convener George Fernandes stated that 'It is unfortunate. He (Shankaracharya) did not deserve that kind of treatment.' Where does the NDA stand regarding the 'treatment' meted to law-breakers in India?

It is not recognised by the BJP, a pure political party, that promoting the cause of a religious 'priest' in public life is very harmful to the secularisation process of Indian society where public/political life has to be separated completely from the private beliefs of religious preachers and practitioners. The BJP is on the horns of a dilemma because it is bound to act as a defender of the rule of law under the Constitution and it is expected to stand by the 'law' and not by the religious affiliation and special status of a citizen who is alleged to be a lawbreaker. The Indian state is on trial. – *Sahara Time, December 11, 2004*

HINDUTVA VS. SECULARISM

Congress president Sonia Gandhi is solely responsible for reviving the party. She had inherited a completely deformed and de-ideologised Congress – indistinguishable in its politics from the casteists and sectarians like Ms. Mayawati and Mulayam Singh Yadav, or the communalists represented by the BJP. Ms. Gandhi accepted the challenge of injecting life into the lifeless party. She believed in a competitive party system, where every party must stand for its belief system, clearly distinguishable from its opponents. This stands in contrast to the political climbers of the Congress during 1990s, who were willing to play casteist or communalist politics for winning elections.

If Ms. Gandhi had to revive a party that was politically comatose, L.K. Advani had successfully brought the BJP to power at the Centre for the first time in the party's history. His Rath Yatras provided an emotive platform where religion and politics became indistinguishable. He organised the Hindutva march on the issue of Ram Janmabhoomi-Babri Masjid, and succeeded in creating a complete political divide in the country. While L.K. Advani (along with the BJP and the Sangh Parivar) had a political mission to transform India into a Hindu Rashtra, Ms. Gandhi was expected to revive an ideologically desiccated party. The Lok Sabha and the Maharashtra State Assembly elections of 2004 witnessed a reversal of political fortunes, and Ms. Gandhi's Congress succeeded in dislodging the BJP. The year 2004 saw Ms. Gandhi move forward in the path of greater success. Mr. Advani, on the other hand, is expected to revive the BJP and consolidate the forces of Hindutva. Both of them are on trial.

Has Ms. Gandhi finally succeeded in bringing the Congress back on rails, or are political victories just freak phenomena? Will Mr. Advani bring back his magic touch of the Ram Janmabhoomi phase of Indian politics, or remain in political wilderness? The BJP's recent movements launched by Ms. Sushma Swaraj and Ms. Uma Bharati, or the agitation against the arrest of Kanchi Shankaracharya, have proved non-starters. Besides, Mr. Advani's inheritance too is not based on a clean slate. BJP-in-power from 1998-2004 transformed the "political culture" of the party of Hindutva. Today, every trait of a party-in-Government can be found in the BJP.

The BJP proclaimed itself as a party-with-a-difference, but six years of Vajpayee Government obliterated all special virtues claimed by the practitioners of Hindutva. Political power in India is a "Great Equaliser" and the BJP-in-Office for six years has become indistinguishable from the politics of its opponents. Mr. Advani has to do a lot of "cleansing" within the party before moving further in his task of reviving the party.

L.K. Advani has re-asserted his ideological commitment before the party. He said on November 27, 2004, "The BJP is really the chosen Instrument of the 'Divine' to take our country out of its present problems and to lofty heights of all-round achievement." He observed at the Ranchi Conference of the BJP national executive on November 27 that the party under his presidentship will oppose the conspiracy to erase "Hindu ethos" from Hindu India. Thus, he gave a clear message to the Sangh parivar that the BJP had not "deviated" from Hindutva. Mr. Vajpayee, too, elaborated the commitment of his comrade-in-arms by publicly stating that there was "no difference between the two (Hindutva and Bharatiyata)".

Thus, they projected to the voter that the so-called "interests" of the Hindus are safe only when the BJP is in power.

Mr. Advani has performed his first task of party's revival by making clear that the BJP is the party of the Hindus, by the Hindus, and for the Hindus. Has Ms. Gandhi delivered an unambiguous message to the Congress or the people that she is opposed to the BJP's ideology, and her party stands for secular, multi-cultural, multi-religious and multi-lingual democracy as enshrined in the Constitution? The Congress was becoming politically irrelevant because it had deviated from its ideological commitment against religion-based politics. In the process, it became the B-team of the parties of Hindutva and casteists. Why should then the Hindu communalists vote for a "counterfeit Hindutva" when the "original" is available?

Ms. Gandhi understood that the decline of the Congress began with the process of complete ideological degeneration of the party. Further, she realised that the party had its own quota of practitioners of Hindutva, who co-exist within the party with the believers in secularism. Many erstwhile political advisers of politically inexperienced Rajiv Gandhi continue to occupy positions of power even today. An important section of the Congress leadership had advised Rajiv Gandhi against annoying Muslims and made him act wrongly on the Shah Bano case. This brought Mr. Advani on the centre-stage, who proclaimed the Congress was pseudo-secular" and pampered the "Muslim minority".

Mr. Advani's logic clicked with the emerging new middle class. He emphasised that the Congress is secular only when it comes to Hindus, and communalist when it has to deal with Muslims. The so-called "old guard" of the Congress advised Rajiv Gandhi to "open" the locks of disputed temple-mosque at Ayodhya and launch his election campaign in 1989 from Ayodhya, with his "infamous" statement of building a Ram Rajya if the Congress was re-elected in the 1989 Lok Sabha elections. But Rajiv lost the elections, mainly because of his failure to grasp the complexities of Indian politics. Post-Rajiv Congress completely buried every "tradition" of the party. It failed to protect the Babri Masjid on December 6, 1992, and the country witnessed communal blood bath.

Ms. Gandhi stepped into such a hopeless situation. She did not carry conviction with the party, and her "foreign origin" was her greatest handicap. It was a repeat story of Indira Gandhi coming to power in 1966, after the sudden death of Lal Bahadur Shastri. But unlike Indira Gandhi, her credentials as a citizen of India were questioned by a section of her own partymen.

The challenge before Ms. Gandhi was to establish her own political credibility along with the revival of the Congress. It was a difficult task. Unlike Mr. Advani, she didn't have solid support of the party organisation. Mr. Advani had "assets" and Ms. Gandhi had personal and political deficiencies. Hence, she should be credited for the electoral victories of the Congress from J&K to Andhra Pradesh. She has been tested, and the legacy of her "foreign origin" lies buried because, like Indira, only she can win elections from both South and North. BJP leader Sushma Swaraj cut a sorry figure by opposing her in Karnataka. The reluctant Congress leaders also came to terms with Ms. Gandhi because none of the self-appointed "old guard" party leaders could win either from North or South, or even from their own local constituencies.

The Rajya Sabha is a sanctuary of defeated and tired "old guard", who are occupying positions of power in the Manmohan Singh-led UPA Government. The "old guard" Congress leaders have been reduced to positions of "courtiers", who are in office solely because of the "courtesy" of Ms. Gandhi. The Congress of 2004 essentially centres round the leadership of Ms. Gandhi. Hence it is not just the Congress, it is Ms. Gandhi who is on trial. Her trial is similar to that of Mr. Advani who has been entrusted with the sole purpose of bringing the BJP back to power. Will his magic work? Will Ms. Gandhi repeat her electoral performances and victories? Indira Gandhi was asked a question: Why do Congressmen treat you as the leader? She answered, "I win the elections for them."

Ms. Gandhi and Mr. Advani are the real political opponents, and they are sailing on the same boat. Both are expected to succeed because in politics, no one mourns a failure. A failed Ms. Gandhi will be dumped by the Congress, and Mr. Advani will take "political sanyas" if he does not deliver.

– *The Pioneer, December 15, 2004*

NDA'S SAME-SIDE GOAL

The UPA Government and the NDA-led Opposition have started a public debate on one year of the Manmohan Singh Government. In a functioning democracy, it is the duty of a ruling formation to defend its record of activities as much as it is the right and obligation of the Opposition parties and groups to expose the weaknesses and failures of the Government. It is the Opposition which keeps the ruling formation on its toes by critiquing parties-in-government. The UPA versus NDA attacks and counter-attacks will continue up to May 22, 2005, the day Manmohan Singh was sworn in as the Prime Minister last year. A very important issue which has long-term implications for Indian democracy is likely to be pushed aside in the noise arising from the boycott of the Lok Sabha by the BJP-led NDA.

Both the UPA and the NDA took public positions on May 12 about the problems in their relationship on the floor of the House. The UPA chairperson, Ms. Sonia Gandhi, said, "For whatever reason, they (the NDA) chose to stay away. They kept inventing one excuse after another to end their boycott. Worse, they tried to justify their actions by spreading canard about the Prime Minister and that too in extremely crude and offensive language." Rebutting the allegations, the BJP spokesman, V.K. Malhotra, said, "We respect the appeals but all the Prime Minister's statements so far have been loaded statements." Since the issue of Government-Opposition relationship in Parliament concerns the future of Indian democracy, it becomes essential to analyse it.

MPs are protected by the Law of Privileges and it is their prerogative to remain out of parliamentary proceedings. It is to the credit of the Indian Parliament that demands for grants for 2005-2006 were approved without the presence of the NDA-led Opposition. Parliamentary democracy emerged in England when people told the king that there could be "no taxation without representation". Indian MPs do not believe that "financial powers" are essential for holding the Government accountable because on April 27 this year, when Parliament was to conduct its most essential function of sanctioning money to the Government for expenditure for 2005-2006, the Leader of the Opposition, L.K. Advani, declared a boycott of the Lok Sabha proceedings. MPs served a notice saying, Money Bill or no Money Bill, they were not going to participate in the debates.

The Opposition is the watchdog of the interests of Indian citizens but between April 27 and May 13, its MPs have been conspicuous by their absence in the Lok Sabha because the UPA Government has not "sacked" Union Railways Minister Lalu Prasad Yadav. It is the right of the Opposition to demand the resignation of Mr. Yadav and it was the duty of the Government to answer the questions raised by the Opposition on the floor of the House. The Prime Minister gave his reply in the Lok Sabha, and the story should have ended there. The business of the Lok Sabha should have continued with the participation of MPs, especially of the Opposition. However, the parliamentary convention of debate and dissent does not seem acceptable to our MPs. The Opposition is miffed because the Government has not agreed to its demand.

The question is, can a Union Minister be held guilty of crime till judicial verdict is not pronounced? The Government has argued that the NDA Government too had followed the same mantra when it was in power between 1998-2004. Else L.K. Advani, Murli Manohar Joshi, Ms. Uma Bharati et al should have been sacked by then Prime Minister Vajpayee because they were charged in the court with the demolition of the Babri Masjid. A worse case was of then Defence Minister George Fernandes, who was asked to quit by Mr. Vajpayee because of the Tehelka scandal. He resigned, but even before the investigations into the Tehelka tapes could be completed, the same Mr. Vajpayee reinducted Mr. Fernandes in the Cabinet.

True, every minister, like Caeser's wife, must be above board in public life – as also every MP and MLA should have a clean public record. Are people's elected representatives in India prepared to legislate that no "under-trial" would be allowed to become a candidate for any elected office under the Constitution? The issue is not of Mr. Yadav or Mr. Fernandes. It is whether violators of the law should be allowed to be legislators. Can enforcers of the rule of law be persons who have broken the law? Pappu Yadav is an elected MP and instead of sitting in Parliament, he is lodged in jail. Lok Janshakti Party has 29 MLAs in the Bihar Assembly and four of them are currently in jail.

Another MLA, Raja Bhaiya, was arrested under POTA by the Mayawati Government in UP. Her successor, Mulayam Singh Yadav, not only released him from jail, he even made him a Minister in his Council. Should the BJP and Congress not sit together and discuss the disastrous implications of the entry of criminals in politics? Parliament is the national forum for a detailed discussion among major political parties with a view to evolve a national consensus on how to deal with problems created by criminals in politics. How can any Opposition party deal with important public issues by boycotting parliamentary sessions? Another central issue is whether Parliament is meant for serious debates and discussions on public policy issues or whether it is a platform for self-publicity by performing non-parliamentary activities by MPs?

Then, does it not amount to contempt of the House to walk out of its meetings? It is serious dereliction of duty by the legislators if they do not attend legislative meetings. They must represent the voters and take their voice to the Government. Parliament is expected to focus attention on people's needs and sufferings. But for the BJP-led Opposition, Mr. Yadav's head is more important. Is there any method in this madness? The BJP, while in power, had a host of ministers who were under judicial trial. However, consistency is not a virtue of Indian politicians. Kalyan Singh as the Chief Minister of BJP-led Uttar Pradesh was accused of "appointing well-known criminals" to remain in power. The BJP then always maintained that "accusations or allegations" against party MLAs, MPs or ministers could not be enough to keep them out of office. Then why such double standards in the case of Mr. Yadav? The boycott of Parliament session by the Opposition is frivolous and irresponsible.

If elected representatives who are under trial must leave office, then L.K. Advani too should be asked to quit as the Leader of the Opposition because, in our parliamentary democracy, his office is next in importance to the Prime Minister's. The BJP-led opposition is running away from its basic responsibility. It is the Opposition's right to participate in parliamentary activities; the BJP-led Opposition has abdicated its own responsibility. The Congress in Opposition during the term of the NDA Government (1999-2004) was rightly castigated for boycotting Parliament sessions. Hence, both the major parties must behave according to the norms of our parliamentary democracy. – *The Pioneer, May 17, 2005*

WHY THE PARIVAR HATES NEHRU

The Sangh Parivar was completely rattled by L.K. Advani's statements on Mohammad Ali Jinnah during his visit to Pakistan in the first week of June 2005 not because Advani was wrong in quoting Jinnah or Sarojini Naidu's statements. Advani's statements were a serious deviation from the basic ideological positions of the Parivar which had been consistently following a policy of anti-Pakistan including anti-Jinnah. Within the country anti-Muslim politics of the Parivar rested on the propaganda that Indian

Muslims were not loyal to India and they were pro-Pakistan. How could Advani dare to deviate a little from the anti-Muslim and anti-Pakistan ideological framework of the Parivar's politics?

Not only this. The Sangh Parivar including Advani have interpreted and misinterpreted Indian history to suit their political goal of dividing India between Hindus versus Muslims. The storm created by Advani's statements in the Parivar had hardly subsided when K.S. Sudarshan, the RSS Sarsanghchalak and the real head of the Hindu Joint Family, again brought history into politics by making outlandish but politically motivated statements on Jawaharlal Nehru and Indira Gandhi. It deserves to be clearly stated that distortion of historical facts is a necessary part of the Sangh Parivar's ideology of Hindutva and its concept of making India a Hindu Rashtra consisting of one nation, one culture, which in reality means Hindu nation and Hindu culture.

This is the reason that Jawaharlal Nehru is considered enemy number one of the Sangh Parivar's ideology of Hindutva and Hindu nation-state. This is why Sudarshan, the RSS chief, stated in Lucknow on June 19, 2005, that Jawaharlal Nehru was responsible for all problems including the unresolved problem of Kashmir. Sudarshan invented a reason for Nehru's failures because of Nehru's English minded approach. Sudarshan further alleged that Nehru conspired to keep Sardar Patel and Subhash Chandra Bose, the favourites of RSS, out of power.

A few facts may be mentioned to substantiate the argument that deliberate misinterpretation and distortion of historical facts and personalities is essential to the anti-secular, anti-Muslim politics of the Sangh Parivar. It deserves to be clearly stated that K.B. Hedgewar and M.S. Golwalkar, the RSS chiefs, had not at all participated in anti-colonial national movement for the independence of India from British rule. The RSS was established and organised to strengthen Hindus against aggressive Muslims and its ideological anchor was provided by V. Savarkar who propounded the doctrine of Hindutva and Hindu nation-state.

According to this theory, Muslim rule over India had to be painted in complete negative terms irrespective of historical facts to the contrary. The RSS and the Hindu Mahasabha were not involved in any struggle against British colonial rulers because their real focus was to sharpen Hindu-Muslim divide and history was a tool and an instrument in this anti-Muslim agenda of the forces of Hindutva. This two nation theory based on separate religious identity of Hindus and Muslims not only kept the RSS-

Hindu Mahasabha away from anti-colonial struggle, it also brought it into confrontation with socially, and culturally inclusive national movement of India. Gandhi and Nehru were real villains for the Sangh Parivar because their ideological positions of socially inclusive India were an anathema to the ideologues of Hindu Rashtra.

This explains Sudarshan's venomous statement against Nehru on June 19, 2005. If the Sangh Parivar believes in one nation and one Hindu state, Nehru fought for a democratic, secular, plural and multi-religious and multi-lingual country. If the politics of Sangh Parivar was to establish a special citizenship for Hindus and a second-class status for minorities like Muslims and Christians, Nehru's political battles were around the concept of equal rights for all citizens of India irrespective of their religion, caste, creed and sex. Sudarshan's anti-Nehru stance led him to repeat the allegation that Kashmir's unresolved problem is a legacy of Nehru.

Kashmir has always been a special part of Parivar's politics beginning with Shyama Prasad Mukherjee, the founder of Jan Sangh with cadre provided by the RSS which included Atal Bihari Vajpayee, L.K. Advani and Deen Dayal Upadhyaya. Mukerjee launched a satyagraha in Kashmir because the Hindu Parivar viewed Kashmir as an integral part of India as it was a Hindu princely stated ruled by Dogra Maharaja Hari Singh. The Sangh Parivar does not accept that Pakistan has any claim over the Hindu princely state of Jammu and Kashmir and they have always held the secularist Nehru responsible for betraying the Hindu state of Kashmir.

This false interpretation of the reality of Jammu and Kashmir is an integral part of politics of distorted historical acts by the Parivar. The cat was out of the bag when Sudarshan, in his same speech at Lucknow on June 19, 2005, praised Indira Gandhi who 'With courage and determination managed to create Bangladesh separate from Pakistan in the war of 1971'. Indira Gandhi, with her 'firmness' and 'determination' succeeded in demolishing a Muslim Pakistan and for such an achievement, Sudarshan gave her a testimonial.

The crux of the issue is that battles on history raging within the Sangh Parivar are an integral part of their politics of social exclusiveness which in reality means that the minorities, especially Muslims and Christians have to be treated as second class citizens in the country. The battle lines have been drawn between Nehru's model of socially inclusive, pluralist and secular politics or the Sangh Parivar's socially exclusive Hindu majoritarian politics of special status for the Hindus and legal discriminations against Muslim and Christian minorities.

Advani got a taste of his own medicine because in the eyes of the Parivar it was an act of sacrilege to praise Jinnah and that also in Pakistan. Advani's guilt got compounded and he became a trailor to the Hindu cause by praising Jinnah in an enemy country like Pakistan. Govindacharya was correct in his statement that Advani's statement on Jinnah could not be swallowed by the rank and file of the Swaymsevaks who had been completely indoctrinated against Jinnah and his creation Pakistan. How could the Parivar accept Advani's statement about a person who had been always held responsible for the partition of Mother India of the Hindus? – *Sahara Time, July 2, 2005*

HISTORICALLY FALSE DEFINITION

The RSS held a chintan baithak at Surat from July 3 to 8 to take stock of the situation within the Sangh Parivar. Of late the RSS has been perturbed by developments within the Parivar because it believes that there is a significant "erosion of ideology" and also "growing personality cult" in the BJP. The baithak was held in the backdrop of an ideological controversy created by BJP president L.K. Advani's speeches on Mohammed Ali Jinnah during his recent visit to Pakistan.

A storm has broken out within the Sangh Parivar because Mr. Advani's "deviation from ideology" has "confused" the Hindutva cadre who have been fed on the staple of "hatred" against Jinnah and his actions that led to partition. How could Mr. Advani, a committed swayamsevak, forget the anti-Pakistan, anti-Jinnah and anti-Muslim ideological baggage carried by his comrades-in-arms?

While the Parivar is involved in its fraternal civil war, terrorists targeted the makeshift Ram temple at Ayodhya on July 5. It provided the much needed ammunition to the Sangh Parivar to target the "incompetent" Governments at the Centre and Uttar Pradesh for their inability to provide security to the holiest of holy places of the Hindus. Mr. Advani and every member of the Parivar found an opportunity to revive the declining BJP by trying to once again play the emotive issue of Ram temple.

Mr. Advani stated on July 6 that the BJP believes in resolving the Ayodhya issue. "... But the Ram Temple will be built right there", he said. The BJP then gave a call for an all-India bandh/ protest on July 6 against the terrorist attack. However, a new reality which the Hindutva forces refuse to accept is that the response of the Hindu masses to the bandh call has been lukewarm.

The crux of the problem within the Parivar is not Mr. Advani's statement on Jinnah, but a complete failure of the entire Parivar to win back the so-called Hindu constituency. Has the Ram temple lost its political appeal for the average Hindu voter? The fact is religion as a tool in politics has limited social reach and this reality is haunting the Sangh Parivar. In a highly religious and ritualistic society, politics of religion is often used to manipulate the voters. But when voters have ignored Hindutva politics as shown in the 2004 Lok Sabha elections, it reveals the rich, pluralist and secular traditions of the Indian society.

The rise and fall of BJP in Uttar Pradesh, the headquarters of social conservatism and religious fanaticism deserves to be explained and analysed for understanding the inherent limitations of the reach of Hindutva ideology among the Hindu masses. Kalyan Singh and Raj Nath Singh among others, became chief ministers of the BJP-led State governments in UP by playing the politics of religion. Now these beneficiaries of Ram temple politics are nowhere in competition with Mulayam Singh Yadav and Ms. Mayawati in 2005.

The march of caste politics has marginalised the Hindutva appeal. The BJP too played caste politics by making a backward, Kalyan Singh, the leader of a "Brahmin-Baniya" party, and this strategy was acclaimed as a great act of social engineering. But even this remained a non-starter.

The developments in UP mean that a "homogenised Hindu" of the Sangh Parivar does not exist, and like all religions, Hindus are internally highly fragmented. The Sangh Parivar's one Hindu Rashtra is a mirage. This is proved by the fact that the BJP is unable to get more than 25 per cent of the vote in the country, where Hindus consist of more than 80 per cent of the total population. The BJP must remember that a Hindu vote-bank does not exist.

Moreover, the Muslim community in normal elections has always shown its internal fragmentation. It is only when they feel terrorised that they vote for some or the other messiah of secularism like Mulayam Singh Yadav or Ms. Mayawati or Lalu Prasad Yadav. It deserves to be stated that all major religions only carry a nomenclature of Christianity or Islam or Hinduism, and except this 'nomenclature' there is nothing like a monolithic religious community in the whole world. When will the BJP accept this hard fact?

The BJP and the Sangh Parivar have refused to accept the logic of highly competitive democratic political processes of India. The Congress is struggling to regain a respectable space in a country where it dominated the post-Independence politics for 40 years. Further, unlike the BJP, a weakened Congress has an all-India presence in the real sense of the term. The Hindus of the whole of India have not accepted the BJP because a monolith Hindu social constituency of the Sangh Parivar is a fiction.

The upshot of above description is that the Hindutva ideology and the logic of competitive democratic politics is involved in a mutually antagonistic contradiction. Also a serious "mismatch" exists between Hindutva of the Sangh parivar and Hindutva of the majority of Hindu believers in India. The BJP is at the crossroads because, as a member of the RSS fraternity with Hindutva ideology, it has also to wear the political mask to win over voters. Here, it finds serious limitations in its political reach even to the so-called Hindus. The RSS refuses to accept that the BJP was really constrained to build the Ram temple in spite of being in power at the Centre from 1998 to 2004.

It must be kept in mind that none of the Parivar members, except the BJP, has had to face democratic elections. The BJP is nothing without the RSS; and the latter has nothing to do with the democratic process. It is impossible for any BJP leader to survive by ignoring the RSS. The BJP is not a "normal" political party, it is just a political mouthpiece of the Parivar.

The current crisis within the BJP and other affiliates of the Sangh Parivar should not lead anyone to conclude that the Hindutva ideology carried on the shoulders of every member of the Sangh is at a dead-end. Every BJP-led State Government, be it in Jharkhand, Chhattisgarh, Madhya Pradesh, Rajasthan or Gujarat, is implementing the Hindutva agenda by breaking or bending democratic norms. The Vajpayee Government from 1998 to 2004, too, did not shy away from using state power to spread and strengthen the Hindu Rashtravad ideology.

The RSS either does not understand the logic of pluralist and competitive parliamentary democracy or it does not have any faith in the democratic process of India. This contradiction between the logic of democracy and the ideological purists of Hindutva is unresolvable by any sectarian and religiously exclusivist party or front. – *The Pioneer, July 12, 2005*

THE BJP IS HARDLY ELIGIBLE FOR THE MORAL HIGH GROUND

Bihar is in the news for both good and bad reasons. This complex admixture has once again been debated in Parliament on August 1 and 2 at the time of the motion for the second extension of President's rule in the state from September 7.

The story of President's rule in Bihar begins with the fractured electoral verdict in the February Assembly election. Neither the RJD alliance, nor the BJP-JD(U) combine was in a position to form the government. After walking out of the BJP-led NDA government on the question of "secularism", LJP chief Ram Vilas Paswan surprised one and all with his performance in the Bihar election. This self-appointed champion of secularism refused to ally himself with other secular forces – the RJD, the Congress and the Communists. The veto exercised by Paswan scuttled the formation of a secular front government in the state in March 2005.

The BJP and the JD(U) could not have formed the government on their own in Bihar. No wonder, they indulged in the politics of "buying" elected MLAs of the LJP and the RJD. Witnessing this, state Governor Buta Singh recommended the imposition of President's rule and the dissolution of the newly-elected Assembly.

The bone of contention, however, is the Governor's report to the President that if the buying of MLAs indulged in by the BJP and the JD(U) is to be nipped in the bud, the Centre should impose President's rule over Bihar. Home Minister Shivraj Patil, while speaking in Parliament on the occasion of second extension of President's rule in Bihar, said that the Governor wrote to the Centre that "the situation is heading in the wrong direction and the House should be dissolved".

The BJP and the JD(U) felt cheated because they had succeeded in luring MLAs from the LJP by offering them lucrative deals for their desertion to the NDA camp. Since the gameplan of the BJP-JD(U) alliance did not succeed, it targeted both the UPA government and the Bihar Governor of disallowing the formation of an elected government in the state despite having sufficient MLAs with it. The cat was out of the bag when JD(U) leader Nitish Kumar stated in the Lok Sabha on August 2: "If MLAs on their own free will want to come to the JD(U), it is termed a horse-trading. Had the MLAs gone to the RJD, it would have been a realignment of secular forces."

The BJP-JD(U) alliance has no leg to stand on because the February electoral verdict was clearly in favour of secular forces who had won a majority of seats in the state. The BJP-JD(U) combine could not have formed the government without engineering "defections" of MLAs from other groups, which would not have been possible without offering them something in return. This is the logic of fractured verdict and the politics of cheap manoeuvring, indulged in by the "extremely principled" parties.

Ram Vilas Paswan killed the very chance of the emergence of a secular government in Bihar. Besides, the allurements offered by the NDA to the greedy LJP MLAs created a situation in which the Governor was forced to intervene. Had the Governor allowed the BJP-JD(U) combine to form the government with the help of new recruits who had been "won" over by these two parties, he would have only legitimised "defections" and "horse-trading" of the MLAs. Singh opted for President's rule because the political stalemate in Bihar could not have been broken without "horse-trading", indulged in by the BJP-JD(U) combine. The two-day debate in Parliament revealed that the BJP-JD(U) combine could not refute the allegation levelled against it by the Governor.

The proclamation of President's rule in Bihar is absolutely justified because the NDA wanted to cook up a majority by following unethical parliamentary practices. If this allegation of the Governor is wrong, the NDA has enough opportunity to expose him in public.

It can be stated that the BJP-JD(U)opposition to the Governor's recommendation of President's rule is not based on principle. Instead, it is the result of opportunistic politics. Since Bihar is always in the news, the parliamentary discussion on August 1 and 2 was not confined to the merits and demerits of the Governor's report to the President. It got extended because of the controversy created by state chief secretary G.S. Kang, who went on "protest leave" because Buta Singh had transferred 17 IPS officers without the former's consent and approval. A chief secretary of a state is the head of the civil services, and it is his responsibility to decide on administrative issues including the "transfer" of the IAS and the IPS officers. This controversy provided an opportunity to the opposition to demand Singh's head. The Governor was charged to have acted in league with the Centre.

But the BJP should know by their own experience between 1998 and 2004 that Governors are "tools" in the hand of party/parties in power at the Centre. The Vajpayee government had appointed RSS activists like Sunder Singh Bhandari, K.R. Malkani, Bhai Mahavir, M.L. Khurana, etc., to serve the interests of the BJP in those states. The BJP, therefore, cannot accuse the Bihar Governor of partisanship. In fact, the water of politics is dirty and every political party is accountable for making it more filthy.

– *The Pioneer, July 6, 2005*

RIOTS AND WRONGS

The Nanavati Commission report on the 1984 anti-Sikh riots in Delhi has been submitted to the Government of India and the Opposition parties have demanded that the action taken by the Government on the report should be placed before Parliament for discussion. The 1984 riots have attracted a lot of public attention because of the popular perception that the local civil and police functionaries allowed the violence to take place because of the active involvement of the then ruling party at the Centre. It deserves to be clearly stated that inter-community conflicts in a plural society like India can sometimes lead to inter-community violence, which is popularly described as 'riot'.

India has a long history of inter-community conflicts which sometimes lead to communal violence. In such times it is expected that the Government will use its law and order machinery to intervene effectively and stop these riots whenever and wherever they happen. The coercive apparatus of the state is expected to maintain law and order in society and effectively deal with any breach of the law. Human society cannot be free from violence and the administrative apparatus of the state is designed to meet the situation created by inter-group or inter-community turbulence.

The 1984 anti-Sikh riots or the 2002 Gujarat riots cannot be compared with normal inter-community strife in the country. In India, large-scale instances of violence are generally inquired into by a commission headed by a judge to determine the culprits. It is well-known that the relationship between the majority and minority communities can sometimes get disrepaired to such an extent that the former may indulge in violence against the hapless minority community, at times even with a view to 'teach them a lesson' for their suspected involvement in 'anti-majority' activities.

This longish description is essential to properly contextualise the problems of inter-community strife amounting to violence. There can be ordinary disputes that sometimes cross all limits of acceptability. It, therefore, becomes essential to understand the reality of extended inter-community violence – the 1984 anti-Sikh riots, the 1993 Mumbai riots or the 2002 Gujarat riots. It is for this reason that inquiry commissions are appointed by the Government. Besides, a democratic and secular state has to ensure that minority communities are not discriminated against by the state functionaries, especially during riots.

The Nanavati Commission was appointed on public demand because it was suspected that an important section of the Congress leadership in Delhi had engineered the 1984 anti-Sikh riots to create a favourable political sentiment among Hindus for the party. A message was given that the Sikh community was responsible for then Prime Minister Indira Gandhi's assassination because her Sikh security personnel were involved in this crime. This is the best manifestation of riots being engineered against the minority community on the basis of purely political calculations. This was the politics of anti-Sikh riots, which differentiates it from other routine Hindu-Muslim riots.

Another important political riot was engineered in Mumbai in 1993. The BJP and other affiliates of the Sangh Parivar had launched a movement for the construction of Ram Mandir at Ayodhya. The Babri Masjid, a bone of contention between Hindus and Muslims, was destroyed on December 6, 1992, by a mob guided by the Sangh leadership. This incident created uncertainty in the entire country, but Mumbai was the worst affected as the city was engulfed in the Hindu-Muslim riots.

An inquiry commission headed by Justice Sri Krishna was appointed to investigate the causes of riots. After all, it was perceived that these had been 'engineered' by Hindu communal forces like the BJP and the Shiv Sena with the active connivance of the State administration. The Mumbai riots too fall in the category of politically-engineered anti-Muslim violence.

Gujarat too witnessed Hindu-Muslim riots in March-April 2002. On the basis of public hue and cry, a judicial inquiry has been ordered to find out the role of the hidden forces behind them. The quick succession of events in Gujarat, beginning with the fire in a railway compartment at Godhra on February 28, 2002, and the BJP-VHP demand for Gujarat bandh on March 1, turned into anti-Muslim vendetta.

The Narendra Modi Government was suspected of playing a partisan role and allowed rioters to go berserk against hapless Muslims in Gujarat. The whole country reacted against the State Government and demanded an impartial judicial inquiry for proper investigation of the Government's role in the violence. The riots in Ahmedabad, Vadodra, and other Gujarat towns were yet another example of 'political riots' because a deliberate message was being sent out: Muslims have to be taught a lesson.

A common element in these three 'political riots' was the total alignment of the state's administrative apparatus with the parties of the majority community against the minority — Sikh or Muslim. The so-called neutrality of the defenders of the law and order was conspicuous by its absence, and the administrative machinery was found to be in the service of the then ruling political masters. The Delhi administration worked as an 'anti-Sikh' force in the hands of the ruling party in 1984. The same story was repeated in 1993 and 2002 in Mumbai and Gujarat respectively.

It is not without reason that the Nanavati Commission has clearly identified the then Lt. Governor and Police Commissioner of Delhi as culprits, along with the Congress leadership. Similarly, the former Chief Justice of India, Justice Khare, castigated the Modi Government by stating, "When Rome was burning, Nero was fiddling." He further stated that victimised Muslims cannot expect justice in Gujarat because of anti-Muslim attitude of the State Government. The trial cases, therefore, were transferred to Mumbai.

How can riots be controlled if the administration itself is involved in fulfilling the political objectives of the ruling parties? Politically-engineered riots have taken place because of the illegal acts of the guarantors of constitutional norms in the country. BJP leader Vijay Kumar Malhotra thundered in the Lok Sabha on August 3 that "the Congress hands are blood-stained" in the 1984 anti-Sikh riots in Delhi. He must be told that the boot also fits the Sangh in Mumbai and Gujarat.

India has witnessed anti-minority violence under the patronage of the ruling power and the reasons are either political expediency (like that of the Congress in 1984) or a product of anti-Muslim psyche of the Sangh. The Nanavati Commission report has once again brought into focus the partisan role of the law and order machinery during inter-community conflicts, whenever political class itself is involved in anti-minority politics. Anti-Muslim riots are a logical culmination of the ideology of Hindu rashtravadis who represent

Muslims as 'the other'. This ideology is the root cause of the politics of riots in India. – *The Pioneer, August 9, 2005*

SECULARISE STATE APPARATUS

The Nanavati Commission in its report on anti-Sikh riots of November 1 to 3, 1984 has unambiguously indicted the political and governing classes of India for indulging in deliberate acts of violence against the Sikh community.

The anti-Sikh riots of November 1 to 3, 1984 were not an ordinary event arising out of Hindu-Sikh conflicts because Hindus especially of Punjab, have inter-cultural and inter-marriage relations with the Sikh community and there is no history of any social distancing between Hindus and Sikhs. It is for the first time that the Sikh minority community was savaged and brutalised by a section of Hindus who decided to take revenge on the Sikh community for the alleged criminal role of Sikh bodyguards in assassinating Indira Gandhi on October 31, 1984.

It could have been a 'spontaneous' reaction by a section of society who felt emotionally quite disturbed on the assassination of a very popular and powerful Prime Minister. This was not the case and the Congress party government at the Centre did not do anything to control the mobs from November 1 to 3 because the anti-Sikh riots were engineered and manufactured by a powerful section of Congress itself. Justice Nanavati has stated clearly and unambiguously that the 1984 riots took place in an 'organised manner' and that 'the systematic manner in which the Sikhs were killed indicated that the attacks on them were organised'.

Justice Nanavati also specifically blames the 'police failure' in performing its basic duty of maintaining law and in order in the city during the riots. The Delhi Lt. Governor, P.S. Gavai and police commissioner Tandon have been specifically identified for their failure to protect the innocent victims of Congress-led mobs in Delhi. It is a well known fact that many a time functionaries of the state operate under the private instructions and guidance of the political masters of the day and Delhi law and order machinery was not an exception.

The upshot of above description is that ordinary 'riots' can be contained by the law and order machinery if there is political will. This is not the first or the last time when a partisan state has refused to enforce law and order when there was tension in the streets.

The practitioners of Hindutva have consistently targeted Muslim and Christian minorities and the ideologues of Hindutva have always exercised state power to terrorise these minorities. A well known and very recent example of anti-Muslim genocide by the ideologues of Hindutva was witnessed in Narendra Modi's Gujarat in March-April 2002. The state government was directly involved, and on these events the then Chief Justice of India, Justice Khare, commented 'when Rome was burning, Nero was fiddling'. Not only this. The Supreme Court transferred from Gujarat to Bombay Courts the investigation of the cases of victims of riots because the highest court of India believed that the witnesses were not free and safe in Gujarat because of the anti-Muslim state government. India witnessed serious anti-Muslim riots after the demolition of Babri Mosque at Ayodhya on December 6, 1992.

The mosque was destroyed by the leaders and activists of Sangh Parivar under the full protection and patronage of anti-Muslim BJP state government of Kalyan Singh in Uttar Pradesh. A government which is committed to the ideology of Hindutva is hardly expected to protect a disputed mosque from a mob led by leaders of the Hindu Parivar.

Justice Nanavati has once again brought into sharp focus the issue and role of a partisan state apparatus during inter-community conflicts. How can a state machinery be impartial when it is itself ideologically committed against a minority community? Political majoritarianism can be contained only by the practitioners of honest secular politics and in the absence of such politics, the state machinery will continue to discriminate against and inflict violence on hapless minorities in a plural country like India. India has to go a long way to secularise its state apparatus to eliminate the state promoted and patronised riots like anti-Sikh riots of 1984 and the frequent killings of Muslim minority community under the shadow of a partisan Hindu state.

– Sahara Time, August 20, 2005

RSS IS THE ONLY REALITY

The ongoing drama in the Gujarat BJP has once again brought into focus the vulnerability of party president L.K. Advani because the RSS has ostracised him. Mr. Advani visited Pakistan from June 4-7, 2005; and his statements on Mohammed Ali Jinnah prompted the RSS to not only denounce Mr. Advani's assessment of Jinnah, but also demand his resignation from BJP's presidentship. This controversy occupied public space for full 43 days of June and July.

The RSS gave marching orders to the BJP chief – who also happens to be the Leader of Opposition in the Lok Sabha – because of his deviation from the ideology of the Sangh Parivar. The RSS, the patron-in-chief of every outfit of Hindutva, cannot accept any ideological deviation from its cadre, which includes the BJP's top leadership. This fratricidal war between the RSS and its political outfit, the BJP, deserves to be analysed. After all, the incident brought into public focus the real face of the BJP and its relationship with the RSS.

An important section of the Indian intelligentsia, especially in the media, projected Atal Bihari Vajpayee as a liberal in the Nehruvian mould during his tenure as the Prime Minister between 1998 and 2004. It was forgotten that Mr. Vajpayee was an RSS pracharak and a product of the Sangh ideology. In fact, the recent controversies only substantiate the argument that the BJP is nothing without the RSS. Besides, Mr. Vajpayee and Mr. Advani are just the carriers of anti-Muslim and anti-Pakistan ideology of the RSS.

There are several reasons for the controversy generated by Mr. Advani's statements in Pakistan. First, by terming Jinnah 'secular', Mr. Advani completely deviated from the Sangh's basic ideological agenda of anti-Muslim and anti-Pakistan. The RSS has, in fact, trained its cadres to believe that Jinnah alone was responsible for the country's partition. Hence he cannot be 'secular', but a villain who divided the Hindu motherland.

Second, RSS pracharaks, including Mr. Vajpayee and Mr. Advani, had preached their followers that Muslims in India were anti-national because their primary loyalty was to Pakistan. The core ideology of the RSS has been built on the basis of hatred towards Muslims and Pakistan. As the BJP is the political face of Hindutva for promoting anti-Muslim ideology in India, how could Mr. Advani deviate from this core ideology?

RSS chief K.S. Sudarshan served notice to the BJP President and asked the party to remove Mr. Advani for his anti-Hindutva pronouncements during his visit to Pakistan. The RSS supremo called a meeting of leaders at Surat on July 3, where he accused the BJP of 'deviations from ideology' and the evil of a growing personality cult in the party. The target was obvious: The Vajpayee-Advani leadership of the BJP. RSS also came out with a resolution on the "ideological erosion and organisational indiscipline of some functionaries of a couple of like-minded organisations", and took serious note of the violations of the Parivar's norms.

When the NDA convenor, George Fernandes, decided to visit the RSS headquarters to convey to the Sangh that it "should not arrogate to itself a political role" – pretending to believe that RSS is a 'socio-cultural' organisation – a storm broke out within the BJP. Ms. Sushma Swaraj, Ms. Uma Bharti and others came out strongly against Mr. Fernandes's statements. Ms. Bharti observed on July 11: "His (Mr. Fernandes's) concern is understandable, but he has no business to comment on the RSS-BJP relationship which is like a mother-child relationship." Mr. Advani, too, made public statements about his commitment to the agenda of Hindutva and the construction of Ram Mandir in Ayodhya.

Finally, the curtain came down when Mr. Advani, accompanied by Venkaiah Naidu, Jaswant Singh and Sanjay Joshi, went to the RSS's Delhi headquarters on July 17 to meet Mr. Sudarshan's two representatives – Mohan Bhagwat and Suresh Soni. There, he reiterated "his commitment to the Sangh ideology". Mr. Bhagwat stated on behalf of RSS: "He (Mr. Advani) expressed that serious efforts be made in the coming days to address the sentiments expressed by us on issues like ideology, conduct, organisation, emergence of new generation, etc."

Mr. Advani has temporarily bought peace with RSS, which is the real centre of power of the Sangh Parivar. The upshot of above narration is that the BJP is just an extension and political face of the RSS, and the BJP-led NDA Government was a carrier of the RSS agenda of one nation, one country and one culture.

Mr. Advani has not only got a temporary extension from the RSS headmaster, but also reaffirmed his commitment towards Ram Mandir. He observed at Rae Bareli on July 28 that "the temple will be built at the same place at Ayodhya" and he asked the UPA Government to perform this job as the Jawaharlal Nehru Government did in Somnath. It must be made clear that the BJP led by Mr. Vajpayee and Mr. Advani has never abandoned the agenda of building a Hindu rashtra. In fact, the BJP cannot abandon its basic anti-Muslim agenda, and even an unimportant deviation will not be acceptable to the real master sitting in Nagpur.

It deserves to be stated that the BJP, as an extension of the RSS, has always caught on any issue that can create division between Hindus and Muslims – Ram temple is just one of them. When the Supreme Court declared the Illegal Migrant (Determination by Tribunal) Act invalid, the BJP jumped into the fray because it viewed the presence of Bangladeshis in Assam as a Hindu-Muslim dispute. Mr. Advani, as the Home Minister between 1998 and 2004, had repeatedly stated in public that Hindu Bangladeshi refugees to India were 'acceptable', but Muslim refugees had to be declared 'illegal' and deported from the country. The Supreme Court judgement has provided the BJP with an opportunity to divide Hindus and Muslims of Assam.

On the apex court's verdict on IMDT Act, Lok Sabha Speaker Somnath Chatterjee observed on July 28: "But how did it arrive at the conclusion that lakhs of foreigners are getting in (from Bangladesh)? What is the basis of its assessment? I am troubled by these questions because (the judgement) does not solve the problem." Mr. Chatterjee further reminded the country that Assam was burning between 1970 and 1980 on the issue of Bangladeshi migrants, when All-Assam Students Union and Assam Gana Parishad had launched anti-foreigner movements that terrorised the minority community in the State.

The IMDT Act was a great compromise because every Bengali Muslim in Assam would have been living under the sword of the AASU-AGP demand of "detection, deletion and deportation" of the so-called Bangladeshis from Assam. The BJP does not agree that migration from Bangladesh is a human problem, which can be solved through negotiations between the governments of India and Bangladesh. How can a party which makes a religious distinction among Bangladeshi refugees miss any opportunity provided by the invalidation of the IMDT Act? Any emotive anti-Muslim issue from Assam to Punjab makes the BJP very active.

The fact is that the RSS alone is real. Every other outfit, including the BJP, is controlled, guided and supervised by the RSS. Neither is Mr. Vajpayee a liberal in the Nehruvian mould, nor is Mr. Advani the Sardar Patel of India. Hindu communalists must not be compared with the heroes of Indian nationalism. Do we need any other evidence than K.S. Sudarshan's July 2005 statement that the RSS nominates its swayamsevaks to work in the BJP? It is obviously to carry on with the RSS agenda through the BJP, which is just an instrument of Hindutva. – *The Pioneer, August 23, 2005*

WHITHER BJP

he real agenda of the meeting of the National Executive of the BJP held from September 16 to 18, 2005 at Chennai was to deal with the controversies around its Party President L.K. Advani which had arisen during his visit to Pakistan in June 2005. The major issue raised by the RSS against Advani's statements in Pakistan was of 'ideological deviation' by the BJP President who not only projected Mohamed Ali Jinnah as 'secular' but also committed a great ideological sin by abandoning the Sangh Parivar's ideology of Akhand Bharat by stating that Pakistan was a reality. Advani's statements in Pakistan in June 2005 and strong reactions from the RSS and other 'outfits' of the Sangh Parivar like the VHP, Bajrang Dal et al about his 'ideological deviations' has led to a great public debate on the real significance of Advani's attempt to distance himself and the BJP from crude and militant Hindutva of the RSS and other shops of the Sangh Parivar. It deserves to be stated that Advani and the BJP had unambiguously implemented the agenda of Hindutva during Vajpayee-led National Democratic Alliance coalition government from 1988 to 2004. It has been suggested that electoral defeat of the BJP in the Lok Sabha elections of 2004 prompted a section of the BJP leadership to project itself as a right-wing and socially inclusive party instead of its image of a fanatic Hindu party which is anti-minority and anti-equality of every citizen before the law of the country. Was it an attempt by the BJP to reinvent itself and abandon its core agenda of fanatic Hindutva with a view to broaden its political and electoral reach to communities which had kept themselves away from the Hindu BJP? It has been surmised that Advani and a section of the BJP leadership realised that a liberal Hindu face is electorally more beneficial than the present ideology of fanatic Hindu Rashtravadis. Political parties in any competitive democratic electoral system try to shift their position on the basis of new challenges and also with a view to respond to the perceptions of the voters. If the BJP has to reinvent itself and Advani's effort is to project a 'liberal BJP' before the voter of India, it has to carry conviction with its parent organisations like the RSS and fanatic fraternal organisations like the VHP, Bajrang Dal et al. The BJP is not a 'Normal democratic party' like the Congress.

The BJP is a party with a difference because it is a political instrument of the RSS and any ideological change with a view to win an election cannot be carried out by Advani or others without the full approval and consent of the RSS. The BJP is just an extension of the RSS and it is a big zero without the RSS and it becomes amply clear from the statements of Advani himself at Chennai meeting where he announced his decision to step down from the post of President of the BJP in December 2005. Advani said that ideologically, RSS and BJP, have 'symbiotic relationship' and 'Both the organisations have benefited immensely from this relationship and together they have succeeded in bringing out ideology of cultural nationalism to the centre stage of India' Advani believes that the RSS and the BJP are 'equal' and 'comrade-in-arms' for the promotion of Hindutva but as a political party, the BJP should enjoy 'autonomy' from its sister organisation. Did Advani get any support from anyone within the National Executive of the BJP on his clarion call for 'autonomy' from the RSS? The answer is a big no. Not only this. Atal Bihari Vajpayee publicly stated at Chennai that the RSS is 'an exceptional organisation, unequal in the world'. Vajpayee observed that the bond between the RSS and BJP is 'unbreakable' and the Jan Sangh/BJP was 'established by the RSS'. Advani himself admitted that the RSS should stick to its mission of 'man-making and nation-building' and also 'train BJP functionaries for politics'. Thus the cat is out of the bag and the argument that the BJP under the leadership of Advani has tried to project a new face of liberal Hindu is unsubstantiated and ill-founded because Advani's departure itself has been commanded by the RSS. A party of the Hindus, for the Hindus and by the Hindus has no capacity to abandon its hardcore ideology because the BJP is just one arm of the RSS and all outfits of Hindutva have to work for the implementation of the ideology of Hindutva as laid down by the RSS. The BJP is an empty balloon without the organisational network of the RSS and it has no independent capacity of its own to mobilise the voters without the Swaymsevaks. The Congress party still continues to win elections in some states and regions inspite of the fact that its party organisation is in a shambles. It is an irony of Indian politics that the Congress without a well-knit party organisation still has electoral and political presence from Kashmir to Arunachal Pradesh and the BJP/RSS, inspite of committed Cadre cannot win an election on all India basis. Not only this. The BJP will be reduced to political cipher without RSS cadre while all regional and castiest parties are able to win region-specific elections on the basis of their 'leaders' or appeal of caste or region. Lalu Yadav or Mayawati or Chandrababu Naidu and other regional and caste leaders are able to mobilise social constituencies on the basis of their social agenda and as leaders of their parties, they have enough flexibility and manoeuvrability to extend their social reach by making multiple social alliances. The BJP is constricted and constrained because

Muslim and Christian minority communities are persona non-grata to Hindutva and a vast majority of secular Hindus keep away from fanatic Hindutva of the BJP. The BJP is unable to motivate and mobilise many social constituencies and groups because it has socially and culturally exclusive agenda and all other parties, all-India or regional or casteist, are open fronts for multiple social groups. It is possible Advani and other leaders of the BJP understood this logic and compulsion of democratic politics and perhaps Advani attempted to broaden and widen the reach of party of Hindutva. But Advani himself is a cog in a wheel and part of a machine and the organisation has clearly shown him the door and made him a zero. The upshot of above description is that competitive democratic politics provides great learning opportunities to parties to adapt and adjust to the new demands of electoral politics. Politics of Hindutva as practiced by the Sangh Parivar has reached a dead end and it cannot cross 20 per cent of national votes limit. Hindutva itself is a limiting factor and the BJP cannot 'reinvest' itself on the model of other parties or groups in India. – *Sahara Time, October 1, 2005*

5

Caste Politics and Reservation

RESERVATION AND CASTEISM

The Common Minimum Programme of the Manmohan Singh-led UPA government at the Centre has stated that it would 'initiate a national dialogue with all political parties, industry and other organisations to see how best the private sector can fulfill the aspirations of the Scheduled Caste and Scheduled Tribe Youth.' The coalition partners of the UPA from South to North India led by ministers like Ram Vilas Paswan, Meira Kumar and D. Maran succeeded in organising a Government of India, ministerial group of seven UPA ministers under the chairmanship of Sharad Pawar to work out the details of reservations of jobs for the SCs and STs in the private sector.

Public discourse has been launched by the caste leaders by supporting such a new opening for SCs and STs by reserving a quota in the private sector, and its opponents, especially the big business organisations and leaders, have raised the issues of 'efficiency and merit' in private sector employment. Hindu mythology and metaphor have been brought by Meira Kumar, the social justice minister in the UPA government, who observed on September 2, 2004, that 'I am sure the industry will rise above the Dronacharya mindset and the Eklavya phobia'. It is a reference to a myth in the Mahabharat that Dronacharya asked for Eklavya's right thumb as *Gurudakshina* (donation) so that the high caste Arjun could win over the low caste Eklavya. V.P. Singh, who started a caste war on the streets of India in August 1990 by abruptly announcing the acceptance of the Mandal Commission recommendations for the reservation of the OBCs in public institutions observed on September 3, 2004 that 'When the state is being privatised, the private sector, at some point, has to share social responsibility, without affecting efficiency.'

A question which deserves to be raised here to shift away the public debate from the stereotyped arguments of the last fifty years is: Has an oppressive caste system been weakened and transformed by the fifty five years of 'affirmative policies' of the central and state governments? Have Indians become less or more conscious of their caste identities because of the changing status of the oppressed and suppressed castes by public interventionist policies of providing new opportunities to the marginal caste groups? The answer to these questions is that the policy of reservations followed by the public authorities has not only failed to bring any change in caste attitudes but the caste label as a brand is projected to corner public resources in the name of public good and social justice. A few facts may be mentioned to substantiate the argument that democratic politics in India have become, in reality, caste politics and casteism is a reality because caste in politics has become a tradable and profitable commodity. First, the anti-Brahmin movement of Ramaswami Naicker in the South began with a reformist agenda for the liberation of Brahman in oppressed caste society; and in the first decade of the twenty first century, Tamil Nadu society and politics are completely fragmented among castes and sub-castes and the DMK, AIADMK and many other offshoots of the Dravidian anti-caste movements are leading small caste-based shops to achieve political power. Such a development in Tamil Nadu politics has created a situation where every caste and sub-caste leader competes for raising the quota of reservations for his/her segment of caste-based supporters. The Supreme Court had to intervene and observe that caste reservations cannot exceed fifty percent of the total vacancies. Second, a lot of misinformation is spread about the success of the so-called Kerala model of development. Behind this drama lies caste and sub-caste based fragmented politics. The Congress-led United Democratic Front and the Left Democratic Front are just 'platforms' for multiple caste-based parties and groups. The Kerala government has to follow a caste based 'quota' policy for any educational project and every caste has to be given permission to open a school or a college on the basis of the strength of the caste-based political groups. Casteisation of politics has completed the full circle of complete mortgaging of public institutions on caste based questions. Third, Lalu Prasad Yadav has proclaimed himself as the invincible Raja (King) of extremely backward Bihar by publicly stating that his Yadav caste is behind him as solidly as a rock. Not to be left behind, the champion of unstoppable ongoing casteisation of Bihar society, politics and government, Ram Vilas Paswan, has floated a caste-based shop known as the Rashtriya Janata Dal and after every election, Paswan or Sharad Yadav or Nitish Kumar are very active commodities for every coalition government at the Centre.

The upshot of the above description is that Indian society and politics are completely cornered by caste and sub-caste leaders, identities and loyalties. Indians have started projecting their caste brand for reserved quota. To sum up, Indians have to choose between casteism and a modern just society where the 'poor' of India are given special treatment by the state, irrespective of the caste brand. The choice is clear.

– Sahara Time, September 18th, 2004

LIMITS OF CASTE POLITICS

The State Assembly Elections held in February 2005 in Bihar and Jharkhand have shown very clearly and unambiguously that the caste-based and religion-based electoral strategies adopted by political parties are showing diminishing returns. It deserves to clearly state that there is nothing like a 'hung' Assembly and electoral verdict has to be seriously interpreted to understand the relationship between society and politics, and political leaders and their social reach.

Political sociology of India has been defined and practiced by political leaders, groups and important individuals and India has witnessed two models of the sociology of politics, i.e., either a confederation of castes or exclusively of a particular Jati and up-Japi playing a role in politics.

The Congress party practiced the model of an all-inclusive social castes and community based 'coalition' for winning an election and also for governance of the country.

This coalitional-platform model of the Congress is challenged by the BJP which claims to be a party of the Hindus, by the Hindus and for the Hindus; in the absence of Muslim vote, it could get only 37 out of 243 seats in Bihar and 30 out of 80 seats in Jharkhand. This proves that party's claim to represent the Hindu majority community does not get translated into majority electoral support as witnessed in the State Assembly elections of 2005 in Jharkhand, Bihar and Haryana.

Further, every claimant of caste-based electoral support could not win an electoral victory because caste-based electoral competition brought the caste versus caste reality in public life. If Lalu claims support of his Yadav caste, Nitish Kumar also follows the same route to politics by confronting Yadav caste-based support structure of Lalu by bringing the Koeri, Kurmi castes behind him; one caste vote bank is challenged by another caste-based support of Nitish Kumar.

This story of elections in Bihar and Jharkhand in 2005 clearly shows that no caste-based party or political formation can win a majority of seats because divided and fragmented castes have found their own shops and leaders. Ram Vilas Paswan jumped into the electoral competition in Bihar to confront and defeat the Lalu Prasad-Rabri RJD-led government but has ended with only 29 seats and the result is that neither Lalu nor Paswan have gained a majority of seats. Bihar has many caste players because if caste is the reference point of politics, there is nothing like it because castes are numerous and many and thus caste-based political shops have to be multiple.

Haryana is also a social laboratory for the practitioners of caste versus caste politics where two clear trends of caste-based politics have emerged in Haryana. First, Om Prakash Chautala of the Indian National Lok Dal and the Devi Lal clan have always projected themselves as 'authentic' leaders of the Jat caste but many other Jat leaders like Bansi Lal or Hoodas et al have also competed for Jat votes in Haryana. Hence one caste can have many competitors among themselves and even-numerically large caste like the Jats in Haryana cannot ensure electoral victory because Jat versus Jat politics has become a normal activity. The evidence from Haryana is clear that it is impossible to insulate a dominant caste from internal competition for winning an election.

Second, inter-caste and intra-caste political competition has contributed only to the fragmentation of society and polity as has been proved by the fact that the Congress party in victory faced serious caste-based tug of war in Haryana while electing a party leader.

The upshot of above description is that caste-based politics has witnessed proliferation of multiple caste-based parties and groups and competition among castes and sub-castes has logically led to fragmented electoral verdict and even if one party gets a majority on its own, caste-based factions within the party continue to compete against one another and the majority party government is weak and unstable because of internal riots based on caste claims and counter-claims.

Resultantly, it has also given birth to complete 'casteisation' and communalisation of society, polity and bureaucracy. Corruption in public life has always engaged the attention of critics, but complete 'casteisation' and communalisation of government led by casteist and communalist parties and leaders has also to be exposed and demystified. – *Sahara Time, March 20, 2005*

LEFT AND CASTE POLITICS

During the CPI(M)'s recent National Congress in New Delhi, the party focused its attention on future political strategies. Two significant facts emerged out of the three-day deliberations: (i) the CPI(M)'s re-conceptualisation of the third alternative in politics; (ii) its desire to expand its base in the Hindi heartland where the party is conspicuous by its absence. Besides, the CPI(M) has recognised the need to grapple with the existing dynamics of caste politics in north India.

The issue of caste will have to be handled politically if the CPI(M) has to break the stranglehold of caste-based parties in UP and Bihar. It deserves to be mentioned that the caravan of caste-based politics, especially after the mandalisation of society, has not only hurt the Congress, but also eliminated the CPI and CPI(M) from north India. This divisive politics has clearly marginalised the forward-looking and socially progressive political formations like the communists and the Congress.

The political line of the CPI(M), as revealed by the party resolution, deserves to be analysed thoroughly. Prakash Karat, the new general secretary of the CPI(M), has clearly spelt out the tasks ahead for his party. Regarding the communists' support to the Manmohan Singh Government at the Centre, he observed: "The onus of keeping the allies united rests with the Congress, which heads the UPA. We are only sentinels of the people." Mr. Karat further said: "We are not supporting the Congress to enable it to pursue discredited policies of the BJP. We will not hesitate to oppose the Congress if it deviates from the CMP." The CPI(M) general secretary seems to have made his position clear: The party's support to the UPA Government is "conditional", and is intended to keep the BJP out of power. He has alerted the Congress to implement the common minimum programme, and that it should not follow in the footsteps of the BJP if it wants to complete its five-year term.

The CPI(M) seems to have learnt its lessons from short-lived anti-Congress experiments at the Centre, which forced the middle class to support the BJP. This was partially because of their disgust for the non-performing governments of V.P. Singh, Chandra Shekhar, H.D. Deve Gowda and Inder Kumar Gujaral. Like their counterparts elsewhere, the Indian middle class too wants security under a stable government. The BJP gained support of stability-oriented middle class by throwing out wavering prime ministers and governed the Centre from 1998 to 2004. It was the issue of stability, not just the rhetoric of Hindutva, that attracted the middle class to the BJP. No wonder Mr. Karat has clearly said that the CPI(M)'s third alternative "should emerge as a result of struggles and on the basis of shared ideology, and not as an electoral strategy".

The CPI(M) has experienced the opportunism of the third front allies in Tamil Nadu, Punjab and Jammu & Kashmir. It deserves to be mentioned that Mulayam Singh Yadav's clamouring for third front is absolutely different from that of the CPI(M). The latter, at its National Congress, discussed the root cause of serious agrarian crisis and reiterated its demand for the implementation of land reforms to ameliorate the living situation of the rural poor. Will the Yadav brothers — Mulayam Singh and Lalu Prasad — accept this? It is unlikely as their traditional vote-bank, the middle class backward peasantry, is the sole beneficiary of agrarian "status quo". Will Ram Vilas Paswan support the redistribution of surplus land to the agrarian poor in Bihar? The Dalit political parties cannot support the CPI(M) in the struggle for land reforms, irrespective of the fact that the poor will be its real beneficiaries in UP and Bihar. Thus, the CPI(M) will find the so-called casteist secular allies, like Mulayam Singh, Lalu Prasad and Mr. Paswan, as social status quoists.

The Indian Marxists have rightly maintained that the caste system plays the role of class relations as defined by Karl Marx. Caste is class in India, but the story does not end with this. Caste identity can never lead to the emergence of class identity because caste is an ideology linked with the Hindu social order. Further, caste in politics has brought into sharp focus the complex reality of caste versus caste and sub-caste versus sub-caste feeling in the public domain. Mulayam Singh Yadav has his own caste-based social constituency and Ms. Mayawati of the BSP has her own assured caste-basis for fighting the elections. Mulayam versus Mayawati is not politics of just two individuals; it is politics of caste versus caste, and the communists have no entry point in such casteist politics.

Caste has become casteism in Indian politics, and parties with assured support from their own castes are competing in politics. It is not a rhetoric when the Yadav brothers claim the support of "MY" (Muslims and Yadavs) and Mr. Paswan challenges Lalu Prasad with an alternative of Dalit-Muslim alliances because Yadavs versus Dalits have become socio-economic and caste-based realities. The BSP and the Congress had contested elections in UP as allies, but Ms. Mayawati claimed that her party had failed to get the upper caste vote, while the BSP's vote-bank was completely transferred to the Congress.

The greatest challenge before the Marxists is demystifying the reality of the casteist ideology. Only then will the basic issues of class emerge on the centrestage of Indian politics. Being practitioners of alternative politics, the Marxists have to unmask casteism. For instance, the new dominant Maratha castes in Maharashtra are equally divided in their support to the Congress, the NCP, the Shiv Sena and the BJP. All the Dravidian parties in Tamil Nadu, whether the DMK, the AIADMK or other splinter groups, have support from different segments of castes. The so-called non-Brahmin movement of the erstwhile Dravidian leaders has got completely equated with caste, and all Dravidian parties get united on increasing the percentage of reservations for various castes in public services.

Casteist leaders are only interested in caste-based reservations in the public services because the caste elite forms their backbone. The increasing demand of reservations for multiple caste groups by these parties keep the poor away from the real crisis created by increasing unemployment in the country. Job opportunities in rural India are decreasing because public investment for capital formation in agriculture has drastically declined. Caste-based parties have not raised these secular issues of unemployment, poverty or food insecurity because caste-consciousness is co-terminus only with reservations in public services. The mantra of quota is also being taken up by the casteist leaders in the private sector.

The upshot of the above description is that the Marxists' quest for alternative politics is dependent on their capacity to expose the casteist ideology in India. Caste-based identities in politics are the greatest obstacles before the emergence of large social solidarity movements around secular issues like land reforms. Caste and casteism go together, and class consciousness cannot emerge unless caste is confronted with class struggles on class-secular issues.

Caste is divisive and always ends up in a "caste versus caste" scenario. Class is a large social identity that can emerge only during people's struggles for secular social causes. This is the task before the Indian Marxists. Hindi heartland politics has been pulverised by communalists and casteists, and alternative politics can emerge only when casteism and communalism are defeated. The heartland has to be liberated from socially reactionary ideologies of casteism and communalism. Socially progressive people's parties and movements will take birth only when regressive politics is buried forever. – *The Pioneer, May 3, 2005*

UP's CASTE CAULDRON IS BOILING

Uttar Pradesh's special place in India's national life is owed not just to the fact that 80 of the country's 543 seats in the Lok Sabha are located here but also because it is bang in the middle of the Hindi heartland. Its proximity to Delhi also makes it the "real" centre of power in India. So much for truisms which should be recalled when important developments unfold. Like the one which happened on June 9 when Mayawati, the uncrowned queen of the Dalits of UP, sought to extend her party, the BSP's, social base by organising an impressive "Brahmin Sammelan" at Lucknow. Not only were Brahminical rituals performed on the occasion, but Mayawati also joined her favourite slogan, Jai Bhim with Jai Parashuram, a Brahminical innuendo.

Mayawati wanted to send the message loud and clear that the BSP also cares for the Brahmin community. Ambiguous slogans such as Yeh haathi nahin, Ganesh hain, Brahma, Vishnu, Mahesh hain were raised. So, was she abandoning her "Dalit-oriented" ideology by joining forces with the Brahmins? After all, Kanshi Ram, Mayawati's mentor, had founded the BSP on April 4, 1984, with "DS4" (Dalit Soshit Samaj Sangarh Sangarh) to fight the domination of the minority upper castes over the majority Dalit Bahujan Samaj. What has happened to Mayawati? Isn't she the one who always targeted the Manuvadis, as the "oppressors" of the Dalits? She emerged as a tall leader of the Shoshit Varg in UP who look to her as their champion and protector. It deserves to be stated that when she became chief minister for the first time in 1993, she had said, "I am not a leader of Bahujan Samaj but of the whole society." But her politics was solidly linked with the distinct social constituency of Dalits and Jatwas. Is it a new avatar of Mayawati when she said at the Brahmin rally "jiski jitni taiyaari hogi, uski utni bhagidari hogi"?

Mayawati has announced that the so-called upper caste will be given party tickets as "partners" of the Dalit castes. This is not the end of the story. Mayawati extended her hand of friendship towards the "poor Brahmins" and she criticised the political leaders drawn from them for not doing enough for their impoverished brethren. She continued that upper caste leaders had only cared for their family and close friends. "What has Atal Bihari Vajpayee done for the uplift of Brahmins in his own state?", she said. In keeping with her new formula, Mayawati unambiguously stated that seats will be allotted to Brahmins on a proportionate basis.

Political holders who are involved in the cut-throat politics of parliamentary democracy do not make shifts or carry out fresh adjustments in an absent-minded manner. Political parties have necessarily got to grow or else they face the threat of extinction. And growth depends on their capacity to adapt and respond to the changing social reality at the grassroots levels.

The Rashtriya Lok Dal of Ajit Singh remains confined to the same agrarian society of Western UP and continues to be identified with the Jats. Every effort made by Ajit Singh, and before him his father, the late Charan Singh, to extend their area of influence outside western UP to the state's other regions failed miserably because the party and its leaders were identified only with the Jat agrarians and that too drawn from a particular sub-region. They raised the demand for the creation of a new state called "Harit Pradesh" to realise their dream of establishing a hereditary chief ministership.

If, on the one hand, one casteist party like the RLD has shown its incapacity broaden its social base, the old Congress of Jawaharlal Nehru, Indira Gandhi, G.B. Pant, Sampurnand and C.B. Gupta have been completely decimated in UP. Its alliance with the upper castes, the Dalits and the Muslims is not only in shambles, every sign of revival eludes it. Mulayam Singh Yadav displaced the Congress in UP in 1980 by creating an alternative social alliance of intermediate peasant castes, particularly the Yadavs, and, in the process, he began attracting other social groups who were completely disenchanted by the Congress after supporting it almost unceasingly from 1947 to 1989 (the exception was in 1967 and 1977).

V.P. Singh, who had been Congress chief minister in the late 1970s-early 1980s, laid the foundation for the burial of the party by dramatically announcing the acceptance of reservations for the backward castes in public institutions in 1990 when he was a purely temporary Prime Minister for only 10 months. Uttar Pradesh witnessed the complete mandalisation of society and polity, and an already caste-divided and caste-conscious society was completely frozen into castes and sub-caste loyalties. The first beneficiary of this was Mulayam because he had organised a powerful intermediate peasant caste of Yadavs and attracted Muslims who completely shifted from the Congress, which was perceived by them to be practicing "soft Hindutva". The Muslims wanted a party with a leader who could take an uncompromising stand against the BJP, and Mulayam emerged as a great champion of their interests.

The ascendancy of intermediate peasant castes like Yadavs or Jats was a danger signal for the Dalits and the landless scheduled castes who were victims of the tyranny of the backward caste peasantry in rural society. A clear political space emerged for the BSP, a party of the Dalits, and Uttar Pradesh politics of the 1990s witnessed the emergence of a political triangle of Mulayam, Mayawati and the forces of Hindutva. In this social trifurcation, the first to be completely marginalised was the Congress. Mulayam Singh Yadav's social constituency is represented by castes which are perceived as "oppressors" of the Dalits in rural UP. Mayawati's BSP filled in the need for a Dalit party to counter the Yadav party of Mulayam. Meanwhile, the Muslims of UP, moved over to Mulayam's side. The emergence of Mayawati as a Dalit party leader also attracted a section of them.

But in 2005, UP politics seems to be shifting away from the BJP-SP-BSP triangle to a contest between two major contenders, the SP and the BSP. The BJP is emerging as a marginal third player. The premise of Mulayam and Mayawati is that the BJP has reached its political plateau in UP and the Ram Temple frenzy is dead. To them the time is opportune to woo the so-called higher castes who had formed the constituency of the BJP. The logic of democratic and competitive politics is that competing contenders for power make calculations about the assets and weaknesses of political opponents. The first signal came from the Rajput/Thakur castes of UP and Amar Singh, a Rajput leader of the SP and comrade-in-arms of Mulayam, made inroads into his caste constituency to wean them away from the declining BJP.

Mulayam launched his present term as chief minister with a shaky support base. Following the principle that an enemy's enemy could be a friend, he released from jail the notorious Raja Bhaiya, an alleged Thakur criminal, who Mayawati had sent to jail. To top it, Mulayam made him a minister by declaring Raja Bhaiya a "liberator"!

Mayawati has proved to be a quick learner in politics and has come to power by keeping her eyes and ears open to the changing scene of UP politics. She reflected deeply on Mulayam's rise and saw through his gameplan. If Mulayam Singh created an electoral bloc with the Yadavs, Thakurs/Rajputs and Muslims, Mayawati had to mobilise an alternative social and electoral base to contain her arch political rival. This explains her strategy to win over the Brahmins who have no contradiction with the Dalits in the rural society of UP. The Yadav, Thakur/Rajput, Muslim supporters of Mulayam have to be opposed by Dalit, Brahmin and Muslim supporters of the BSP. This was the message of the Brahmin Maha Sammelan of June 9. The BSP leadership has launched Brahmin mobilisation rallies in the districts as well. The state is now witnessing a very deft game of caste-based political strategies.

The upshot is that India's largest state is caught in a bog where politics is purely caste-oriented. It is a situation that criminals are manipulating to their advantage by backing one side or the other. The bureaucracy and police are also divided on the basis of caste identity and caste loyalty. Every institution of civil society is involved in the battle to win advantages. Truly, UP is in the dark ages. – *The Pioneer, July 2, 2005*

WHITHER CASTE POLITICS

The 1990s had witnessed a political upsurge in UP and Bihar because the direct beneficiaries of V.P. Singh's dramatic announcement in August 1990 on the Mandal Commission report on backward caste reservations came to occupy the seats of political power on the slogan of 'social justice for the hitherto neglected backward castes.' For the first time in India, the new backward caste leaders became crucial in the making and unmaking of coalition governments at the Centre. This new phenomenon of backward caste assertions was hailed as the empowerment of the backwards who had succeeded in displacing the high caste political leadership of UP and Bihar.

A few questions deserve to be answered about the real meaning of post-Mandal politics of UP and Bihar as actually witnessed during the last one-and-a-half decade of backward caste rule in these states. The limitations of backward caste and Dalit politics deserve to be stated because it seems that Lalu, Mulayam, Mayawati et al, the champions of 'social justice movement', are all struggling to keep themselves afloat. What has happened to the formidable social constituencies of these 'leaders' who felt politically invincible?

Mulayam Singh Yadav and Mayawati have experienced electoral victories and defeats from 1990 to 2005, the golden period of backward-Dalit rule in Uttar Pradesh. Mulayam Singh Yadav came to power in 2003, not on the basis of his formidable Muslim-Yadav (M-Y) social constituency but by engineering a split within the BSP and also with the outside support of the Congress. Mayawati has been CM and has also faced political challenges in spite of her claims of majority support of the Bahujan Samaj along with a section of Muslims in UP.

Lalu Prasad Yadav is fighting a grim political battle for his survival in 2005. His ruling RJD was decisively defeated in the February 2005 Bihar assembly elections in spite of his boastful statements that "there are 16% Yadavas and 17% Muslims in Bihar. That is 33% votes for me." This is the solid M-Y support on the basis of which he ruled over Bihar. Lalu Yadav is facing an uphill task to regain power in the October-November 2005 elections in Bihar.

Not only this. Every casteist political leader in UP and Bihar is experiencing the complete fragmentation and hierarchisation of the backward, most backward and Dalit castes. This has compelled these caste leaders of yesterday to secure alliances with other 'caste groups' to win elections in UP and Bihar.

The hysterical pro-Mandal Commission movement and the euphoria of the agitation have died down. Now the basic and antagonistic contradictions between the backward caste peasantry and the untouchable Dalits have come back into politics and the Yadavas find it difficult to win elections on the basis of M-Y vote bank. That is why Lalu Yadav needs the Congress party to get the support of higher castes, since Bhumihars, Rajputs and Brahmins had completely abandoned M-Y led alliance. It is not only Lalu Yadav, even the Janata Dal (United) led by Nitish has aligned with the BJP counting support from upper caste voters who are aligned with the Sangh Parivar in Bihar.

The self-appointed messiahs of social justice have realised that elections cannot be won on the basis of "pure" segments of divided castes and this has led them to form alliances with other castes. But even this exercise has created a situation of fragmented electoral verdicts as witnessed in Bihar and UP. The argument is that the post-Mandal casteisation of politics led by intermediate backward caste parties of Lalus, Mulyams, Nitishes and Ajit Singhs has reached a plateau and its potential to win elections is quite limited. Mulayam, like Lalu, has brought along with him Rajput leaders like Amar Singh, criminals like Raju Bhaiya to win upper caste support without which he cannot win an election in UP.

Mayawati of the BSP has also realised that she too has to make caste alliances between untouchable Dalits and high castes in UP. That's why she organised a Brahmin Mahasammelan at Lucknow on June 9, 2005 where she publicly admitted that her slogan against Manuvadi forces "was to keep the upper castes away from the BSP". She announced that henceforth the BSP will nominate Brahmin and Bania candidates. The BJP has also realised that its upper caste Hindu constituency is not adequate to win elections in UP and Bihar.

The whole post-Mandal phenomenon of caste versus caste and sub-caste versus sub-caste has led to the emergence of caste and sub-caste based assertions in UP and Bihar. The politics of divided and fragmented caste hierarchies has led to the fragmentation of parties: every caste leader is competing against another specific-caste-based leader. Mayawati versus Mulayam or Ram Vilas Paswan versus Lalu Yadav is a testimony to the fact that caste divisions and caste-based assertions have led to sectarianisation and complete casteisation of politics and every institution of governance in UP and Bihar.

The virus of caste-based politics has spread like a killer disease in the body-politic of UP and Bihar and the slogan of social justice for the oppressed, suppressed Dalits and backwards has remained just a slogan. The backward caste peasantry has wielded its power to protect its landed property rights and any talk of land reforms for the benefit of the poor in UP and Bihar is taboo. The only hope against hope is that a modern economy at the national level will help in the creation of modern productive and social relations which will make people transcend caste.

An industrial culture of modern science and technology is a necessary condition to transform the existing social relations which are based on medieval categories of caste. Politics has solidified caste identities, and a modern science-based economy can create the material and social situation necessary to bury the caste structure of India. Till then UP and Bihar are in a prison house of 'caste versus caste' and 'sub-caste versus sub-caste' public life.

– *The Economic Times, November 19, 2005*

NOT MINORITYISM BUT JUST ENRICHMENT

The joint Hindu family of the Sangh Parivar survives and thrives on the ideological politics of hatred against minority communities, especially Indian Muslims, who are always projected as anti-Hindu.

It is not surprising that the Hindu Rashtravadis are always inclined to describe any activity of the Indian State concerning the welfare of minorities as "appeasement". The BJP has always targeted the secular policies of the Congress-led governments as attempts to pamper the Muslim minority community.

Logical thinking is not a virtue with the Swayam sevaks of the RSS, whether L.K. Advani or Narendra Modi. The Sangh Parivar is not trained to distinguish between the lunatic fringe of a community and a community of 150 million. Terrorism in Punjab in the 1980s can never be attributed to the Sikh community because it was an activity of a small group, which had appointed itself as the guardian of the Sikh community. The upshot is that any act of violence is appropriated by the Sangh Parivar to create Hindu-Muslim division and any localised inter-community riot is also converted into a Hindu versus Muslim dispute, irrespective of the fact that a section of lumpen Hindus or Muslims may be responsible for creating a situation leading to violence and riot.

It is not just that terrorism or riots are attributed to the policies of appeasement and pro-minorityism. Any welfare or development activity undertaken by a Congress regime is promptly categorised by the Sangh Parivar as "pro-minority". The Congress-led government in Andhra Pradesh had decided to "reserve" a minuscule percentage of seats in public institutions for the "backward Muslims". The Sangh Parivar made it a big issue because any "idea" of reservations or special concessions to the minorities is not only opposed, it is perceived as pampering.

Allahabad High Court has decided that Aligarh Muslim University is not a "Muslim minority" educational institution. This judgement has divided the Muslim intelligentsia and the UPA government has decided to amend the Aligarh Muslim University Act and provide it a "minority community status". The Sangh Parivar does not draw any conclusion that the Muslim intelligentsia is divided on the issue of status of AMU because its main project is to demonise any secular intervention by the government. It is of no concern to the BJP ideologues that in a functioning democracy community opinions can be of many colours and shades.

Further, the Constitution of India has provided for special educational and cultural rights for the minorities. The Supreme Court has upheld the right of the minorities to maintain their own educational and cultural institutions to cater to their specific educational and cultural needs. A multi-religious and multi-cultural society like India has got to take care of the special educational and cultural requirements of diverse community groups and the Constitution is fully reflective of such needs and sentiments. The Constitution accepts that India's unity is based on diversity and such a unity cannot be maintained or protected without protecting and promoting cultural diversities.

The Sangh Parivar resents and opposes steps, even the most limited ones, to provide representation to minority communities in the public services. The Justice Sachar Committee had asked for just facts about community-wise representation in the Indian armed forces, but the Sangh Parivar and the BJP launched a campaign against the fact-finding activity as "anti-national". The Manmohan Singh government has been castigated by the BJP for it, but is it not the duty of the Indian State to identify social differences among various communities for undertaking special redressal steps for meeting their special reasons for backwardness? It deserves to be clearly stated that it is the duty of any democratic government to respond to the special needs of multiple diverse social groups.

Why does the Sangh Parivar smell a rat at every action of a secular government in response to minority rights? The Sangh Parivar cannot accept that the minorities have special rights or status in a "Hindu Rashtra" because the RSS ideology is built on the principle of Hindus versus the others, and any concession to the minorities is considered threatening to the Hindus.

The BJP's attack against the UPA government's policies is a product of its own anti-minority ideological position. How can the UPA government's so-called pampering of minorities lead to bomb blasts in a city? Were there no bomb blasts in India from 1998 to 2004 when the BJP was in power? The answer is that the

Sangh Parivar cannot think without targeting the Muslim community about every action of sectional violence in India. The Sangh Parivar thinks, breathes and smells only in terms of Hindus versus Muslim and all its activities are directed towards the goal of dividing India on religious basis.

Hence, Indian Muslims are "terrorists" because they "target the Hindus". Have the Indian Muslims not made any contribution to the socio-cultural and economic development of India? What is the relationship between the bomb blasts at Varanasi and the UPA government's approach towards Aligarh Muslim University? Can there be any connection between policy of reservations for Muslims and the so-called Muslim involvement in terrorism? The real objective behind the Advani-Rajnath Rath Yatra, therefore, is not national integration but accentuating divisions for political and electoral gains. – *The Pioneer, March 18, 2006*

THE DIVIDE AND RULE GAME GOES ON

The Constitution has been twisted and subverted to serve political interests. Politicians take refuge behind declarations of constitutional loyalty when rich electoral dividends are assured.

Arjun Singh has, of late, been heard proclaiming from the rooftops that he is duty bound to implement the new reservation policy, and not doing so would mean betraying the Constitution, which after its 93rd amendment ordains 27% quotas of OBCs in central educational institutions mandatory and irrevocable. The Union Human Resource Development Minister did not stop at that, though. He went on an offensive against the National Knowledge Commission, pointing out to its members, most of who had criticised the government's recent quota move, that they were not above the Constitution, and could not afford to be "unaware" of the existence of "a Parliament" or the law passed by them.

It is, indeed, gratifying to note that our political class has at least woken up to its constitutional obligations. For, in the past 60 years of Independent India, the Constitution has, for our politicos, been the most dispensable article of both political practice and governance. Had that not been the case the Supreme Court would not have repeatedly asserted that action of the government" are in violation of the basic structure of the Constitution". Virtually, every party in power can be held guilty of violating some or the other fundamental principle of the Constitution.

Such violations are most in evidence vis-à-vis the Directive Principles of State Policy and the scant attention that the political class of free India has paid to them. Our national would have been completely different than what it is today only if proper attention had been paid to the constitutional provisions of Articles 41, 45 and 46 in the years that immediately followed India's Independence from colonial rule. Article 41 explicitly mentions "Right to work, to educational and to public assistance in certain cases".

Article 45 asks for "provision for early childhood care and education to children below the age of six years"; and Article 46 mentioned the need for "promotion of educational and economic interests of scheduled castes, scheduled tribes and other weaker sections".

It requires neither genius nor exceptional intelligence to see the people who were obliged to uphold the Constitution never cared to implement those three key articles. The framers of our Constitution had made Directive Principles non-justiciable probably because of the paucity of financial resources available to the Indian State at the time of Independence. But the judiciary has now given "legal teeth to these Directive Principles" because the resource base of the Indian state has expanded considerably. The Indian economy has in recent years broken through the barrier of the infamous Hindu rate of growth to achieve a healthy 8% annual growth rate.

The State is levying a special cess to fund its campaign to universalize elementary education - the Sarva Shiksha Abhiyan - despite the expansion of its resource base. This indicates its lack of commitment: the backlog of illiteracy among poor children cannot be tackled by taking recourse to a paltry "special cess" and without any direct state intervention.

Singh's argument that all political parties are bound by the 93rd Constitutional Amendment to implement the new reservation policy is, at best, disingenuous and, at worse, politically paradoxical verging on the suicidal. For, if constitutional obligations had been fulfilled, Indian children would have been liberated from the cruse of illiteracy, malnourishment and exploitative and oppressive bonded labour.

But to argue that our political class failed to enforce the Directive Principles merely because they have been non-justiciable would be inaccurate and even fallacious. Successive governments have been unable to even enforce chapter III (on fundamental rights) of the Constitution, which is "legally binding". Why have governments done no more than pay lip service to Article 21A, inserted by the Constitution (Eighty-sixth Amendment) Act 2002, which makes it mandatory for the state to provide free and compulsory education to all children between six and 14 years.

So, if the HRD Minister is obliged to enforce the new reservation policy because the 93rd Constitutional Amendment mandates it, should the minister not, by the same logic, be equally committed to Article 21A (Right to Education)? Or, is one constitutional obligation more important than the other in his scheme of things?

How does one explain the double standard of our political class vis-à-vis the sanctity of constitutional provisions? The Constitution has been twisted and subverted whenever such acts serve short-term political interests. By the same token, politicians take refuge behind declarations of constitutional loyalty when rich electoral dividends are assured.

The Right to Education is, therefore, expandable. It won't, after all, help politicians in pandering to retrograde social sentiments and dispensing political patronage to make a quick vote. Its path is the long and arduous way of social transformation. The 93rd amendment that provides for reserving seats for OBCs in central institutions is, on the other hand, a sure-fire recipe for electoral success.

Its enforcement would help in conservation of the socially fragmented and polarized status quo. An effective weapon is the vital though, narrow battle for state power. The upshot is that if Yadavs can have parties and leaders, the Congress too can hope to woo other backward caste denominations by flaunting its purported concern for the academic and professional future of their children. Enforcing the 93rd amendment, it believes, can help achieve that. The game of divide and rule goes on.

–Economic Times, May 27, 2006

6

Political Parties and Issues before the Nation

EXPLOSIVE AND BURNING

The Northeast witnessed ghastly violence on October 2, the birthday of Mahatma Gandhi, the apostle of peace. Bomb blasts ripped through Dimapur Railway Station and a market in Nagaland, killing innocent persons including children. While the Central and the seven State governments were on alert following the explosions, innocent Assamese continued to die at the hands of ULFA and the National Democratic Front of Bodoland (NDFB) throughout the first week of October.

These were not the only instances of violence. Manipur had burnt for full three months from July to September after the death of Manorama Devi. What has been the response of the Centre towards the issue of militancy in Northeast, especially during the last four months when the UPA Government has been in power? How have major political parties reacted to the violence? How have the immediate demands put by different groups in the Northeast been responded to by the Indian political class?

It deserves to be stated that political solutions in the broadest sense of the term would help us to get rid of the dark clouds hovering over Northeast. The incompetence of political leaders to provide solutions to the complicated ethnic, linguistic and territorial disputes in the Northeast can be seen in the manner the Central Government has handled the demand of the Manipuris to withdraw the controversial Armed Forces Special Power Act. The anger of the Manipuris was directed against the draconian Act as it was felt that the atrocities committed by the Armed forces against ordinary Manipuris could not be judicially challenged and investigated, and the Manorama Devi episode brought the pent up rage of the Manipuris on to the streets.

The Manipur Government, the Centre and the Army have all made extremely confusing statements on the demand of the Manipuris regarding the withdrawal of the Act. Have any lessons been learnt from such a confusion while dealing with delicate issues facing the Northeast? The Indian political class is still giving contradictory signals on the issues currently faced by Assam and Nagaland.

The Central Government is on tenterhooks because violence in Dimapur occurred when there is already a ceasefire and the NSCN of Isak Swu and Th Muivah are negotiating with the Centre. Who is responsible for disturbing peace in Nagaland when powerful insurgent groups like the NSCN(I-M) are not involved? Further, it is a well-known fact that "militancy" in Northeast or elsewhere can operate and succeed if they have a safe sanctuary to retreat. The UPA Government and the Opposition BJP have pointed their fingers of suspicion involving Bangladesh and Myanmar as the villain of the piece.

A note of caution: Whenever sovereign neighbouring countries are accused of "hostile neighbourly activities", governments should be very cautious and solutions among neighbouring countries should be sought through diplomacy. Political brinkmanship on the part of Indians while dealing with difficult problems with neighbours can be counterproductive. Not only this, public opinion in the country may become extremely hostile and volatile if the leadership accuses neighbouring countries for their domestic problems.

It is not being suggested that the Indian Government should not make sincere diplomatic efforts to convince the neighbouring countries to not provide sanctuaries to militants. In fact, this should be done while ensuring that Indians do not develop a "hostile" and "enemy" kind of attitude as a result of repeated public statements against the neighbouring countries. The BJP, the main opposition party, has not risen to the occasion and statements by its leaders have been extremely unconstructive in dealing with the problems of the Northeast. The Leader of the Opposition, L.K. Advani, washed his hands off by accusing the UPA Government of being "callous". His "chargesheet" against the Congress went further when he alleged that "vote bank" politics of the Congress was responsible for the current situation. Mr. Advani alleged that the soft policy followed by the UPA Government "towards terrorists and separatists" is responsible for the crisis because the

Congress has been "hobnobbing" with such elements for electoral gains. The Congress and the BJP have always adopted very different policies while dealing with Northeast militants or the Naxalites. The Congress has always used the "coercive power of the state" against militant groups but is prepared to negotiate with them in "public" or in "secrecy".

Home Minister Shivraj Patil rushed to the Northeast on October 4 and said that "doors for talks with militants were always open, but they should be unconditional". Mr. Patil unambiguously elaborated the approach of the UPA Government by stating, "We are prepared to sit for talks, but we cannot talk to a group demanding independence." In the same tone, Assam Chief Minister Tarun Gogoi on October 2 offered for talks with the ULFA and the NDFB.

A very significant development in the Northeast is that the Naga leaders and the All-Assam Student Union (AASU) have openly come out against the insurgents. The NSCN(I-M) has announced a reward for tips that will lead to unravelling the mystery behind the Dimapur blasts. Naga groups, committed to peace and negotiations, have taken great offence to the violence. AASU gave a "bandh" call on October 5 against the violence by the ULFA and the NDFB.

This is a silver lining in the otherwise dark situation that many important local civilian groups have come out against the insurgents. Further, AASU, in one of its four demands on October 5, wanted preference for "sons of the soil" while recruiting employees for Central Government agencies operating in Assam. The employment situation in Assam is grim and the Centre should tackle the situation differently.

The Government and the Opposition have to tackle the problems of the Northeast with a "united national consensus". The BJP has not learnt any lesson from its own experience of managing complex "regional" problems during its rule from 1998 to 2004. A mix of coercion and negotiations is the only approach which deserves to be followed by the Centre while dealing with Northeast insurgents. Further, policymakers should abstain from blaming neighbouring countries for their alleged connivance with insurgents. They should also expect that any meaningful dialogue with neighbours would succeed. Since the United States has made "anti-global terrorism" the main plank for its aggressive military occupations, every neighbouring country of India is aware of this changed global situation.

Hence, Bangladesh or Myanmar, like Pakistan, are not oblivious of American interests in South Asia. It was not absentmindedness of the American Ambassador to offer on October 5 the support of FBI to deal with insurgency in the Northeast. If India can be given unsolicited help by American FBI, smaller countries can always be cowed down by US imperialists. National consensus, which is the need of the hour, cannot be created if Muslim Bangladeshis are viewed as mischief-makers by a section of Indian policymakers.

– The Pioneer, October 07, 2004.

CALLOUSNESS TOWARDS NAXALISM

The Cabinet Committee on Security of the Congress-led UPA government raised high hopes on September 15, 2004, when it endorsed the Andhra Pradesh model of "dialogue" with the Naxals or the People's War Group or the Left extremists. Home minister Shivraj Patil announced that he would hold a meeting of the chief ministers of Naxal infested states like Jharkhand, Chhattisgarh, Bihar, Orissa, Madhya Pradesh, Maharashtra, Uttaranchal, Uttar Pradesh and West Bengal on the basis of the CCS meeting of September 15. He announced that "The Centre is of the view that there should be a long-term strategy to tackle the Naxal problem instead of merely reducing it to a law and order situation." This announcement of the home minister raised hopes that the new government would adopt a positive and socially reconstructive approach to the agrarian crisis which has given birth to Naxalism and it will be a decisive break from the past policies of former home minister L.K. Advani who only adopted a "law and order" approach towards a genuine social problem of agrarian misery.

However, Patil, during his meeting in Hyderabad with chief ministers on September 21, 2004, took an about turn and announced that the states were "at liberty" to decide the manner in which they would control extremism. He continued that "we do not want to advise you. Whatever you are doing, if done in a proper manner, we will stand by you." This policy statement of the home minister led to total confusion among the assembled chief ministers. The Jharkhand, Chhattisgarh and Bihar governments insisted at the meeting that "the centre hold talks as the Naxal menace was spread over several states and different approaches to curbing the menace could cause a law and order problem." The home minister abdicated and said "you (states) are in a better position to handle the matter" and "if need be we will stand by the state."

Patil gave a very disingenuous and specious argument to escape from the responsibilities of the central government by saying that "if the centre issued a directive, it would be confusing as the centre's and the state's area of jurisdiction was clearly demarcated". The 'directionless' state governments announced their own approaches at the meeting which was convened to adopt a 'unified policy' towards a 'social problem' which at the present affects at least nine states of India. Naveen Patnaik, the chief minister of Orissa, announced a policy of 'dialogue' with the Naxal outfits and he has followed it up by ordering the release of many Naxals from prison. Y.S. Rajashekhar Reddy of Andhra Pradesh announced the continuation of his government's policy of 'dialogue' which he had announced in April 2004 during the elections. Reddy has invited Naxal/PWG leaders for talks on October 2, 2004. The Chhattisgarh home minister's plea fell on deaf ears when it was stated that 'the guerrillas were seeking shelter in Andhra Pradesh' and 'this was the reason the nine different states were sharing the forum' for evolving a common approach. Bengal chief minister Buddhadeb Bhattacharya sanctioned one crore rupees for the rehabilitation of "50-odd extremists of the Kamtapur Liberation Organisation who have surrendered since last year".

The upshot of the above narration is that any change of government at the Centre from the Vajpayee-led NDA to the Manmohan Singh-led UPA has hardly brought about any change in the sensitivity of the rules towards an essentially social and political problem created by serious agrarian misery in backward areas and especially poor tribal dominated states. It is an estimate of the government of India that 125 districts and nine states are facing Naxal violence which is a direct product of agrarian neglect by the post-independence governments during the last fifty years. A dramatic example may be given to substantiate the argument that Left extremism can be tackled if the agrarian crisis is directly tackled by the government. The story of West Bengal may offer many lessons for policy makers. It was only the programme of agrarian reforms and agrarian development launched by the Left Front Government of Jyoti Basu from 1977 that liberated Bengal from Naxal violence.

The Naxal movement is supported by people who have been completely marginalised and socially ejected from the economic development of the last fifty five years. Bengal showed the way and it is clear that guns are not the answer to an essentially social problem. – *Sahara Time, October 09, 2004*

RESTRUCTURING BUREAUCRACY

A restructuring of bureaucracy has been on every PM's agenda, and the latest in the queue of reformists is Manmohan Singh. In his Independence Day address he had declared that "despite more than a decade of liberalisation, the state was here to stay; the government was necessary to improve the lives of the vast majority of Indians." The Hota Committee Report on Civil Services Reforms was tabled too in August. And, speaking of reforms, the PM himself spoke of the need for a better implementation of public programmes and policies, and to target social groups such that they benefit from officially sponsored anti-poverty programmes. He followed that up by assuring the Federation of Small Scale Industry of the elimination of the inspector raj as that obstructs the SSIs' growth potential.

It should also be noted how India's post-Independence leadership has always recognised that the so-called 'steel frame' of the civil service India inherited was out of sync with the new development challenges facing the rural poor. The Hota Committee Report was, for example, preceded by many others, like ones by Gorwala (1951), Gopalaswami (1952), Paul Appleby (1953), Mudaliar (1956), Krishnamachari (1962), Kothari (1977, on Administrative Reforms), and Satish Chandra (1989). Therefore, successive central governments have gathered much wisdom from these committees and commissions. But, despite all their suggestions, however, prime ministers still recite the old litany of bureaucratic bottlenecks that impede the implementation of public programmes. Clearly, there is little to hope for from yet another committee, which also applies to the Hota Committee.

Its recommendation that recruitment for the higher civil services may be made after children have completed high school is laughable. That is because school-children lead sheltered lives under their parents and have little, or no, exposure to complicated social realities. Can a pubic servant serve society without undergoing the tough and tumble of actual life, encapsulated in day-to-day social reality?

The Hota Committee suggests that they be educated, and trained, by an academy of education/training to be officially set up along the lines of the National Defence Academy. But what it ignores is that the young acquire training for the army, engineering or medicine to become specialists, whereas the key need for entrants to the civil services would be a high level of social consciousness, and awareness of India's social problems and realities. Meanwhile, higher education equips students to understand and analyse the social universe, and imparts a threshold level of maturity so essential for entrants to the higher civil services.

But the imperative of restructuring India's bloated bureaucracy cannot be brushed under the carpet just by rejecting the Hota Committee's suggestions. The first step in any reform must start at the top – especially in India, where the higher is a person's authority the more is his influence over functionaries who are lower down. And, bureaucratic bosses can either expedite, or stall, implementation in India's status-conscious society. This is the reality of the higher civil services that needs empirical analysis; and the suggested cure will bring relief from none of the ills if the problem is diagnosed wrong. Reforms will remain on paper unless we highlight some old characteristics of the bureaucracy. Next, therefore, we examine some of its salient, 55-year old traits.

First, India's higher civil service is an 'autonomous' power centre, fully protected by the Constitution and judiciary. That the bureaucracy is self-assured, self-centred and very conscious of its importance also increases the social distance between itself and the masses. So it is neither inefficiency, nor lack of motivation, but a feeling of 'superiority' which impedes them from implementing pro-poor programmes and to regard them with indifference.

Secondly, India's bureaucracy, as a centre of power, is linked with other power centres in society. Given India's parliamentary democracy, it has discovered the power of elected representatives like MLAs, MPs, ministers, chairmen of PSEs, and the like. Through trial and error, it has also learnt to establish fraternal links with its political masters; and the bureaucracy gets the licence to enjoy power once those linkages are in place. That is what orients officials towards politicians instead of ordinary citizens. (Serving the latter is a thankless job, but a quid pro quo with politicians rewards both).

Thirdly, by being so co-opted, the lifestyle of bureaucrats has drawn closer to the components that govern political life. Politics here is caste-based, and so too are the alliances which the bureaucracy quickly makes. Thus, bureaucrats are eager to implement ideologically discriminatory policies when their political masters go by a religion-based ideology. Hence, it is not just that casteist parties, and leaders, attain power via caste loyalties; bureaucrats too discover their own caste-based identities to link-up with such politics. They are just as quick to abandon them before the altar of linguistic, or sub-regional, identity should regional chauvinists, or aggressively local parties, attain power. The myth of an all-India service is fully exposed. It got distorted, ever since a politicised, communalised, caste conscious, and regionalist, bureaucracy took birth, thanks to the prevailing political categories of winning elections.

Thus, we must conclude that the agenda of the cleansing of politics and of bureaucracy must go hand-in-hand – especially in its higher echelons. The latter is the fountainhead of unprofessional and discriminatory administration. Thus, although the PM wants to make it development oriented, the reality is that the bureaucracy has long ceased to be the impartial guardian of the rule of law. That is the crux, and neither the Hota Committee's recommendations nor Manmohan Singh's platitudes will salvage the crumbling of India's bureaucracy. We need a political consensus to rid the bureaucracy of its evils, to make it adhere to the rule of law and for it to impartially protect every citizen.

– *The Economic Times, December 18, 2004*

REVOLUTION AND CRIME: AGRARIAN DISCONTENT

The Left-extremists – or Maoists (MCC) or members of PWG – who believe in the politics of annihilation have been able to operate in a democracy like India because the country's institutions have failed to liberate the masses from the stranglehold of the feudal-landlord classes. It must be clearly stated that the politics of bullet, guided by a complete misunderstanding of the Marxist-Leninist theory and praxis, has found acceptance in India because the country has failed to implement the much-needed land reforms in the agrarian sector.

Bihar, Orissa and parts of Andhra Pradesh or Jharkhand are the States that have splinter groups which have been able to sell a convoluted ideological and theoretical framework to the receptive oppressed sections of society. Naxalism in India has grown in areas that are well known for agrarian underdevelopment and landlord oppression. The question is, should the state too respond to this social problem in the same manner? The answer is "no". If it is the social situation that leads to the growth of violence, the state must first address the socio-economic issues.

It is correct on the part of the Chief Minister of Andhra Pradesh to open doors to negotiation with the representatives of MCC-PWG to find a political solution to the agrarian discontent that has strengthened the so-called Leftist adventurists. The Congress has announced its policy of negotiation and dialogue with the socially alienated groups that are operating in Andhra Pradesh, Jharkhand, Orissa, Bihar, etc. Home Minister Shivraj Patil spelt out the Union Government's agenda on January 18, 2005. According to him, "dialogue" was a "better option to deal with the problem." He further said, "Dialogues have succeeded in the past and efforts should be made to make them successful now."

Patil also declared that if talks failed the state will have to "do its duty". "We would like them (States) to hold talks, but if they decide to act, they have the Centre's full support." While admitting that Naxalism was a "national problem", Patil maintained that the "path of negotiations and dialogue" should be followed as decided by the Andhra Pradesh Government. It is a fact that neither a coercive State apparatus nor 'private armies' of landlords can deal with the challenge posed by groups which have won the confidence of the socially oppressed marginal sections in rural society.

The West Bengal Government could blunt extreme Left adventurism by implementing land reforms. It simply struck at the root of the problem–rural discontent in West Bengal. The question is, why did Kerala remain unaffected by Naxalism? The first communist State Government led by E.M.S. Namboodiripad in 1957 brought the agenda of agrarian restructuring to the centre-stage. Successive State governments have consciously adopted policies to create conditions which would be completely inhospitable to the Left adventurist groups.

The politics of bullet followed by the numerous fractured Naxal groups is indigenous to India and its solution lies in eradicating the social causes of rural deprivation. Another social reason for the emergence of Naxalism has been identified by J.K. Sinha, Director General CRPF, whose 23 battalions have been permanently involved in confrontations with Naxalites. Sinha asked for an "investigation into the source of finances of naxalites". According to him there seems to be a "nexus between criminal mafia and Left-wing extremists". He stated on January 29, that,

"Either the Naxal cadre is being used or the money is being shared." According to him 'kattaha' was smuggled from the Chatara forest in Bihar and the "local forest officials, Naxals and the organised mafia were all involved in this operation."

It is well known that an ideological umbrella can be used and abused by criminals too particularly when protection to mafia groups is provided by a section of bureaucracy. The upshot of the above description is that Naxalism is neither an all-India phenomenon nor motivated by the love for gun by criminals. An inequitable agrarian social order has in some States led to disenchantment with the system. A section of society resorts to violence if it loses faith in democracy and its institutions. Naxals too are no exception to this general rule of social behaviour. The solution lies in resolving the causes of social discontent prevailing in some States, especially those which have failed to implement land reforms. Any ideology, even if it is misguided or socially pervert, never prevails in a vacuum.

It is nourished and nurtured by existing social situations in a specific historical context. This applies to Naxalism as well. India has been able to resolve many complex social issues by identifying the genesis of those problems. The root of Naxalism is in the widespread agrarian discontent. – *Sunday Pioneer, February 6, 2005*

ELECTIONS, PARTIES AND DEMOCRACY

Prime Minister Manmohan Singh said on February 12, "I would be the last one to deny that corruption is a problem in the country." He maintained that parties need funds to fight elections with, and this "paves the way for black money". Mr. Singh suggested that "state funding of election" would ensure transparency and check corruption in politics. Election in a democracy is the villain of the piece because the need for money to contest elections makes parties approach "private fund-givers" who, in turn, are provided political patronage by the elected leaders. Indian democracy is under siege not only because of corruption but also because of serious distortions in the party system. The growing control of the mafia over public life is a threat to the very survival of Indian democracy.

Elections and parties are the pillars on which the functioning of a strong and successful democracy depends. However, elections are often reduced to farce. The Assembly polls in Bihar, Jharkhand

and Haryana this month have once again brought into sharp focus the weakness of the multi-party system and the difficulties faced by the election machinery in holding free and fair polls. A few facts may be mentioned to substantiate the argument that, irrespective of the electoral verdict in these three states, parliamentary democracy will not become healthy.

The party system in these three states is almost non-existent. Major political contenders in these provinces "belong" to families and are private shops masquerading as parties. In Bihar, Lalu Prasad Yadav of the RJD and Ram Vilas Paswan of the LJP have publicly stated that if one of them is depending on the support of Muslims and Yadavs, the other is attracting support of Muslims and Dalits. In Bihar, elections are being contested not by democratic party organisations but by leaders dependent on sectional support of Muslims or Yadavs or Dalits. The Congress, in spite of its pretensions, is a marginal force and the sickness prevailing in the Bihar Congress party organisation is not at all different from either the RJD or LJP.

The Congress is in a shambles. Bihar PCC president Ram Jatan Singh refused to file his nomination papers because he was not given the constituency of his choice. Not only this, the former Bihar PCC chief, Sarfaraz Ahmed, quit the party and joined the RJD.

In Haryana, leaders of Om Prakash Chautala's INLD and the Congress distributed tickets to their family members and relations with abandon. Mr. Chautala, who is the real manager of INLD, has given tickets as have his sons, Ajay and Abhay. In this situation how can the Congress abandon families of important leaders when "family tree" is worshiped at the Centre? The Congress is contesting in 90 seats and the family members of Messrs Bansi Lal, Bhajan Lal, Samsher Singh Surjewala et al are all in the race as a "family team".

Jharkhand, too, is following in the footsteps of Bihar and Haryana. JMM chief Shibu Soren (like Mr. Yadav in Bihar) is a permanent fixture in Jharkhand politics, and the JMM shop is owned by him. Stung by the criticism that he was promoting his sons, Hemant and Durga, he said, "For decades I led the Jharkhand movement. My sons learnt from me, now they want to lead from the front. What is wrong if someone from my family who is young, capable and has the party's backing is given a chance? Ask Lalu? Won't he allow it?" The BJP is in no better situation because in the last four years, the party had to change its Chief Minister because of internal revolts.

If strong and viable party system is almost non-existent in these three states, the political vacuum is filled by families, mafias and criminals. Chief Election Commissioner T.S. Krishnamurthy stated this on January 22. He said, "Conducting elections in Bihar, Jharkhand and Haryana is a challenge in view of the criminal-politician nexus. The free movement of criminals was spreading fear in the voters' mind." Further, he said that free and fair elections were not possible if the management of elections was in the hands of partisan, casteist and communalist bureaucrats.

"Personalism" has substituted party system, and the actual winning of elections has nothing to do with the so-called party manifestos. It is an extremely worrisome situation because chief ministers, ministers and MLAs who claim to be the voters' representatives are not bound by any party ideology, and instead of enforcing the rule of law, they themselves happen to be practitioners of lawlessness.

A democratic form of government is superior to every other known type of governance because in such a system, the rulers are elected on the basis of party competition and they go through an "accountability test" on the basis of regular and periodic elections. George Bush (Jr), after his re-election as US President, said on January 16, "We had an accountability moment. It was called the 2004 elections. The American people listened to different assessments made about what was taking place in Iraq, looked at the two candidates, and chose me."

Gujarat Chief Minister Narendra Modi made the same statement after winning the Assembly elections in 2002. The critics of Mr. Bush's policies on Iraq or Modi Government's role in the post-Godhra communal holocaust were dismissed as people of no consequence, because the voters had re-elected the much-maligned Bush or Modi. Incidentally, fascists and dictators like Hitler or Mussolini too have staked claim to power on the basis of popular verdict. The electoral mandate provides legitimacy to every pretender and saboteur of democracy — as is observed in some Assembly elections in India. Indians should know that politics of bullet has replaced politics of ballot and elections have become a farce when managed by the State.

The staggering of elections in three phases in Bihar or the redeployment of security forces from one place to another has not worked in safeguarding the sanctity of the vote. These facts clearly substantiate the argument that parliamentary democracy in India has been hijacked by pretenders and freeloaders who have misused and abused the democratic electoral system. Elected representatives are not accountable to any one except the party dictator who controls the party finances and elections. How can such representatives practice accountability in governance?

What is the explanation for the growth of serious distortions as observed during elections? Politics has become a very profitable business, and without winning elections politicians cannot reap the benefits of power. Personalised party finance and patronage of power in the hands of political families and a coterie is the best way to keep politics under "private family control". Political office is a sure guarantee for prosperity, and hence such families, along with criminals, want to win elections at all cost. The Prime Minister has not grappled with the threats facing Indian democracy from political class per se. His simplistic perception of "state funding of election" will not help in restoring the health of Indian democracy. – *The Pioneer, February 22, 2005*

IS THE EC ALWAYS RIGHT?

The Election Commission (EC) is a constitutional authority to organise and supervise Lok Sabha and State Assembly elections and ensure that "free and fair" polls are held and the sanctity of ballot is maintained. In normal circumstances, the task of the EC should not involve any public controversy. Political parties should ensure that the rules of democratic politics are followed under the supervisory umbrella of an independent, impartial and multi-member EC.

Are we living in normal times? The EC issued a statement on February 19 that it was "pained and anguished" over Haryana chief minister Om Prakash Chautala's accusations. He had dubbed the EC as an "agent" of the Congress. Chautala's outburst is not the first instance of the impartiality of the EC being questioned by political leaders.

A former CEC, J.M. Lyndogh, and Gujarat's chief minister Narendra Modi were involved in a slanging match. The then prime minister, Atal Bihari Vajpayee, had to make a public statement – "Constitutional authorities should maintain civility in public debate." – to rein in Modi.

The source of differences that arise between the EC and political parties is the Code of Conduct of elections. Political leaders do not want any interference in the way they want to campaign. It must be pointed out that the EC often finds itself caught in a crossfire because of its intent to enforce a level playing field to all contestants.

First, the ruling party in a state or at the Centre has a natural advantage over the opposition parties because it can make announcements and pronouncements that can influence the voters in their favour.

Lalu Prasad Yadav, as minister for Railways, appointed Justice U. C. Banerjee to inquire into the cause of fire in a railway compartment at Godhra on February 27, 2002. Since Godhra and its aftermath has generated immense public controversy, the Interim Report which Justice Banerjee submitted on the eve of the Bihar elections attracted much public attention.

Lalu, as leader of the Rashtriya Janata Dal, campaigned against the BJP and he did not think that public discussion of the Banerjee report was a violation of the Code of Conduct. On the contrary, the EC observed that this report should not become an issue during the campaign. In Haryana, Chautala, as chief minister, thought that it was his prerogative to conduct his duties and the EC stopped him from making "government appointments" before the elections.

Second, the central government is trapped. On the one hand there is this imperative to decide whether or not to enhance the rate of interest for the Employees' Provident Fund and, on the other, the EC has asked it to defer the announcement until after the Bihar, Jharkhand and Haryana elections are completed.

Third, the state governments have followed a policy of posting and transferring pliable officials during the elections so that ruling party candidates can violate the rules to their advantage. Every ruling party candidate has a list of "favourite" officials who it prefers to be located in his constituency.

This malpractice has been stopped because after the announcement of the election schedule, the election machinery of every state comes under the supervisory jurisdiction of the EC. A tug of war results between the EC and the state governments over transfers. Clearly, the enforcement of the Code by the EC becomes a Herculean task because ruling parties do not cooperate with it.

What is the explanation for the recurring conflicts between the EC and the political parties? Winning an election is a matter of life and death for any political leader, especially when politics has become a lucrative and profitable business. It is not only that every family member of important political leaders is engaged in the race for winning an election, well known criminals have also realised that a favourable election campaign is an immunity from the law.

If it were not so, the EC and some honest "local officials" involved in the conduct of elections would not have ordered the large scale "externment" of powerful and influential criminals on the eve of elections.

A weakened and delegitimised EC suits unscrupulous politicians and criminals to successfully "capture" the ballot. A leading newspaper, on the basis of statistics provided by the EC, reported that as of February 22, about 20 per cent of the 1,038 candidates contesting for the 243 seats in Bihar had criminal charges ranging from murder, arson, looting and kidnapping against them. On the basis of affidavits submitted by the candidates to the EC it is clear that criminals cut across party lines.

Every party has its own share of bahubalis (strongmen) and those who could not get tickets from any political party went ahead and nominated themselves as "Independents". Incidentally, one thousand "Independents" are contesting in Bihar, and the political class is not worried about these "footloose" candidates because, either way, they will end up being bought over if they are elected. On one occasion, Lalu himself alleged that his arch rival, the LJP leader Ram Villas Paswan, had nominated well known criminals as his party candidates.

Democratic politics in India has many areas of "darkness", and hope is sustained by a vigilant watchdog like the EC. It invited Chautala's ire for implementing the Code of Conduct. On February 20 he said that "the state has been deprived of central funds in the name of enforcing the Code which has remained in force in the state for a long period".

But he is evading the questions: Why is the election period so long in India? Why are elections not completed in a single day for the whole country in the case of the Lok Sabha? What is the need for fully armed paramilitary forces to keep vigil? Why are repolls ordered after the day of actual polling?

A multi-purpose constitutional body is a buffer between the lawless political class and the voter who wants to exercise his constitutional right through a free, fair and fearless process. It is often alleged that the National Conference and the Congress always "rigged" elections in Jammu and Kashmir.

It created a situation where people took to the "politics of bullet" because "politics of ballot" had become a fraud. If "fair, free and fearless" elections are not held, democracy will be replaced by gun-wielding individuals and groups. The real complaint against the EC arises only from the ruling parties because they are not allowed to "indulge" in malpractices during elections.

Human judgement can be wrong at times. The EC brought forward the dates of counting in Haryana from February 27 to February 23. However, on an appeal in the Supreme Court on February 22, the status quo ante was restored. Similarly, Lalu was right in his claim that the Interim Report of Justice Banerjee is a public document and hence can be publicly discussed during elections. Also, the EC gave confusing signals about the Railway minister's right to make Justice Banerjee report a document for public discussion. But does this give a Chautala or a Narendra Modi the right to use "interpretative" language against the Commission whenever an inconvenient decision is reversed in favour of these "worthies" of Indian politics.

The role of the EC should be seen and evaluated in the prevailing political context of India where democracy is under threat, and is seized by those who claim to be the elected representatives of the people. Indian democracy is not threatened by any foreign enemy; every institution of democracy is under attack from elected political representatives.

In this context, the Election Commission of India has always performed the yeoman's task of defending the sanctity of the ballot from the enemies of democracy. Thus it is not surprising to see that political class is engaged in emasculating this watchdog.

– The Pioneer, February 26, 2005

PARTY BEHAVIOUR AND MISBEHAVIOUR

Parliamentary democracy and the sanctity of the Constitution depend on the behaviour of the contenders for political power. The current political events in Goa, Jharkhand, Bihar and Haryana deserve to be discussed keeping in mind the short and long term impact of these political developments on the future of Indian democracy. Some well-known facts may be mentioned to properly understand the direction of political development in India.

First, the Goa Assembly witnessed party splits, defections and the involvement of high constitutional functionaries like the Speaker and the Governor. The events created an atmosphere which led to the imposition of President's rule on March 4. Second,

Jharkhand and Bihar have begun a difficult political journey because the voters did not give a clear verdict in the Assembly elections. The governors of these two states, like their predecessors, have exercised their "discretion" and "judgement" in determining the viability of the fractured parties, groups and individuals to combine and form a stable coalition government. Past experiences and the present developments in Jharkhand and Bihar clearly prove that if the voters throw the ball in the court of MLAs of a fractured Assembly, all norms of political behaviour are subverted for capturing power. The Governor has always been at the receiving end with the losers in the game of forming a successful coalition in a fragmented Assembly often accusing him of playing a partisan role.

Third, Governors, as in Goa, Jharkhand and Bihar, are not considered impartial and neutral while deciding on the merits of claims of various combinations to form a government. The Morarji Desai Government of the Janata party in 1977-79 and the Vajpayee-led NDA governments at the Centre in 1998 to 2005 followed the Congress's practice by appointing partisan governors. Party activists and political psychophants were appointed as governors by every party in power at the Centre, be it the Congress or the BJP.

Fourth, the Central Government is the final court of appeal in the event of shifting party alliances in a fractured State Assembly, or when a party in power is reduced to a minority because its own members or supporters have walked to another camp. The BJP is on the war path against the UPA Government because it is convinced that the Governors are working at the behest of the Centre and depriving the party's legitimate right to govern Goa and Jharkhand. In 2000, the opposition in Bihar had accused the Vajpayee Government when Nitish Kumar, an ally of the BJP, was administered the oath of office of Chief Minister. Then Lalu Prasad Yadav said it was an illegitimate intervention by the BJP.

It deserves to be recapitulated that all major parties and prime ministers have behaved in the interest of their own parties while dealing with State governments formed by parties which are not represented at the Centre. The Centre's partisan nature becomes visible when State governments are formed on the basis of fractured mandate; and this often generates controversy.

A close look at Jharkhand and Bihar electoral verdict clearly shows that the root cause of the present controversies, as in the past, is fragmented politics and a fractured verdict. In Jharkhand,

JMM with 17 seats; Congress: Nine; RJD: Seven; UGDP: Two; Forward Bloc: Two; Stephen Marandi: One; NCP: One; CPI(M): One; and independents, Enos Ekka and Harinarain Rai, have declared themselves as UPA partners with 42 seats. The BJP with 30, JD(U): Six; AJSU: Two; and along with Ekka and Rai have declared themselves as NDA combine with 41 MLAs in an Assembly of 80 seats. In the post-election scenario in Jharkhand, both the JMM and the BJP have to manufacture a majority to form the government. In such a situation of claims and counter claims, the Independents or rebels are a precious commodity. They are extremely shifty as they are accountable to none except themselves.

Why are political parties not demanding a ban on Independent or rebel candidates from contesting elections? Parliamentary democracy functions on the basis of parties and not footloose individual candidates. Parties allure such Independent MLAs in case of a need to form or topple a government. Electoral politics is not just a game of numbers. Elections are held to elect a majority to form a government and a minority to play the role of opposition to check the arbitrariness of the ruling party.

The electoral process in Jharkhand and Bihar today – and many a time in other states in the past – has been vitiated and subverted by political adventurists. The rules of the game of parliamentary democracy are followed if a majority party is reduced to a minority status in subsequent elections. However, the rules of the game are completely abandoned if one party rules for as long as the Congress did: For 40 years. It is also clear that in the phase of non-Congress Central governments the rules of the game have always been massacred. The BJP is making noises against the UPA and against the role of partisan Governors in Goa, Jharkhand and Bihar simply because it is out of power. When in office, the BJP and its earlier shadow, the Jana Sangh, indulged in the rape of democracy by using partisan Governors and by appointing party favourites to the office.

The Bihar Governor is paralysed because the verdict is totally fractured. The Bihar Assembly of 243 elected members now consists of RJD: 75; Congress: 10; BSP: Two; NCP: Three; CPI: Three; CPI(M): One; LJP: 29; BJP: 37; JD-U: 55; CPI-ML Liberation: Seven; SP: Four; and, Independents: 17. Here, every major group is unable to form any alliance to manufacture a majority to form the government. The worst fraud has been played by Ram Vilas Paswan of the LJP. Parties contest elections to form a government, but Mr. Paswan wants an anti-democratic arrangement with President's rule in Bihar. Political parties participate in a democracy to strengthen the institutions of democracy, but Bihar, Goa and Jharkhand are witnessing parties and leaders bent on subverting democratic institutions.

The Congress has emerged as a marginal player with only 10 seats in Bihar and nine in Jharkhand. The party's dream of regaining its lost glory lies shattered. Also, notwithstanding the Congress's outstanding performance in Haryana, the party is a completely divided house. Its revival still remains a pipedream.

Democracy in India cannot function according to the letter and spirit of the Constitution because every political party or group is engaged in cut-throat competition to capture power. The phenomenon of political misbehaviour is not the prerogative of any one party; the Congress, the BJP, and the so-called regionalists – each one of these has abused and misused power while in office.

– The Pioneer, March 8, 2005

INDEPENDENTS' DAY: SHOW THEM THE DOOR

Jharkhand BJP leader Arjun Munda approached the Supreme Court to quash the Governor's decision to make Shibu Soren the Chief Minister of the State. The bone of contention between the NDA and the UPA was the support of two Independent MLAs, Harinayan Rai and Enos Ekka. In the State Assembly of 80 MLAs, the magic number of 41 members cannot be achieved without their support. After all, the State's electoral verdict is fractured between the NDA and the UPA.

Earlier, former Goa Chief Minister Manohar Parrikar too had approached the Supreme Court to quash the order of State Governor S.C. Jamir, who invited Congress leader Pratap Singh Rane to take the oath of chief ministership on the doubtful loyalties of Independent MLAs. These legislators were earlier supporting the Parrikar-led-BJP Government. Such a murky situation was, at last, settled by the imposition of President's rule in the State. In the Assembly of 30 MLAs, shifting loyalties of the independent MLAs have become a part of Goa's political culture. No doubt, the State has witnessed a quick succession of different regimes.

The Jharkhand and Goa incidents have created a crisis for every constitutional institution, like the President, Supreme Court, Parliament, Prime Minister, Leader of Opposition, etc. The acts of omission and commission of a few MLAs in the State Assembly have violated the very norm of parliamentary democracy. What is the cause of such political crises in India? This is not the first time that the shifting political loyalties of a few legislators have led to political deadlocks. In small States like Himachal Pradesh, Haryana, Goa, Jharkhand, etc, the strength of the House depends on the State's size because a few legislators can make or break a Government. The electoral verdict of 2005 Jharkhand Assembly elections shows the difficulty in forming a stable Government in the Assembly of 80 MLAs, where the UPA has 33 pre-election alliance legislators and the NDA has 36. In this situation, neither the BJP-led NDA nor the JMM-led UPA could have formed the Government. Hence, they have to manufacture and manoeuvre a majority with the support of Independent legislators like Stephen Marandi, Enos Ekka, Harinarain Rai, etc. Not surprisingly, these Independents have become the most precious commodity for both the contenders for power.

The issue of the relevance of these Independent or unattached candidates has assumed significance in the wake of current constitutional crisis. After all, parliamentary democracy is based on political parties, and not on individuals. The logic of parliamentary democracy is that political parties mobilise voters on the basis of their well-defined ideologies, belief-systems and distinct programmes. Political competition in democracy is not among isolated individuals, but among parties — the BJP versus the Congress, the BJP versus the communists and federalists versus centralists.

Political parties provide programmatic and ideological alternatives to the voters who can make a choice between one or the other contending political claimant to power. Is there any place for the so-called Independent or unattached candidate in such democratic order, where contesting mega-ideologies followed by major political parties are involved to win the voter's support? The upshot of the above description is that the involvement of scattered independents is absolutely against the meaning and practice of parliamentary democracy. The voters' mandate has to be the only criterion in the formation of a majority Government or an Opposition. Independent candidates in the body-politic are like cancer in human body that can be cured only through surgical operation.

The Constitution and the Representation of People Act clearly say that only a political party can contest elections. The dirty political record of the so-called Independent candidates are enough to completely "debar" them from contesting an election. The unattached MLAs get attached to a party or group on the basis of political bribe, and they offer themselves to the highest bidder. After all, they are not responsible to anyone. Generally, a party is formed when people agree to its programmes and are united together to implement their manifesto. Besides, a party member is bound by the party constitution that maintains strict discipline on him. The so-called Independent "law makers" are not bound by any legal or constitutional obligations. They are their "own masters", and are devoted to their own personal welfare. They enjoy powers without sharing any responsibility. Should not these individuals be shown the door with a view to cleanse the country's body-politic? – *Sunday Pioneer, March 13, 2005*

SEVEN SISTERS' PARLIAMENT

The Constitution of India has provided a very rich framework for the governance of plural society and many institutional models are in operation for dealing with specific cultural and ethnic needs and demands of an extremely diverse and varied society. Assam, Manipur, Mizoram, Meghalaya, Nagaland, Tripura and Arunachal Pradesh have been under different arrangements for governing Hill Tribes or people from the plains who have asserted their ethnic identity. In spite of multiple experiments to govern the ethnically and tribally divided Northeast, inter-ethnic rivalry has not ended and is dramatised by Naga leaders who have demanded the creation of a Greater Nagaland by merging Naga inhabited areas in Assam, Manipur etc. It is impossible for any democratic government to concede the Greater Nagaland demand.

Apart from the fact that new remarking of a territory along ethnic lines is not acceptable to any other state, even Greater Nagaland will be troubled as other groups will not like to be part of it. Ethnic identity linked with claims on specific territory creates difficulties because every group asserts its territorial claim for self-rule that is always directed against other groups. It has led to ethnic cleansing and violence in the Northeast.

The Naga, the Kuki-Chin-Mizo tribes and the Meiteis in Manipur or Bodos or Karbis in Assam are involved in a continuous struggle and no solution has been or can be found to satisfy the specific territorial claims of competing ethnic groups. If this Hobbesian war of all against all has to be tackled, the seven Northeast states should be governed by a 'supra-federal system of governance'. The Indian federal system provides for a Central and State government and areas of autonomous jurisdiction and inter-relationships are clearly laid down in the Constitution. This arrangement of 'dual government' should be extended to the seven states. They should continue to exercise powers under the Constitution but a supra-regional government should be constituted for the Northeast for common activities. A Parliament comprising an equal number of elected representatives and a Council of Ministers representing the seven states can be created as a 'sub-federal supra government' which will be responsible for tackling problems faced by the region.

The advantage of creating a supra-regional government for the region is that the responsibility for harmonising the conflicting demands of multiple groups will devolve on them. Another advantage is that an effective supra-government will be nearer the scene of action than the distant Centre. A feeling of distant and unresponsive Central government among sections of disturbed society can be effectively responded by devolving some of the Centre's powers to the supra-regional government Innovative federalism is the need of the hour to deal with intense rivalries among ethnic groups by removing the link between territorial claims and ethic identity. –*Tehelka, April 2, 2005*

FEDERALISM AT CROSSROADS

A claim has been made that cooperative federalism has replaced and displaced a highly centralised and authoritarian Union government that had made Indian federalism more unitary in form and in substance too. Is it so?

It is worth examining the political developments in Goa and Jharkhand to substantiate the argument that the claims of re-federalisation and genuine decentralisation of power structure in the 1990s and the first decade of the 21st century is not only premature, but Indians have to take many more steps to achieve a proper system of federal checks and balances.

The shifting loyalties of the MLAs in Goa and Jharkhand brought into focus the role of State Governors and Assembly Speakers that was attacked as 'partisan'. The President of India, the Union Government, the Supreme Court, the pro-term Speaker of Goa, the Speaker of Jharkhand and the Speaker of the Lok Sabha were all involved in the disputes in these two states. The telling example of exposing the argument of the winds of change blowing in the federal balance of power is provided by he role of the Governor – because from 1950 to 2005, Governors have been accused of being partisan in every situation of political fluidity in any State of India.

The Supreme Court vs. Union of India in the Bommai case (1994) has commented: "Since the Constitution came into force, the President has taken action under Article 365 on nearly 100 occasions. On not a single occasion has the action has been constitutionally proper. The motivation has uniformly been to displace governments (almost always belonging to rival political parties) and substitute others in their place. The Sarkaria Commission has noted that most of the instances of exercise of power under Article 356 were wholly improper".

The champions of the emergence of the New Federalism ignore the fact that every party at the Centre whether it be the Congress, or Janata, or the BJP or coalitions supported by the regionalists at the Centre, have been accused of using the State Governor for purely partisan purposes.

The story does not end here. The office of the Speaker, whether at the state or the Centre is also involved in controversies and it is not the first time that Supreme Court and Speakers have come to clash on the role of the Speaker of a State Assembly. The controversy erupted when the Supreme Court on March 9, 2005, directed the pro-term Speaker in Jharkhand to hold a 'trust vote' on March 11, 2005 and not on the date to be decided by the Speaker himself. A storm broke out when Somnath Chatterjee, Speaker of the Lok Sabha, expressed his strong views on the issue of jurisdiction of the Court. The Lok Sabha Speaker, who occupies a position of primus inter pares in relation to Speakers of the State Assemblies decided to call a meeting of all Speakers on March 20, 2005 to formally discuss the conflict of jurisdiction between the judiciary and the legislature. But such an important all-India meeting was publicly boycotted by the BJP and the party's Speakers from Gujarat, Madhya Pradesh, Rajasthan, Chhatisgarh and Jharkhand who did not attend the meeting. Is this official boycott an example of cooperative federalism? This is an evidence of abnormal functioning of the federal system of which no party can be said to be over the board.

Another example in recent times is that of the BJP asking its State governments of Rajasthan, Madhya Pradesh, Jharkhand, Chhatisgarh and Gujarat not to implement the Value-Added Tax that was to be implemented from April 1, 2005. The whole issue of VAT has been discussed in the best traditions of a federal system and where state governments have actively participated in the decision-making process to evolve a uniform tax policy. And yet the BJP has obstructed a healthy federal system making its point in the case of VAT.

The upshot therefore is that India has miles to go before any claim on cooperative federalism can be made. India's federal system will face many challenges because the politics of the 21st century is not 'coalitional' but 'polarised' - between the Congress and the BJP. Regional parties and groups are at the back and call of one or the other. How can federal system be smooth when politics is 'polarised' as revealed from the events in Goa, Jharkhand, and VAT? – *Sahara Time, April 16, 2005*

FEDERATION AND COALITION

The Manmohan Singh-led UPA government at the Centre is a coalition or 16 parties and groups, and except the Congress party all other parties and groups are confined to a specific region or a state. Every region or state-based party or group is always interested in receiving maximum benefits from the Central Government for specific state represented by a group or party in the coalition government at the Centre. This is a new political reality of India and it is a break from the past when the Congress party ruled over the whole country whether at the Centre or the states. This one party dominated political system for 40 years was characterised by all the evils associated with the centralisation of power and Indian federal system had become a farce because in reality it was "unitary system in spirit and federal in from only".

Since the domination of one party rule over the whole country has been replaced by a coalition of multiple parties and groups at the Centre, it has directly impacted the actual functioning of federal system in the country. The UPA government consists of very important regional groups like the DMK of Tamil Nadu, Lalu Prasad Yadav and Ram Vilas Paswan of Bihar, Sharad Pawar of Maharashtra et al and sit in the Central council of ministries in their own right and they occupy equal and many a time more than equal status than the ministries of the Congress party.

A very contentious issue regarding the appointment of governors for the states was raised by Sharad Pawar, when he demanded that governors should also be appointed from the parties and groups of the UPA partners. The Congress party led by Manmohan Singh followed its old practice of appointing state governors from its own party only and Sharad Pawar reminded the Congress party leadership that coalition parties have equal share in the appointment of state governors.

It is for the first time in the history of post-independence India that a "quota" for coalition partners has emerged as a demand for the appointment of governors by a coalition-led Central government. Further, the UPA government, again for the first time in India, has not been able to appoint "advisors" during the President's Rule in Bihar because Ram Vilas Paswan and Lalu Prasad Yadav are at loggerheads on the issues concerning Bihar and the UPA government will collapse if it does not accept the conflicting opinions and views of its two coalition partners at the Centre.

The story does not end here. It is not only Paswan and Lalu. Shibu Soren of Jharkhand Mukti Morcha, a coalition partner of the Central government, brought great discomfiture to Manmohan Singh because the state Governor of Jharkhand, a Congress party nominee, created controversies for his alleged partisan attitude in inviting Shibu Soren to take the oath of office of the chief minister. It created a furore in the country, the President, Parliament, the High Court and Supreme Court were all involved in a political storm created by the action of the Jharkhand state Governor who was seen to be favouring the JMM because it happened to be a coalition partner of the Congress-led Central government. The upshot of above description is that Indian federal arrangement of governance has always been crises-ridden because either the regions feel neglected by the Centre or regional parties represented in the coalition government at the Centre exercise pulls and pressures for their specific region-based demands.

A telling example of the story of conflicts among the partners in the coalition government at the Centre has been the portfolio of railways because a railway minister can show to the public of gains for his state during his stewardship of the railway ministry. Nitish Kumar of Janata Dal(U) was a railway minister in the Vajpayee-led NDA government at the Centre from 1999 to 2004 and both Ram Vilas Paswan of the Lok Jan Shakti Party and Lalu Prasad contested against one another for the post of railway minister as members of the UPA coalition government. The railway ministry is the bone of contention because Nitish or Paswan or Lalu are primarily representatives of Bihar state and all these three are competing against one another in Bihar and its impact is felt at the coalition government at the Centre whether it be of the NDA or the UPA.

The logic of coalition government at the Centre is that either the Central government defends the deeds and misdeeds of its regional or coalition allies or it provides "special benefits" to the regions which are represented in the coalition at the Centre. Chandrababu Naidu of the Telugu Desam was the convenor of the United Front governments of H.D. Deve Gowda and Inder Kumar Gujaral from 1996 to 1998 and he completely shifted support to the BJP-led Central government from 1998 to 2004 for the sole purpose of getting "special benefits" from the Centre for his own state. If Chandrababu Naidu used his political stint with the coalition governments at the Centre from 1996 to 2004 for "special benefits" for his state, Mayawati of the Bahujan Samaj Party, a supporter of the UPA government at the Centre, has a complaint against the Central government for not defending an ally from CBI investigators in cases related to corruption in public life. Lalu Prasad Yadav created an artificial storm by not only levelling wild charges but also made a demand for the dismissal of the Election Commission because he perceived them as their "opponents". Lalu Prasad is the minister in the Central Government and he is expected to defend the autonomy of a constitutional authority like the Election Commission, but as a minister of the UPA coalition government, he has a "license" to ask for the "dismissal" of the Election Commission. The law minister of the UPA Government defended the integrity of the Election Commission in Parliament, while a railway minister of the same government, but of another party, asked for action against Election Commission.

What is the implication for the failure of coalition governments at the Centre to run the Indian federal system smoothly? In India, the Central government is the real centre of power and every state government has to adjust with the politics of the Central government. Not only this. The party in power at the Centre can provide many special benefits to a political favourite state government and it can also punish a politically hostile government of the state leading to the dismissal of a ministry of a political party which is hostile to the Centre.

Coalition partners understand this central logic of Indian federal system and they are maximising gains by becoming a partner at the Centre. It is not without reason that Jayalalitha of the AIADMK is always accusing the UPA government for neglecting her "interests" — because her arch rival the DMK is a "partner" of the Central government. It deserves to be stated that the DMK was a very active supporter of the BJP-led NDA government at the Centre and Karunanidhi walked out of the NDA just before the elections not because of any ideologies, but because if an alternative coalition is formed at the Centre, the DMK should be very much present.

The greatest advantage of a coalition system at the Centre is that every regional party has participated in power at the Centre whether with NDA or UPA, and in this process they have realised that the support of the Central government is required for 'regional uplift and benefits'. The all India parties like the Congress and the BJP have also realised that "regional groups" are a necessity for their survival at the all India political level. The UPA, like the NDA, has been accommodative of its regional partners and a politics of federal give and take has come to stay in India.

At the same time, Indian federal system will always be confronted with challenges as narrated above because coalition partners have a "localist" approach which comes into conflict with an "all India national approach". The UPA government has experienced many moments of anxiety as a result of demands and behaviour of its own ruling coalition partners.

– Sahara Time, May 28 , 2005

TIES OF CONVENIENCE

The Lok Sabha elections of 2004 brought to an end the Hindutva led regime of the NDA, and secular political forces represented by the Congress, the Communists and others formed a United Progressive Alliance government led by Manmohan Singh. It was never expected that cooperation between the Congress and the Communists will be a smooth journey because both the parties have serious political differences at the same time ideology of secularism has brought them together on to a common platform. The 'uneasy' political co-habitation between these two political opponents is quite visible and at the same time the 'unity of these two secular forces' is likely to continue because neither the Congress nor the Communists will like to hand over power to the BJP. In this context, it is important to discuss the journey of the UPA government in 2004-05.

The Manmohan Singh-led UPA coalition government at the Centre celebrated one year of its rule with great fanfare in the middle May of 2005 and hardly a month after their self-congratulatory functions, the Congress party received a stern message by the Communists that they will not attend the UPA-Left Front Coordination Committee meeting. The proposed boycott of Coordination Committee meeting by the communists has rattled Sonia Gandhi and Manmohan Singh who are negotiating with the Left Front leaders with a view to win over their active support for the Congress-led UPA coalition at the Centre.

Prakash Karat, the General Secretary of CPI(M), announced on June 26 that the "boycott" of the Coordination Committee Meeting was because of serious policy differences between the Congress and the Communists. In a letter to the Prime Minister from the Left Front partners, he stated, "Right now we want to give a serious message to the coalition leadership that we cannot be taken for granted on economic policies, specially disinvestment". The announcement by the Manmohan Singh government that "it will go ahead with disinvestment in Bharat Heavy Electrical Limited and other Public Sector Undertakings" was the last straw that completely alienated the Communists from the UPA.

The Left Front partners are concerned that Manmohan Singh, P. Chidambram, Montek Singh Ahluwalia and other economic reformers in the Congress Party by following the policies of disinvestment of the Navratnas are laying the foundations of "gradual privatisation" and the Left cannot accept this "creeping privatisation" of the profit making public sector undertakings. Not only this. The Communist parties have shown their complete unhappiness with the UPA government on price hike of petroleum and its dilly dallying policy on National Employment Guarantee Scheme which has yet to receive parliamentary approval. All this led Prakash Karat to state on June 26, 2005 that not only disinvestment of BHEL is "the first serious violation of the common minimum programme", the "UPA has not been able to ensure adherence to the CMP". Karat concluded his stem statement that "they will continue to extend support to the government but we do not want to give an impression to the government that there is coordination because there is no coordination".

The crux of the matter is that political understanding between the Congress-Led UPA government and the communists has come to a breaking point because the agreed national Common Minimum Programme is not being adhered to by the government and "violation" of the CMP has created a deadlock between the Congress and the Communists.

Jyoti Basu stated on July 3, 2005, that the Congress should 'introspect' on whether it could continue with the policies of 'indiscriminate liberalisation and privatisation.' Even before the dust could be settled on policy differences between the Congress and the Communists on disinvestment of BHEL, Pranab Mukerjee and Donald Rumsfeld signed a ten year India-US Defence Agreement on June 29, 2005 in which India and US have sated their 'shared security interests.' This India-US Defence Agreement has miffed the Communists who cannot accept India tying itself so closely with American strategic interests and differences between the Congress and the Left have come into the open on the basic directions of foreign policy.

What is the real meaning of the withdrawal of the Communists from the meetings of UPA-Left Coordination Committee? It is complete lack of understanding by the critics of the Communists who have maintained that the Communists are distancing from the Congress because in the forthcoming 2006 state assembly elections in West Bengal and Kerala, the Communists have to contest elections against the Congress. Any linking of Communist parties's decision to "suspend" their cooperation with the Congress because of the forthcoming state assembly elections is a complete trivialisation of the Communist economic philosophy which is fundamentally different from Manmohan-Montek thinking. Manmohan Singh's decisions have directly hit the poor workers and peasants who happen to be the main social constituency of the communists. How can anti-poor and anti-labouring classes policies of the gungho liberalisation regime led by Manmohan be accepted by a party of the mass of the poor of India?

Unlike the Congress and other bourgeois parties, the Communists cannot act as the "gatekeeper" of the capitalists and prosperous middle classes of India. Prime Minister, in the Development Council Meeting of June 27-28, 2005, admitted that the country was facing serious agrarian crisis but the communists cannot be a party to such a verbal rhetoric of a Prime Minister when the rural poor are in distress. It is not only starvation deaths or the suicide of the small and marginal farmers reeling under debt that are a testimony to the deep agrarian crisis, it is callousness and inaction of the UPA government towards these suffering classes that the communists cannot accept.

Yet Congress and Communists are 'Cooperating' with one another for the common purpose of fight against Hindu communal politics of the BJP. Sonia Gandhi's Congress has emerged as an important political force and, with the support of Communists, it can confront the Hindutva of the BJP. This political marriage of convenience is expected to continue, in spite of zig zag journey, to contain the march of a common enemy. – *Sahara Time, July 23, 2005*

THE TUG OF WAR IN BIHAR

A political storm has hit Bihar over the transfer of seventeen IPS officials by Governor Buta Singh. He has supposedly been working under the directions and guidance of Lalu Prasad, whose party is an important component of the Congress-led UPA coalition government at the Centre. These transfers of police officials have become controversial because G.S. Kang, the Chief Secretary of the state, has gone on long leave in 'protest' against the Governor's arbitrary action involving a matter in which a Chief Secretary has to give his consent. The Bihar association of the IAS officials held a meeting in support of their Chief Secretary who had lodged a protest against the Governor on the issue of transfer of officials. The formal position is that President's rule in any state is imposed for a very temporary period to place a state government directly under the command of Central Government.

The Governor is a constitutional representative of the Central Government and during the period of President's rule, he is assisted by "advisors" appointed by the Central Government to carry on the work of day-to-day administration. Another important formal position is that the Cabinet Secretary at the Centre or the Chief Secretary of a state government is "head" of the civil service and he is the final administrative authority to deal with the postings and transfers of officials at the Centre or at the state level. During the President's Rule, a Chief Secretary has to work with Central Government appointed "advisors" to manage the affairs of the state. Hence Chief Secretary remains at the "apex" of the civil service, whether during the President's Rule or during normal periods of democracy in the state. The Chief Secretary's public protest against the Governor's action had to become a matter of serious political controversy and the opposition parties naturally jumped into the fray especially at a time when the monsoon session of Parliament is underway.

The Central Government, President, Parliament, the Supreme Court, the Bihar High Court, Election Commission, Political Parties and every component of democratic politics is involved in the controversy because Bihar State Assembly elections have to be held during the next few months. How can politicians keep themselves away from any serious or non-serious issue during the election season?

It deserves to be clearly stated that the collapse of one party rule of the Congress has led to the formation of chaotic and short-lived coalition governments at the centre beginning from 1990. It was expected that the successors to the Congress party would follow the rules of the game which, they always alleged, had been violated by the Congress during its forty years of rule over India. The office of the Governor has always been a matter of controversy. While the Congress ruled at the Centre every opposition party alleged the party of appointing political yes men as Governors of states.

The BJP, a real ideological opponent of the Congress, followed the practice of appointing RSS activists as Governors. Not only this, the BJP-led Coalition Government at the centre from 1998 to 2004 worked under the 'extra unconstitutional' authority of the RSS whose K.S. Sudarshan was an official RSS link with the Vajpayee Government. Every important appointment made by the Vajpayee Government was specifically cleared by the RSS; and RSS activists like Bhai Mahavir, K.R. Malkani, Late Sunder Singh Bhandari, M.L. Khurana et al were all appointed Governors of States by the RSS-led BJP Government.

In fact, the Bihar politics in particular has certain negative tendencies that are also found in different degrees in the whole of India. Indian politics has been communalised and plural, secular and participatory democracy is threatened if the constitutional institutions of governance like bureaucracy, police and judiciary are allowed to be penetrated by Hindu communalists, or casteists or well known criminals. The Election Commission of India has issued instructions to officials of Bihar to serve warrants of arrest absconding criminals who happen to be active in politics. Pappu Yadav, an alleged criminal, who happens to be an MP, had to be shifted to Tihar jail in Delhi because even in prison in Bihar, he was suspected to be absolutely free because of his political connections. Ram Vilas Paswan floated Lok Janashakti Party against Lalu Yadav's RJD, and nominated even criminals for Assembly Elections; especially those who had been denied nomination by Lalu Yadav. The BJP-JD(U) alliance partners have brought those criminals away from the collapsing LJP of Paswan, and Nitish Kumar, the JD(U) leader has publicly stated that these criminals will be given tickets to contest elections with the support of the BJP and JD(U).

Should Bihar be allowed to become a heaven of criminals in politics? Shahabuddin, a RJD MP from Siwan, has been in prison and the police officials during President's Rule have seen to it that this criminal-turned-MP is treated according to the strict principles of rule of law. The transfer of IPS officials from Siwan broke the camel's back and the Chief Secretary, as head of his team, launched a protest against this action of the Governor. It is only a firm, fair, legality-oriented civil and police bureaucracy which can uphold the rule of law and stand in between the criminals and their political protectors. The events in Bihar have once again brought into sharp focus the theory and practice of relationship between elected political representatives and permanent bureaucracy in democracy.

This is an all-India issue. The post-Godhra riots in Gujarat in March-April 2002 witnessed the complete blurring of any distinction or boundary between the Narender Modi-led Government and bureaucracy because both acted hand-in-hand when the riots were taking place. The events in Bihar or Narendra Modi's Gujarat have alerted the conscience keepers of the values of pluralist, secular democracy of India to put their heads together and cleanse the stable by restoring the majesty of constitution.

– Sahara Time, August 13, 2005

A JUDGEMENT MISUNDERSTOOD

The Chief Justice of India, Justice R.C. Lahoti, was quite upset with the Attorney General of India while announcing his order on quota in private unaided educational institutions and he remarked, "If this is the attitude of the government, then wind up the courts, and do whatever you want." All hell broke out in Parliament against the order of the seven-judge bench headed by the Chief

Justice; parliamentarians, irrespective of party affiliations, demanded enactment of a special law or even an amendment of the Constitution for modifying the judicial order on reservations'.

It needs to be clearly stated that it is not the first time the highest court of the country and Parliament have differed on public policy issues but the tone and temper of language used by parliamentarians gave an impression of 'confrontation' between the government/parliament and the judiciary. It was a storm in a tea cup which assumed the colour of confrontational politics in the country. The simple fact is that the Chief Justice castigated the government for 'criticising the apex court's judgments without 'understanding' them. The litigation against the policies and percentages of reservations announced by the Central and various state governments has been quite frequent because different social groups approach the judiciary to 'interpret' the decisions of the governments on reservation. Not only this. Minority community-maintained institutions have special constitutional rights to reserve seats for their community and appeals have been frequently filed by different groups against the rights of minority community maintained institutions to reserve seats for their own community.

Parliament and Legislatures have a right to 'legislate according to the provisions of the Constitution and the Judiciary has a constitutional right to 'review' these laws with a view of either upholding them or declaring them null and void. Judiciary is always involved in disputes among citizens and the Constitution of India guarantees 'right of judicial review' and Parliament has to either accept the verdict of the courts or amend the laws accordingly. This is the constitutional position in India. Why did Chief Justice Lahoti lambast the government for not 'understanding' the judgment of 'quota' as announced on August 12, 2005? The Chief Justice himself stated that "Every judgment (Pai, Islamic and the August 12 One) says that there's a need for a law on the matter. Yet the government says the judiciary is being confrontationist..." The government and Parliament were protesting too much and making noises against the honourable judges without reading the judgment. Chief Justice Lahoti was presiding over a seven-judge bench and the Pai case had been decided by the full bench of eleven judges and a seven-judge bench cannot overrule the judgement of a full bench of eleven judge. This was the reason that Chief Justice Lahoti asked Parliament to pass a new law or amend the Constitution if it desired 'quota in unaided private institutions'. Why did Parliament and the government react strongly against the judgment on the basis of perfunctory newspaper reporting of the orders of the Chief Justice?

It is a well-known fact that 'the policies of reservations in India are politically very emotive and every party wants to project itself as the champion of 'social justice' which gets equated with 'reservations' for the Dalits and the backward castes. Political parties try to win over multiple caste constituencies by offering them 'quota-based reservations'. V.P. Singh, a Prime Minister for ten months only, created a political storm in August 1990 by accepting Mandal Commission Recommendations on Reservations for the Backward Castes. Many unemployed persons of the 'high caste' felt insecure and undertook 'self-immolation'. Tamil Nadu state governments of the DMK or the AIADMK competed against one another by raising the percentage of 'reservation of seats' for the Backward Castes and the situation became ridiculous because 80 to 90 per cent of public services were 'reserved' and the Supreme Court had to intervene and slash it to 50 per cent only. If the Supreme Court had not imposed a ceiling of 50 percent reserved quota, every state government would have played havoc with the percentage of reserved seats in public institutions. The Supreme Court also intervened by stating that reservations should be 'rotational' and 'creamy layer' of the Dalits and backward castes should be disqualified from the quota of reservations.

It is not surprising that the state governments have been demanding that they alone should be given the power to determine the percentages of quota based reservations and there should be no ceiling over the limit imposed over them by the Constitution. A demand for quota in private sector is of recent origin because the government employment opportunities have become very limited and Ram Vilas Paswan or Ms. Meira Kumar or other representatives of Dalit interests have launched a campaign for 'quota based reservations' in the private sector. Private sector is resisting it and in this ongoing public debate the latest judgment of the Supreme Court sparked a controversy because the proponents of reservations in private sector are quite vehement in their demand. Since democratic politics is competitive, every party projects itself as a champion of quota-based reservations not only in the public sector, but also in the private sector. The private sector is refusing to be regulated by the government laws in its recruitment politics. Hence Chief Justice Lahoti's judgment nailed the stand of the supporters of reservations in the private sector. The judiciary simply wants that Parliament should legislate on 'quota issue' according to the Constitution of India. No more and no less. Where is the confrontation? It is a figment of imagination of politicians who are emotionally involved in the issue of quota-based reservation. – *Sahara Time, September 10, 2005*

POLITICS ALONE CAN TACKLE NAXALISM

India is witnessing an armed struggle against the State in 150-odd districts spread over 14 states. The response of the State to such an armed struggle has been episodic and ad hoc because the state functionaries have treated this large-scale social unrest as a mere law and order problem.

Naxalism is quite active in states like Andhra Pradesh, Chhattisgarh, Jharkhand, Bihar, Orissa and Maharashtra, while some elements of it can be found in West Bengal, UP, Tamil Nadu, Uttaranchal, Kerala, Karnataka and Madhya Pradesh. The Naxal phenomenon of armed struggle against the State began in the '60s and was confined only to West Bengal and the Telengana region of Andhra Pradesh. But today, the practitioners of armed struggle have spread their network in 14 states and more than 150 districts of India. Significantly, they are very active in the tribal areas and districts suffering from acute agrarian crisis.

The BJP-led coalition government at the Centre, from 1998 to 2004, followed a policy of ruthless suppression of Naxals. Andhra Pradesh chief minister Chandrababu Naidu implemented this policy of suppression as advocated by the then Union home minister L.K. Advani. But home minister Shivraj Patil of UPA, unlike his predecessor, clearly stated on September 23, 2005, that the government in Naxal-infected states should reduce dependence on arms by these groups and encourage "conditional or unconditional talks with them."

Mr. Patil further elaborated: "Orissa was willing to do it. Jharkhand said some consensus should be evolved and if the Centre took the lead, it would be useful. Others thought that some principle could be followed. We told them they should spearhead the peace dialogue. We can come in whenever they feel they need us." In other words, every political party which has an agrarian social base, including the Congress, has recognised that the Naxal problem is not merely a law and order problem and has social reasons which need to be addressed on the basis of a "dialogue" with the People's War groups. The UPA government's policy of "dialogue" with Naxals was practised by the Congress government of Andhra Pradesh for full one year and it has been reversed on August 17, 2005, after the assassination of a state minister by the Naxals.

It deserves to be clearly stated that the ideologues of Naxalism were absolutely wrong in characterising the Indian State as "neo-colonial and unpopular". This faulty theoretical formulation led them to launch an "armed struggle" against the 'anti-people' State on the Maoist model. Naxals were absolutely wrong when they proclaimed "chairman Mao is our chairman." Charu Majumdar and others did not recognise the strong democratic social essence of the bourgeois Indian State and they failed to launch popular democratic struggles in support of agrarian restructuring of India. This led the Naxals to challenge the armed might of the State through the power of gun. This faulty ideology and strategy of armed struggle against the State failed and democratically-elected West Bengal government completely marginalised Naxalism by undertaking large-scale land reforms.

Actually, the genesis of Naxal problem lies in the "unfinished agenda of land reforms" and the Indian State's insensitivity to tribal exploitation by contractors, bureaucrats and politicians in the remote tribal belts. Naxalism in India has a social origin. Gunnar Myrdal in his classic *The Asian Drama – an inquiry into the causes of Indian poverty* – had alerted the Indian State, as early as the '70s, that it has not been able to implement basic land reforms in many parts of the Indian states. But it does not mean that land reforms have not been on the agenda of the Indian State.

India has abolished traditional rent seeking "absentee landlordism" but surplus land has not been distributed to the landless. Moreover, the backward caste – middle peasantry – which has been the beneficiary of the much-maligned land reforms are behaving like "neo-landlords" and are ruthlessly dealing with the Scheduled Caste, landless agricultural workers. The Yadavas of UP and Bihar, the Jats of Rajasthan, Haryana and western UP or Khammas and Reddys of Andhra Pradesh have captured the state machinery and they are hardly interested in undertaking any land reform. It is not a question of land reforms alone, even minimum statutory wages are not paid to the landless workers. However, state governments, controlled by the backward caste, middle peasantry, are not at all committed to implement the policies concerning the amelioration of the living conditions of tribals and Dalits. The government of Bihar (and its successor Chhattisgarh) has turned a blind eye to private armies of high caste landlords, like Ranveer Sena, which are inflicting private vendetta against the oppressed and struggling landless. The Naxals have to face the bullets of the armed constabulary and the landlord's armies in these states.

The agrarian crisis has become more pronounced in the '90s. Government data clearly show that capital formation in rural India is declining and unemployment in rural areas is increasing at an alarming rate, affecting not only the landless but also millions of marginal and small-holding farmers. Rural industrialisation can provide new opportunities to the surplus army of the rural unemployed but the state governments do not have any agenda for creating rural employment opportunities. But the new National Rural Employment Guarantee Scheme adopted by the UPA government could help tackle this problem, albeit in a gradualist manner.

It deserves to be stated that Naxal method of armed struggle against the well-armed Indian State will not succeed. At the same time, the state managers should know that the Naxal problem is the result of serious acts of omission and commission by those who have been elected to serve the masses. A social problem like Naxalism can be resolved only if the Indian State follows social welfare policies. For, violence by the State breeds more violence by the weak and helpless groups. A socially activist and interventionist State can tackle the Naxal problem. Fanon's 'Wretched of the Earth' need succour and not suppression by the state. – *The Economic Times, September 10, 2005*

AN UNCARING SOCIETY

It is a sign of changing times that through Public Interest Litigation, the old parents are asking judicial intervention to seek succour from their own progenies. In one such case the Supreme Court has even ordered that old parents should be given maintenance by their grown up children. The Indian 'Joint Family System' had worked as a social insurance for dependents including parents or widows but the fast pace of modernisation is impacting very negatively the old system of social security without creating a new system of maintenance for the old parents where they can live with dignity.

If the 'old people' feel unwanted by their own kith and kin the state should take the responsibility of the growing number of the senior citizens. After all, senior citizens have served the country when they were capable of working in various sectors of social and public life. The senior citizen of today has been an extremely 'useful' pillar of society and it is the duty of the state to make contribution for the happiness of their immense contribution to nation building and social development.

The advanced western societies created a well developed institutional system for the felt needs of the old citizens who had been once active and working during their life. The Twentieth Century Europe and North America established a developed system of welfare state which took complete care of the felt needs of the senior retired citizens. The idea of "welfare state" is based on the principle that it is the duty of the state to protect the lives of those who have been active in the service of their society. The concept of 'charity' for the needy was replaced by the concept of "legal obligation" of the state to look after the health and financial need of the retired citizens. The concept of the rights of man in democracy has always been evolving by including more rights in the list of "freedom for the citizen including senior citizens". It deserves to be clearly stated that the welfare programmes of the state for senior citizens is not based on either "charity" or "sympathy" but on the concept of "rights" of citizens in a democracy.

Yet the former President of United States Ronald Reagan and former Prime Minister of England Margaret Thatcher were the ideological and political "wreckers" of the social security state; Thatcher ridiculed the whole idea of a caring state as a "nanny" activity. The last decade of the Twentieth Century and the first decade of the Twenty First Century have witnessed the emergence of an ideology based on the concept of the "retreat of the state" from the area of social welfare. A large vulnerable section of society which consists of senior citizens are now asked to face the tyranny and cruelties of the free market economy on their own. European countries are involved in a grim social situation because it is not easy for them to dismantle the developed system of social security and the recent elections in Germany have clearly shown the crisis of German politics. The Social Democrats are reluctant votaries of anti-welfare state and German Conservative Party is for dismantling of Social Security network. The electoral results have been fractured and both of these major parties are not in a position to form the new government on their own.

The Constitution of India has also laid down the foundation of a welfare state in its Chapter IV on the Directive Principles of State Policy. The Chapter of the Constitution provided for many guarantees to the citizens who are old and need help by the state. The Central Government Health Services Scheme was established by the Government of India to take care of the health requirements of the old citizens. Of late, pension scheme for the retired persons has been evolved to take care of the financial needs of the old people. Inspite of this India has miles to go in the direction of establishing a caring welfare state.

An alternative to the non-caring family is the state because it has to recognise that the senior citizens have certain 'rights' in return for their "services" rendered to society. If the old people are considered a "burden" on joint family and the state also washes its hands away from its social obligations to senior citizens, the only option left for the "old people" is to beg on the road for their livelihood. The state has a right to impose taxes on its citizens and out of such public money a few essential services can be provided by the state to the growing population of senior citizens. The judgments of Court directing the children to take care of their old parents is throwing the old to the wolves. Courts are not offering solution to the problem. The idea is to ensure that the old persons do not have a feeling of being "unwanted burden on family or society". Hence the role of the sate as a promoter of healthy social life assumes importance. – *Sahara Time, October 15, 2005*

TOWARDS SOAP-BOX POLITICS

The following is excerpted from a news report in a national daily on November 25: "The Winter Session of Parliament began on a stormy note on November 24, with an unrelenting Opposition forcing the adjournment of both the Houses over Iraqi oil pay-off scam and demanding the resignation of Union Minister K. Natwar Singh and Congress president Sonia Gandhi." Every session of Parliament gets disrupted because of the incapacity of the Government and the Opposition to discuss the issues, howsoever contentious they may be, on the basis of well laid down parliamentary procedure. Is it a healthy phenomenon for a democracy? Is it essential for the Government and the Opposition to scuttle 'debates' in Parliament?

Political developments in a functioning democracy are determined by the interaction between the Government and the Opposition. A few facts may be mentioned to substantiate the argument that the Congress-led UPA Government and the BJP-led Opposition are determined to 'confront' each other — both inside and outside Parliament.

The roots of confrontational politics lie in the 2004 parliamentary election. The very possibility of Ms. Sonia Gandhi becoming the Prime Minister brought a sharp reaction from the BJP. The latter had decided to 'boycott' the swearing-in-ceremony in 2004, if Sonia Gandhi were to become the Prime Minister. BJP leader Sushma Swaraj announced that she would shave her head to show public disapproval of a 'foreigner' becoming the Prime Minister. Govindacharya and Uma Bharati, the then Chief Minister of Madhya Pradesh, also jumped into the bandwagon of 'anti-foreigner' campaign to save 'Bharat' from an 'Italian Sonia'.

The preparations undertaken by the BJP to launch a great public movement against Ms. Sonia Gandhi, however, collapsed like a house of cards when the latter withdrew her candidature in favour of Manmohan Singh.

Not prepared for such a 'rebuff' from Ms. Sonia Gandhi, the BJP soon took the issue of 'tainted' ministers (like Lalu Prasad Yadav) to confront the UPA Government. It served 'notice' on the UPA Government either to 'drop' the 'tainted' ministers or face the music of parliamentary boycott. The BJP translated this political rhetoric into reality by not allowing Prime Minister Manmohan Singh to make his first speech in Parliament on the vote of thanks for President's address. Never in the 55-year-old parliamentary history of India had the Prime Minister been boycotted so disgracefully. The greatest discomfiture of the BJP on this issue came when some of its own allies disapproved of such boycotts of parliamentary procedures.

The BJP was completely isolated on the issue of tainted ministers. After all, tainted ministers have been present in several cabinets both at the Centre and in the States, but parliamentary proceedings are never 'paralysed' on this pretext. The BJP leadership was found without clothes in public eye, as it could not sell its strategy of the 'disruption of parliamentary proceedings' to uphold the great cause of 'ministerial integrity'. The show flopped.

Parliament witnessed confrontation between the Government and the Opposition on the removal of the BJP-appointed Governors of Uttar Pradesh, Goa, Haryana and Gujarat. This stand- off came to an end after BJP president L.K. Advani and Home Minister Shivraj Patil debated the issue on the floor of the House. The same story has been repeated during the ongoing session when the BJP-JD(U) combine disrupted parliamentary proceedings on the issue of the Volcker report, despite the Prime Minister's willingness to discuss the issue in Parliament.

Why did the BJP abandon its normal parliamentary path to scrutinise the working of the Government? Is it reasonable to expect that their relationship would remain normal during the current Lok Sabha? The immediate hostility of the BJP towards the UPA Government seems to be the result of the most unexpected electoral defeat of the NDA Government in the 2004 parliamentary election. The 'India Shining' campaign had convinced the party leadership that the voters would enthusiastically flock back to the BJP. No wonder, the electoral reverses left the party in complete disarray. Several contradictory voices were heard within the Sangh parivar about the causes of the BJP's electoral defeat. While some blamed Gujarat Chief Minister Narendra Modi for the party's poor performance, a few others held the loss of BJP's ideological identity responsible.

If the BJP is in disarray, the health of the Congress is also not very encouraging. Indeed, the 2004 parliamentary election gave no reason for either party to celebrate. The BJP (with 138 Lok Sabha seats) and the Congress (with 145) have yet to establish their absolute dominance in the House. Also, their individual vote percentage is less than one-fourth of the total votes cast.

The two national contenders for power also represent two ideologically opposite poles of battle in India. It is only in the 1990s that the terms 'de-saffronisation' or 'detoxification' entered the idiom of Indian politics. It is also for the first time that both the Government and the Opposition are levelling allegations of 'ideological penetration' of pubic institutions, including high constitutional offices of the country.

It is good that the 'Secularism vs. Hindutva' debate is not being brushed under the carpet. Not surprisingly, the political class has been compelled to take public position on the issue. This is the explanation for confrontational politics between the Congress and the BJP, as both of them have either to expand themselves or wither away. Politics of the last decade of the 20th century and the beginning of the 21st century has brought India face-to-face with certain basic issues of nationalism.

The political situation in 21st century India demands greater interaction between the Government and the Opposition at every fora of democracy, including Parliament. The situation, however, is just the opposite. A few explanations have been offered for this turn of events. It has been suggested that the entry of 'new social groups and constituencies' in Parliament has brought a new socio-political culture, which is different from the elite-dominated Lok Sabhas of the 1950s.

Today, parliamentary procedures are not considered sacrosanct by the peasant class-dominated political parties of the backward castes, which have come to occupy the corridors of power. Why do we expect these groups to honour parliamentary procedures developed by an old ruling elite?

Another line of argument is that the spread of mass media in the 1990s has made some MPs take to theatrics. Media, after all, is more interested in sensational news than serious political debates. Besides, politics of polarisation between the 'secularists' and the 'Hindu rashtravadis' is being reflected in Parliament. Maybe the media has tempted the politicians to voice their opinion in TV channels and newspapers with greater vigour than in Parliament.

– *The Pioneer, November 29, 2005*

DEMOCRACY DISGRACED

The country was in for a rude shock on December 12 as it watched over TV screens 11 Members of Parliament accepting what is ever since known as cash-for-questions. This turned out to be far more serious than the ongoing drama of 'oil-for-food' controversy raised by the opposition parties in Parliament. The BJP was completely taken off guards as its six MPs out of eleven culprits were identified in the 'cash-for-questions' scandal. This is more so since it had taken holier than thou position on the issue of corruption in pubic life by paralysing Parliament accusing Natwar Singh on 'oil-for-food' scandal. It was not for the first time that 'camera' had caught the BJP stalwarts accepting bribe. Earlier party president Bangaru Laxman and its minister Dilip Singh Judeo were caught in similar circumstances.

So it is, indeed, a sad day for parliamentary democracy that six MPs of the BJP, three of the BSP, one of the Congress and the

RJD each accepted 'cash-for-questions' ranging from as petty an amount as Rs. 10,000 to Rs. 1.1 lakh. This scandal involving eleven MPs who were paid money to ask 'sponsored' questions in Parliament is of a very different nature than the cases of bribery involving pubic functionaries. Every case of misuse and abuse of authority by public functionaries does not merit equal treatment because the public status occupied by bribe-takers is based on a differential scale of social prestige and social expectations from the actors involved in cases of misuse of their public authority. Members of Parliament are expected to act as role models in setting the high standards of public life in the whole country and the public belief is shaken completely if an MP can accept bribe to ask a question at the behest of private interested individuals. Parliament is a pillar of Indian democracy and if citizens lose faith in this fundamental pillar, their faith in democracy is shaken completely by the misdemeanour of its own members.

Further, it has been commented that Indians should learn from England when the British Parliament not only took a swift action against its own members Neil Hammilton and Tim Smith who had accepted 2000 pound a question on behalf of Harrods department store run by Mohammed All-Fayed. It also undertook an exercise of cleansing the public life by reforming the political process. It is not essential to look for guidance from the British Parliament because India was faced with a similar situation when a Congress MP H.S. Mudgal had taken Rs.10,000 each on two occasions from the Bullion Merchants Association to ask questions suggested by it. The Mudgal episode had unfolded on September 24, 1951 and he wanted to resign from the Lok Sabha for this grave breach of Parliamentary code of conduct. Jawaharlal Nehru did not agree with the idea of just a resignation by the guilty MP, and he himself moved a resolution in the Lok Sabha that the house 'resolves that Mudgal deserved expulsion from the House and further that the terms of the resignation letter he gave to the Deputy Speaker at the conclusion of his statement constitute a contempt of this House which only aggravates his offence'.

Nehru emphasised the exceptional nature of corruption involving MPs in the performance of their legislative duties and this facilitates us to ask a Question: Why are MPs of 2005 not guided by the highest standards of morality as laid down by the founder of the Indian Republic? It is legitimate for a MP to take assistance from different sources to deal with a matter of public importance for discussion and debate on the floor of the House.

Feroze Gandhi, a Congress MP during Nehru phase of politics, raised Mundhra case alleging Congress Finance Minister T.T. Krishnamachari, for showing 'undue favours' to an adventurist industrialist Hari Das Mundhra. It was a hot rumour in the corridors of Parliament that Feroze Gandhi was supplied relevant and confidential documents and files concerning Mundhra deal by civil servants who were not expected to assist an MP in a case like this. Krishna Menon, Defence Minister in Nehru Cabinet, was faced with barrage of questions and criticisms by J.B. Kripalani, an opposition MP, on the partisan role of the then Defence Minister while dealing with the armed forces. Krishan Menon had alleged on the floor of the House that Kripalani was in contact with 'disaffected Military Generals' who were supplying him with confidential files in a clandestine manner. Parliament did not attach any importance to the allegations of consulting confidential files either against Feroze Gandhi or Kripalani because it was considered quite legitimate for MPs to explore every source of information while performing their legitimate role in the two Houses of Parliament. The moral of story is that a distinction has always been maintained between legitimate areas of activity and illegitimate actions of MPs.

An explanation for the galloping corruption in public life is offered by the political class itself which holds extremely expensive elections as the fountain source of corruption in the country. The need for funds for contesting expensive elections leads to the creation of a 'nexus between politicians and fund givers' in return for political patronage which is provided by MLA, MPs and Minister to the 'fund givers'.

Criminals are in politics because politicians. Politicians cannot shift the responsibility of politics and business and politics and criminals 'nexus' because politicians have themselves created such a 'nexus'. Why blame electoral democracy for the evils of elections in democracy? An elected office 'holder considers himself completely immune from the constraints of legality and morality in India because power acts as an intoxicant for the power wielder in a completely hierarchical and unequal society like ours. Mudgals, Bangarus and Lodhas represent this new reality of corrupt and power drunk political class of India of 2005.

– Sahara Time, December 24, 2005

BANISH ILLITERACY

The UPA has been trying to put a benevolent face by embarking upon developmental schemes like the National Employment Guarantee Scheme; National Rural Health Mission; National Urban-Rural Mission; National Highways Development Programme and Sarva Shiksha Abhiyan, including mid-day meal scheme. The government data clearly show that the country has very badly missed on its programme of educating a larger majority of children, including both boys and girls especially belonging to the poor and under privileged strata of society. The country recognised the need to tackle the problem of mass illiteracy and the Constitution (Eighty-sixth Amendment) Act 2002 added to Article 21 A says that "The State shall provide free and compulsory education to all children of the age of six to fourteen years in such manner as the state may, by law, determine. This amendment led to the birth of Sarva Shiksha Abhiyan (SSA) as a "flag-ship programme for achievement of universal Elementary Education in a time bound manner." This mission is "being implemented in partnership with state governments to cover the entire country."

India has entered the 21st century with a baggage of 192 million children, as notified by the government, who have never seen the face of school and it is in spite of the fact that the directive Principles of State Policy enshrined in the Constitution of India of 1950, recognised through Article 41 that the State shall secure Right to Education and Article 45 refers that "The State shall promote with special care the educational and economic interest of the weaker section of society" ; it has taken half a century for the governments of independent India to realise that they have completely failed to perform their constitutional obligations to provide 'Elementary Education' to children born after Independence of the country. The worst indictment came from the Supreme Court of India of February 2, 2006. While adjudicating on Public Interest Litigation concerning 'Child Labour' the Honourable Judges stated that 200 million children in the age group of 6 to 14 "almost are engaged in child labour and are out of the school". It is shameful state that these millions of children who are "out of school" are "forced to do manual work." The central Government provides 75 percent of funds for the SSA scheme to the states and the HRD ministry at the Centre has asked for an increase to Rs. 11,000 crore for 2006-07 compared with Rs. 7,156 crore of 2005-06.

Is the Himalyan failure of governments at the centre and the states to ensure elementary education to children born after Independence of the country attributable to just sheer neglect and inertia of the bureaucratic machinery of India? It deserves to be clearly stated that education for the poor children has never been a priority for democratically elected central, state and local government institutions. Hindu society has always distinguished between 'mental activity' and 'manual workers' and education was always meant for the children of high castes and the absolute majority of children of 'other castes' were never expected to get education. The Indian Caste system is completely responsible for keeping a large majority of children deprived of literacy because education is meant for the privileged children of high castes only. Further, post-Independence India witnessed the phenomenon of commodification of education and parents with financial resources are able to 'purchase' education for their children in the form of a marketable commodity. A democratic government has to be pressurised by its own citizens to provide education which can be bought by those who have purchasing power, any social pressure on government will be minimal.

The central and state governments are not at all committed to the idea of providing education to the children born after independence of India. While in 2002 the Constitution was amended, in July 2004 the UPA government decided to levy 2% education cess on all central taxes to finance primary education and mid-day meal scheme to children of the poor. The Prarambhik Shiksha Kosh has been set up and in 2004-2005, by levying this cess for education, government collected Rs. 5000 crore. The moot point is that the government is searching for excuses while dealing with the problems of mass illiteracy. Manmohan Singh in his Press Conference held on February 1, 2006 stated that "Whether I am the weakest Prime Minister or not should be judged by my actions" and it can be unambiguously stated that he would be remembered in history if he can make Indians feel that national illiteracy is a thing of the past. – *Sahara Time, February 18, 20066*

GOVERNANCE AND ACCOUNTABILITY

The common minimum programme of the Congress-led UPA regime is a reformist manifesto as revealed by the introduction of the National Rural Employment Guarantee scheme and the Right to Information Act, 2005. Besides, Ms. Sonia Gandhi-led National

Advisory Council is engaged in the task of identifying programmes and policies for the uplift of the poor. At the same time, the Congress president's personal preferences for the views and opinions of non-government voluntary agencies have provided non-bureaucratic feedback to the Government.

The Indian political class is aware of the fact that globalisation, privatisation and liberalisation is a sure recipe for electoral defeats, as experienced by the BJP-led NDA Government in 2004. The 'India Shining' policies of the BJP liberalisers and economic policies followed by TDP leader Chandrababu Naidu led to their defeat in 2004. Ms. Sonia Gandhi must know that the Congress cannot be an exception to the rule.

Being great learners, politicians are expected to abandon policies that do not bring electoral dividends. Ms. Sonia Gandhi seems to be aware of the pitfalls of economic policies of gung ho liberalisers like Manmohan Singh, P. Chidambaram and Montek Singh Ahluwalia. Not surprisingly, a few welfare programmes have been included in the CMP of the UPA Government.

Politicians are adept in playing tricks on voters by pursuing anti-people policies with a few charitable concessions focussed on the poor. It is difficult to suggest that the politics of liberalisation is consciously mediated by Ms. Sonia Gandhi's pro-poor postures of the National Advisory Council. It is possible that the NREG scheme or RTI Act may just be paper tigers with a view to provide cosmetics to the ugly face of liberalisation.

The UPA Government is engaged not only in providing 'humane' face to economic reforms, but also shown commitment to political and administrative reforms. Its CMP says, "As part of its commitment to electoral reforms, the UPA will initiate steps to introduce the state funding of elections at the earliest." It deserves to be stated that any electoral reforms will have a positive impact on the Government's performance. It is a known fact that every well meaning economic programme, like the NREG scheme, is bound to fail in the existing situation of largescale corruption in pubic life.

The Government is not the first to emphasise the need for electoral reforms. The Election Commission, ir its voluminous report, has called for such reforms in India. Last year became memorable in the political history of the country because a few MPs were expelled for accepting "cash for asking questions" in Parliament. This was soon followed by another allegation that a few MPs had misused MPLAD funds. The quick succession of events involving grave misconduct of the people's representatives led to the demand of electoral reforms, besides the need for the state funding of elections in India.

Leader of Opposition L.K. Advani has been a champion of the state funding of elections on the flimsy plea that highly expensive elections have become the root cause of corruption in politics. Our political class seems to have become a parasitical 'rent-seeker' that wants a pound of flesh from the state exchequer for all its activities, including the basic function of fighting elections. Can the absence of the state funding be the reason for our politicians to indulge in corrupt practices? What is the guarantee that corruption will come to an end, if elections are funded by the state?

Every political party is well funded and its leader is the one who controls the treasury. The control over purse provides him an unchallenged authority within the party. How could Rajnath Singh be made BJP president without any election in the party? Why are Mulayam Singh Yadav, Lalu Prasad Yadav, Mr. Karunanidhi and Ms. J. Jayalalithaa unquestioned leaders? Ms. Sonia Gandhi presides over the Congress by destroying internal democracy within the party. Mrs. Indira Gandhi had always asserted that the Congress needed her, as she was the only vote-catcher for the party. Mrs. Gandhi's observation was only partially true, as she also owed her supremacy to the fact that she was the chief controller and distributor of party funds.

Every political party is unabashedly following the footsteps of Mrs. Indira Gandhi. No wonder, today, tinpot leaders control party funds to elicit blind obedience from its members. Political parties and their front organisations have a legitimate right to collect funds for their multiple public activities. The only condition is that funds should be "publicly collected and publicly audited". Corruption in public life cannot come to an end unless political parties are compelled to operate openly.

How can India maintain democracy with the help of closed and secretive party system? It deserves to be stated that industrialists, entrepreneurs, traders, lobbyists and middlemen have vested interest in maintaining secrecy while funding politicians. After all, it guarantees a confidential quid pro quo between the public actor and the private fund-giver.

It is to the credit of the RSS to declare openly that its swayam sevaks offer money in secrecy. The Sangh Parivar's method of collecting funds is a hallmark of every closed organisation. Our political parties, however, cannot act like the RSS. They are, after all, expected to ensure transparency in governance.

The promoters of the state funding argue that elections are the biggest source of corruption for the "god-fearing" politicians. The country, however, is already spending a lot of money in organising elections. Though the deployment of armed forces during polls is expensive, there seems no way out—thanks to criminalisation the of politics. Can the criminalisation of politics be controlled by the state funding of elections? Such demands are a diversionary technique adopted by politicians to evade the real issue of the lack of transparency and accountability of political parties to the people.

Economic gains of any welfare programme undertaken by the Government cannot reach target groups without reforming the body politic, which is plagued with corruption. The state funding of elections is not a remedy for tackling the cancer of corruption in public life. The only way of dealing with the problem is to make public every internal activity of our political parties.

The NREG scheme or food-for-work programmes are essential for the poor. The UPA Government is on the right-track, if it links welfare programmes with electoral reforms. After all, economics and politics are two sides of the same coin. Economic development with equity is bound to get derailed, if political parties are not made accountable for funds they receive.

– *The Pioneer, January 10, 2006*

INTO 2006 AND ALREADY STUCK

The Manmohan Singh-led UPA Government commenced the New Year with a heavy agenda of foreign policy. Kashmir, Iran and the West were three major areas of focus.The ball was set rolling by President Pervez Musharraf of Pakistan who, in an open-ended interview to TV commentator Karan Thapar on January 8, proposed 'the concepts of self-governance and joint management' of the disputed territory of Kashmir. Gen Musharraf told Thapar his proposal of 'self-governance is a dilution of sovereignty'. In efforts to continue dialogue, the Manmohan Singh Government has met with multiple Kashmiri groups.

Undeniably, the Kashmir dispute is a multi-dimensional and indivisible part of India's domestic and foreign policies. The

Manmohan Singh Government has abandoned the earlier positions of the Indian Government and has involved the so-called pro-Pakistan secessionist Kashmiri groups in finding an amicable solution. Also, many CBMs have been taken by both India and Pakistan to improve their bilateral relationship and the latest step in the people-to-people contact is the train service between Amritsar and Lahore.

The foreign secretaries of India and Pakistan during their 3rd round of composite dialogue not only discussed the issue of cross-border terrorism but also the disturbed situation in Pakistan's Balochistan and Waziristan provinces. The Government of India had to assure the Pakistanis that problems in Balochistan were absolutely their internal issue and Indians were not at all involved there. Dialogue between these two countries is essential to improve the levels of trust and mutual confidence.

Furthermore, Indian foreign policy makers are expected to take a position on Iran's nuclear strategies because Germany, France and England have informed the United States about their failure to find any solution to this contentious issue. India is very keen to have Iran-Pakistan-India oil pipeline and foreign policy makers will have to make difficult choices because neutrality in this dispute is just not possible. Further, the Communist parties, which are 'outside' supporters of the UPA Government, are absolutely opposed to any anti-Iran policy of the Centre on the issue of nuclear Iran and its referral to the IAEA or UNSC.

India is already involved in serious negotiations with the Americans on the issue of separation of civilian nuclear plants from its military nuclear plants because it is a pre-condition for getting American recognition of Nuclear Weapons State by India. The proposed forthcoming visit of President George Bush in March has brought an element of urgency in negotiations on the issue of separation of nuclear energy plants by the Indians because our hawkish nuclear establishment wants to celebrate a nuclear weapon state status, which will be accorded by Mr. George Bush only if the clauses of agreement of July 18, 2005, are implemented.

US Under Secretary of State for Political Affairs Nicholas Burns, during his visit to Delhi on January 20, and German envoy Michael Schaefer, too, during his visit on behalf of the European Union on January 19, have both approached India to support the Western position on nuclear Iran at the meeting of the IAEA's Board of Governors and also during the discussion in the UNSC.

While Iran has been in denial over allegation that it is involved in making nuclear bombs, Western countries are determined to bring Iran before the UNSC.

Mr. Schaefer and Mr. Burns have both assured India that "We have simply entered another phase of diplomacy". It can be a sweet talk to persuade India to support the West against Iran both in IAEA and UNSC. Mr. Burns' negotiations with Foreign Secretary Shyam Saran on India's nuclear separation programme did not meet Indian expectations and the US official Burns threw a douche of cold water by stating that nuclear separation was 'challenging' and 'complex'. He clearly suggested that 'it was unrealistic to expect Bush's visit to be a cut off point by which the agreement would have been worked out.'

However, though Pakistan, Iran and the US are on Indian foreign policy agenda, the Manmohan Singh Government is completely paralysed in dealing with the diverse pulls and pressures of these three countries. Pakistan is convinced that India has nothing to offer but increased people-to-people mobility through bus or railway services, while a real solution to the Kashmir dispute is nowhere on the horizon. President Musharraf's latest proposals including 'demilitarisation' of Jammu and Kashmir along with 'self-government and joint management' have been completely cold-shouldered by the Indian Government. One wonders whether or not President Musharraf is offering concrete proposals and, if so, whether Indians are stuck in the past. Regardless, negotiations seem stymied.

Evidence of this nostalgia is the BJP's revival of its old dead horse campaign for the abrogation of Article 370 of the Constitution, which provides special status to Jammu and Kashmir, without realising that the issue died long ago. As the old mindset of the BJP on Kashmir is visible, the Manmohan Singh Government is also found lacking in generating fresh ideas. Indian foreign policy has not moved even an inch closer to solving the Kashmir dispute and even the expected softening of the Line of Control between India and Pakistan has remained purely cosmetic.

Similarly, Indian foreign policy makers are at wits end on the nuclear issues concerning Iran. Indian foreign policy makers cannot aggravate the Americans, their strategic partners, but it will definitely hurt India's national interests if Iran does not get Indian support in its struggle against Western nuclear bullies. The Manmohan Singh Government is also evading a parliamentary debate on the July 18, 2005, agreement between Mr. Bush and Manmohan Singh on the serious matter of separating nuclear plants in the country. It is ironic, however, that while the American Congress is fully involved in investigating the Bush Administration's nuclear policy concerning India, the Indian Parliament has steered clear of discussing such a serious policy issue as the nuclear plants of India.

This proves the extent to which the Manmohan Singh Government is deadlocked on vital foreign policy issues concerning the country. The very first month of 2006 has shown complete foreign policy paralysis of the Government on interrelated issues of Pakistan, Iran and the US. The explanation for such indolence might lay in Manmohan Singh's pro-Americanism and the realities dictated by geographical proximities between India, Pakistan and Iran. – *The Pioneer, January 24, 2006*

SECULARISM: ZIG ZAG PROCESS

The Constitution of India has not only guaranteed the Right to Freedom of Religion, it has also protected 'cultural and educational rights and interests of minorities'. The sum and substance of the Indian Constitution is that not only will the State not discriminate against any citizens on the basis of religion, language, culture or race, it will also protect and promote special cultural and educational rights of minorities.

The Constitution has to be worked by elected political representatives and it is possible that either the ideology of secularism, as enshrined in the Constitution, is not acceptable to the ruling parties or that politicians may offer tokenist concessions to the minorities keeping in tune with the formal letter of secularism in order to garner their votes. The crux of the issue is: can any democratic secular state reconcile the demands of secular equality of every citizen and also evolve public policies to meet the aspirations of groups engaged in religion-based identity politics?

Is reservation of seats in public institutions for backward class religious minority groups an act of 'minorityism' or 'appeasement' or an obligation of the democratic state towards the historically underdeveloped and backward minority groups? Do the Muslims of India have the right to express solidarity with Muslims in other countries or are their rights subject to an approval from the Hindu majority community?

It will be a truism to suggest that the Hindu majoritraian party is hostile towards the Muslims because the idea of Hindu majority has been constructed by projecting the Muslims as the 'other' and 'different'. Hindu versus Muslim is a staple diet of the Sangh Parivar and it is not unexpected if the practitioners of Hindu identity politics not only discriminate against Muslims when in power, but also campaign against Muslims when out of power.

Further, if on the one hand, Muslim demands are opposed by the Hindu Rashtravadis, on the other, articulation of Muslim demands by Muslim leadership is confined to a few limited concerns of the community. For instance, the Shahi Imam of Jama Masjid of Delhi, Syed Ahmed Bukhari, brought together on March 18, 2006 Jamat-e-Islami, the Jamat Ulma-e-hind and floated the All-India Muslim Representative Conference to chalk out an agenda of economic uplift of the community. The agenda prepared by Muslim leadership consists of a mix of religion-social and politico-economic demands concerning the community.

Does this 'agenda' go into the heart of problems faced by highly socially diverse Muslim minority living in a secular India? Has it not occurred to the Muslim leaders that some of the important socio-economic demands of the community cut across the prevailing status of deprivation of the poor of India, irrespective of their religion or caste? Does the Alladin's lamp of 'reservations' in public institutions and services help to increase substantially the representativeness of secular institutions of governance?

The electoral representative system based on first-past-the-post cannot be an answer to Muslim representation in elected legislatures. However, proportional representation will only institutionalise permanent minority-majority representation in legislatures. How does one increase minority representation in secular elected democratic institutions for creating a sense of belonging to the minorities?

Political empowerment by representation of Muslims in elected representative bodies will strengthen the fabric of Indian secularism because the voices of the Muslims in legislatures will be heard as equals to the others. This central issue of political empowerment of minorities, by increasing their 'representation in elected legislatures, brings us to examine the role of secular parties in promoting national integration in post-Independence India.

The Congress-led UPA government has interpreted the electoral verdict of Lok Sabha elections of May 2004 as a defeat of religion-based politics of Hindu Rashtravadis and the victory of the secular political formations. The Congress in its traditional style has undertaken a few tokenist steps in response to some of the felt needs of the minorities.

The minority representation in elected legislatures should increase and secular political parties are expected to identity 'authentic' community leaders who can win an election with the support of secular parties and voters. It is high time that 'authentic community voices' are heard in decision-making legislatures and it can be achieved only if secular political parties identify and project 'community leaders' as elected representatives of the people of India. Minority communities will develop a feeling of active participation in democratic nation-building processes if they have a sizeable representation in democratically-elected bodies.

Further, the upholders of secularism have to recognise that many a time, minority communities are treated in an unjust manner because the state functionaries, especially the bureaucracy and police, suffer from the disease of social 'biases' against minority religious communities. Many Judicial Commissions of Inquiry into riots have found the presence of 'bias and prejudice' in the conduct of bureaucracy and police against religious minorities. A citizen of a secular and constitutional democracy has the right to be treated 'equally' by the state functionaries but the religious minorities are many a time denied this right by the bureaucracy and police.

The upshot of above description is that while religion-based identity politics is conducted on the basis of Hindu versus the 'others, the practitioners of secular politics are expected to project an 'alternative' model of non-discriminatory governance in India. The secular political forces have to take the bull by its horns, and instead of the present tokenist interventions, they have to create a real political and administrative system in which the minorities can actively participate in democratic politics and also enjoy their fundamental rights of citizenship.

– *The Economic Times, March 25, 2006*

THE NATIONAL AS LOCAL

The ongoing assembly have highlighted the inter-permeability of state-level and national issues. Regional parties are seeking votes on not only local issues but also on matter concerning national policy.

The Lok Sabha and the state assembly elections in India of the twenty-first century have all-India significance because neither the

Congress nor the BJP, the two claimants for an all-India political space are unable to form a central government on their own electoral strength in the Lok Sabha of 545 members. The BJP had to seek the support and cooperation of about 23 regional parties, groups and popular local leaders to stay in power at the Centre from 1998 to 2004. This story is repeated in the case of the Congress which has been in power at the Centre since 2004. A new dimension has been added to the Congress-led UPA government because its 14 allies are dependent on the "outside support" of more than 60 Left MPs in the Lok Sabha.

It is only part of the story to state that the weakening of the all-India national parties has led to the emergence of the coalition governments at the Centre. The real significance of the emergence of this phenomenon is that national parties have not only to work in cooperation with regional and sub-regional groups but the real impact of such a coalescing of national and local arties is felt both at the national and state level politics. This becomes clear if we focus on the ongoing assembly elections.

The Congress party and its major allies in the UPA government are either competing or cooperating with one another in the assembly elections of Assam, West Bengal, Kerala, Tamil Nadu and Pondicherry. The Congress-led Untied Democratic Front government in Kerala is involved in a bitter electoral struggle against the Communist-led Left Democratic Front. The Communists have extended an "outside support" to the Congress-led UPA government at the Centre, but in Kerala no-holds-barred electoral better is being fought between the Congress and the Communists. Sonia Gandhi launched her party's campaign against Kerala Communists and stated on April 18: "The United Democratic Front alone can ensure social harmony and development". Sonia further asserted that "Only the UPA has a positive agenda for the state". Prakash Karat, the Secretary General of the CPI(M), stated that the Communists are contesting the elections in Kerala and West Bengal "to reverse the anti-people politics of the UPA".

Karat raised issues of national significance during election campaigns in Kerala and West Bengal and stated that the UPA government at the Centre has been following the US agenda and asserted, "India had thrown to the wind the basic tenets of the Non-Aligned Movement". Is foreign policy of India an issue for the state elections or is it in the domain of the Central Government?

The purely regional and state based parties are seeking votes on not only local or regional issues but also on matters concerning national policy. The Congress party is contesting elections in Assam against Asom Gana Parishad, a regional formation, which is supported by the Communists. A very critical issue in Assam is the infiltration of Bangladeshis. Regional parties like the AASU-AGP and the newly established Muslim Assam Untied Democratic Front and the Congress have to deal with the complex and emotive problems of Bangladeshis and the law dealing with illegal migrants has to be enacted by the Centre. The AASU/AGP has been opposed to the central law on migrants, the illegal Migrants (Determination by Tribunal) Act. The Congress, during elections has promised that "minorities will be protected against harassment" and the BJP has communalized the issue by championing the cause of Hindu Bangladeshi migrants as opposed to Muslim migrants. Assam's electoral politics has clear All-India dimensions and national and regional parties are engaged in finding solutions to this emotive issue.

The DMK- and the AIDMK-led alliances have occupied the centre stage of Tamil Nadu electoral politics and the Congress is contesting the election in alliance with the DMK, a UPA coalition partner at the Centre. An interesting electoral issue in Tamil Nadu is the role of the DMK ministers in the central government because of J. Jayalalithaa main electoral and political agenda is to attack the DMK by pointing out that its 13 ministers in the central government have failed to protect and promote the interests of the state. She has maintained that it is legitimate expectation from a regional party to take care of its own state's interests by its presence in the central government.

The upshot of the above description is that India federalism has been qualitatively impacted by the growing involvement of purely regional or local political formations with the problems of governance of the whole of India on the basis of their direct presence in the central government. The Centre makes its national and international politics by taking along regional parties. Regional parties compete and cooperate by involving themselves in decision-making processes at the central level.

Manmohan Singh himself accepted this fact while addressing the CII meeting on April 12, 2006. "I derive courage from the fact that our civilization has always been based on the libertinism and pluralism of "unity in diversity' and the central government is a 'unifying' factor by taking along 'diversities' represented by regional parties". The central government with the support of regional parties can effectively take a stand against extremist movements and their demands because the Centre can claim national legitimacy based on the support of regional parties. The PM could assert on April 1 that, "The ULFA can raise the issue (sovereignty of Assam) but that does not mean that we will discuss it." He could also tell the NSCN-IN on their demand for Greater Nagaland that, "the question of compromising territorial integrity without the consent of the states does not arise".

If, one the one hand, the regional parties sensitise the central government about their political needs and compulsions, regional parties, on the other hand, can come out of their local ghetto politics by their association with national politics. The federal balance of power can be safeguarded if the Centre is responsive to the demands of the states and the states, represented by regional formations are able to shed their excessive baggage of parochialism and localism.–*Economic Times, April 29, 2006*

7

The Foreign Policy of India and US

KERRY, BY GEORGE: VOTE FOR CIVILISED WORLD

George W. Bush is seeking a second term for US presidentship, and his challenger, Democrat John Kerry, is involved in a political battle to liberate America and the Third World by defeating the incumbent President. Bush is a practitioner of American imperialism; he fanatically believes the US is a "hyper power" and, hence, it can act as the sole global "policeman". He is the "chief political executive" of that segment of the ruling class which defined its ideology in the "Project for the New American Century" in 1997. And it is not an ordinary occurrence that his military-industrial establishment – represented by Dick Cheney and Donald Rumsfeld among others – has been the author of this project, which has been described by US scholars as an ideological programme of "neo-conservatives" of US politics.

Bush cannot be understood without demystifying the imperialist pretensions of neo-conservatives. They believe America is threatened by an "axis of evil" represented by Islamic fundamentalists and global terrorists and Islam is identified as villain of the piece because these neo-conservatives are also believers in and practitioners of fanatical Right wing Christianity. This makes them righteously believe that the "civilised world" (or Western values) must be protected by the armed might of the sole superpower of the 21st century. The "doctrine of pre-emptive war" as practiced by Bush is a logical extension of their firm belief that the superior Western values of free market, democracy and individual rights are under threat from the satanic forces represented by global terrorists.

These fanatical neo-cons sell their imperialist agenda by reminding the Americans and the world of the terrorist attacks on American symbols of power on September 11, 2001. Bush has justified every illegitimate war in the name of "fight against global terrorism". It does not matter to him and his imperialist establishment that it was a great lie to justify the war against Iraq in the name of eliminating (the imagined) weapons of mass destruction in that country. Neo-cons under the political leadership of Bush do not have any respect for international law while pursuing their ideology of pre-emptive wars.

The election campaigns of Bush and Kerry have brought into sharp focus the ideological differences between the two contenders. Thomas L. Friedman sums up the political distance between the self-assured neo-con imperialist, and the others, in his article, 'Addicted to 9/11' (The New York Times). He writes, "The President (Bush) has exploited the terrorism issue for political ends – trying to make it into another wedge issue like abortion, guns or gay rights – to rally Republican support and push forward his own political agenda." It is not only The New York Times or The Washington Post that have openly come forward in support of Kerry; even The New Yorker has broken its 80-year tradition of neutrality by coming out in support of Kerry and by stating that it was not sacrificing partisan independence. "We just felt that this was an important election to take a stand on," wrote the paper.

The argument put forth by Kerry's supporters is that President Bush's aggressive and interventionist policies in the name of "war on terrorism" have made Americans insecure and the country unsafe. His policies have created great hatred against America, and instead of containing the threat of terrorism he has succeeded in exposing America to global hostilities. The so-called high technology war against Iraq ended in May 2003, but American soldiers and their allies are still dying every day.

The American project of "democracy from above" in the case of Afghanistan and Iraq is plain adventurism, because minimum security conditions have not been established in these societies. Not only this, the neo-cons have exempted rich Americans from paying tax and the state has withdrawn from its role of providing social security to ordinary citizens. America has been handed over to the corporate world and Bush's team is controlled by the Wall Street and New York Stock Exchange. Also, Bush's "no-liberal free market economy" ideology wants to project this image to the whole world without caring about the threat that this free enterprise doctrine poses to the poorest of the world.

A vote for Kerry is a vote for a relatively "civilised" world, which at present is threatened by Washington-based imperialists and militarists. The imperialist, pro-rich, anti-poor President deserves to be vanquished. His defeat would be a rejection of the dangerous neo-con policy of establishing democracies at gunpoint. It is not an ordinary incident that America was "isolated" in its war against Iraq which has been described by UN Secretary-General Kofi Annan as an "illegal war". It is expected that Kerry will restore some normalcy in global affairs and rescue the world from the ideological lunacy of Bush and his friends.

– Sunday Pioneer, October 31, 2004

TREAD WITH CAUTION IN BUSHLAND

Indian foreign policymakers have to understand and grapple with the real political meaning and significance of the re-elected President Bush. His November 4 electoral victory is based on specific ideological beliefs of 51 per cent American voters, who expressed specific preferences in the elections. In this context, the Foreign Minister, Natwar Singh, made a childish observation while alluding to India's future relationship with America. He was unnecessarily euphoric in his statement of November 25, 2004, which says that the Government accords "high priority to developing relations with the US". He further said, "It is in our interest, in the interest of the region and for global peace, security and goodwill that the two great democracies of the world have a steady relationship."

Natwar Singh observed that India-US relations were "beginning to acquire a degree of stability and predictability and a willingness to work together on shared concerns." It has never been suggested by anyone in India that reciprocal and mutually beneficial relationships should not be built with America. In spite of many ups and downs during the last 55 years, US and India have continued to interact with one another. However, Mr. Singh's statement lacks the basic understanding about the reality of Mr. Bush's America after the presidential election.

A layman can be euphoric about "two democracies" coming closer, but a Foreign Minister should acknowledge the reality of US democracy as represented by President Bush and his neo-conservative team of Dick Cheney, Donald Rumsfeld, Condoleezza Rice and others. It is essential to bring out clearly the political and social implications of the new Bush regime. By not understanding the real meaning of Mr. Bush's victory, we may fall into a trap as shown by Mr. Singh's hyperbolic praise of US democracy and its shared concerns with India. However, he forgot to mention Iraq to the US.

President Bush has come to believe that his re-election is an endorsement of his foreign policy by the Americans. The most important component of his policy is to "protect the civilised world from Islamic terrorists" and establish "democracies" in Iraq and other West Asian countries. Mr. Bush has emerged as a new messiah of "democracy" for the dictatorially ruled Islamic world and he would launch a "pre-emptive" war to get rid of tyrants like Saddam Hussein. Unlike Natwar Singh, French President Jacques Chirac made a "balanced and cautious" statement on November 17, 2004, during his meeting with UK Prime Minister Tony Blair. Mr. Chirac said, "There is no doubt there has been an increase in terrorism... To a certain extent Saddam Hussein's departure was a positive thing, but it also provoked reactions such as the mobilisation in a number of countries of men and women of Islam which has made the world more dangerous."

The Arab-Islamic world is seething with anger against American aggression in the name of war on "terrorism". Within America, Mr. Bush and his campaigners raised the ghost of September 11, 2001, during the elections and the "terrified" Americans voted for warmonger Bush and his neo-cons. India should carefully listen to Colin Powell, who interpreted Mr. Bush's election as "a mandate to pursue American national interests in international affairs". he added, "The President is not going to trim his sails or pull back. It is a continuation of his principles, his policies, his beliefs." Mr. Powell has not only enlightened the world about the real meaning of the second term of President Bush, he has himself withdrawn from the scene because of his revulsion for his "aggressive and warmonger" colleagues in the Bush team.

The crucial point to be understood by Indian foreign policymakers is that America, after September 11, 2001, has become fanatically committed to the idea that its Judeo-Christian belief is superior. This belief has made Mr. Bush's supporters "self-righteous". The 2004 American presidential elections are a definite move towards Christian conservatives with a belief in so-called

Christian "moral values". Mr. Bush is considered the embodiment of this value system, which will condition his domestic and foreign policy. It is not surprising that the American voter said "Yes on Iraq war" because after 9/11, Americans have come to believe in "us and good" and "them and evil".

A conservative consensus, which exists in America, says Mr. Bush has to crush the "axis of evil" represented by Islamic terrorists and any foreign policy of a "hyper power" conditioned by "religious fanaticism" is bound to be dangerous for world security. Will Indians feel safe if Americans keep fighting wars against Afghanistan or Iraq or so-called nuclear Iran? This is not a figment of the imagination. The Post wrote that many religious groups "have asserted that Mr. Bush owes his victory to value-voters." It went further to say that for the first time "vast numbers of evangelical Christians showed their clout at the grassroots level without being organised by national groups such as the Christian coalitions or the moral majority."

Indian foreign policymakers have subordinated their interests to the American project on Iraq from 2003 to 2004. It was expected that the Congress-led UPA Government would follow an "autonomous" policy on Iraq by distancing itself form imperialist America. Unfortunately, this has not happened, primarily because of Ms. Sonia Gandhi's ignorance of the Nehru-Indira-Rajiv world view of autonomous foreign policy for India. We seem to have accepted "hegemonic" US's right to build the world in its own image, howsoever faulty it may be. Further, terrorism and religious fanaticism have emerged as new challenges to public policymakers, and India is involved in a fight against mindless "terrorism" indulged by multiple groups in society.

Terrorism is not the issue. How has President Bush's approach to Islamic terrorism helped in containing this challenge? The French President has alerted every one that America's war against Saddam Hussein has made the "world more dangerous" because new groups in different countries have taken to terrorism. American foreign policy has helped in "proliferation" and not "containment" of terrorism. After all, it is easy to fight a high technology war against visible object like Saddam Hussein, but it is impossible to root out the anger of dissatisfied groups ready to sacrifice their lives by fighting against their ideological enemies. India has 150 million Muslims and traditional economic and cultural linkages with Islamic countries which are becoming centres of anti-Americanism.

The Government succeeded in getting the abducted Indians released from Iraqi kidnappers because India has goodwill among Arab countries. How can Indians accept the ideology of demonised Islam as propagated by the US? The US and India have fundamental differences in their "global outlook". Hence foreign policymakers should get rid of euphoric approach towards American democracy and concentrate on Indian national interests.

In pursuit of such a policy, Indians will find "areas of convergence" with America and they should never hesitate to take up an independent stand on clash of opinions with the US. The UPA Government's foreign policy should be guided by the fact that America is imperialist while India a democratic. It is to be hoped that India draws some lessons from American and other Western countries' interventions in the Ukrainian elections. George Bush's America is "interventionist" while India believes in "co-existence". Can we go together? – *The Pioneer, December 1, 2004*

OUTSIDERS ARE MEDDLING

Prime Minister Manmohan Singh has been involved in fire-fighting exercises on the foreign policy front, thanks mainly to the confusion created by his own Minister for External Affairs. If it had been a one-time lapse on the part of Natwar Singh, it could have been ignored. However, he has made it his habit to make foreign policy announcements, especially during his visits abroad, and the Prime Minister is compelled to clean the mess.

One such example was on December 15 when the Foreign Minister offered unsolicited advice to the South Koreans: "North and South Korea should not follow India's example in becoming a nuclear power." Manmohan Singh had to intervene in the Rajya Sabha the next day by stating that "India is a nuclear power and a responsible nuclear power... India's defence and strategic affairs have to be decided upon on the basis of continuity and national consensus with due deliberations. These are issues but kept above partisan politics." Not only this. Will any sovereign country accept pontification from a Foreign Minister of a nuclear power state? After all, India has lost its political and moral standing on the nuclear issue, thanks to Indira Gandhi, the Hindu communalists, and the Indian bomb lobby.

Manmohan Singh, in his detailed intervention in the Rajya Sabha on December 21, clearly responded to all the major issues concerning the UPA Government's foreign policy. On the membership of the Security Council, he said, "There is no ambiguity in our stand. There is no confusion... We don't believe there should be any discrimination in the Security Council on veto rights." Russian President Vladimir Putin's statement on India's membership of the UNSC excited some officials from the Ministry of External Affairs or the PMO to make a statement that India would be ready to accept a non-veto UNSC status. Hence, Manmohan Singh was forced to observe that there was "no clarity on what shape the Security Council reforms would eventually take". He further said, it was "premature" for the Government to "pre-judge" the issue at this stage. It seems Indian policy makers have predicted the real gender of the baby even before the child is born.

Every Prime Minister has performed the job of not only making the foreign policy but also educating the citizens on India's relations with Pakistan. It's essential because these two neighbouring countries have been continuously involved in disputes. India cannot have any autonomy in its foreign policy without de-linking itself from a hostile Pakistan. Manmohan Singh has unambiguously stated the Government's approach towards Pakistan by maintaining that cross-border terrorism is not acceptable and that the present boundaries between the two countries will not be "redrawn". In his talks with Pakistan President Pervez Musharraf in New York in September 2004, Manmohan Singh had observed that "possible options for a peaceful negotiated settlement of the J&K issue would be explored in a sincere spirit and a purposeful manner." The Prime Minister reiterated this stand in his meeting with his Pakistani counterpart, Shaukat Aziz, on November 23. It is hoped that the framework for India-Pakistan relationship under the UPA Government as defined by the Prime Minister himself is rigidly followed.

The Prime Minister will have to follow the real spirit of his foreign policy statements by coming to terms with the policies of the Bush regime in America. The signals from the US under the re-elected President Bush are quite disturbing. America's relationship with Pakistan has always adversely affected India, and Pakistan has never shown interest in purposefully negotiating with India whenever it has received "military" and "political" support from the US. India and Pakistan have never been allowed to negotiate on their own because Americans, on the pretext of Cold War politics or currently under anti-terrorism crusade, have always pumped arms into Pakistan. More, US foreign policy has always intensified an arm race between India and Pakistan. How can any CBM between the two neighbours succeed when a superpower is patronising one country?

It is unfortunate that the Manmohan Singh Government has not learnt any lesson from the blunders committed by the Vajpayee Government from 1998 to 2004 while dealing with the US. Mr. Bush signed a Bill on December 20 that clearly stated its "long-term commitment to Pakistan, a stalwart ally in the war on terrorism." US arms sale to Pakistan worth $3 billion was to help stabilise and secure Pakistan. The Vajpayee-led NDA Government refused to draw correct lessons from US foreign policy designs which had projected September 11, 2001, terrorist attack as an alibi for world domination.

If, on the one hand, President Bush stated on December 21 that the "Iraqi troops were unfit for battle", on the other, he warned that he doesn't "expect the process to be trouble free" because the "democratic process" in Iraq will be "disrupted". Anti-terrorism of America and continuing war against Iraq from March 2003 to December 2004 is only one part of the militarist approach of the Americans to world affairs. It deserves to be stated that the American economy is in deep crisis and it is in decline. President Bush has no solution for economic revival and he has responded by the militarisation of America with a view to make US capitalists earn huge profits from the sale and export of weapons of mass destruction to every part of the world including Pakistan.

President Bush declared on December 20, "We will submit a budget that fits the times. It will provide every tool and resource to the military, will protect the homeland, and meet other priorities of the Government." The statement provides a key to understanding the growing militarisation of America, not only for internal security, but also for strengthening the armed might of its allies, including Pakistan. The Indian foreign policy-makers must understand the global implications of a declining economic superpower and the emergence of sole military superpower in the first decade of the 21st century. A unipolar new world order led by a militarist hyper power has been witnessing "wars" against countries America perceives as "hostile" or "unfriendly". Its war against Iraq is not the first and nor is it the last pre-emptive military intervention.

President Putin said on December 23, "America is trying to isolate his country." Mr. Putin's bold statement against US policy goes against the "national interest" of Russia. The Indian Foreign Minister, who claims to be a Nehruvian, has made pathetic appeal to the Americans on the issue of Pakistan's militarisation that has adverse effect on security balance in South Asia. Natwar Singh, while replying in a Rajya Sabha debate on December 22, observed: "It may also erode the goodwill and friendly feelings that exist for the US in India, both as a sister democracy as well as a strategic partner." Is it an adequate Indian response to US machinations in the India-Pakistan bilateral military balance of power?

Manmohan Singh has straightened out many confusions about Indian foreign policy created by his own colleagues. India and Pakistan can never have smooth bilateral relationship if America continues to play one country against the other by following overt and covert policies of acting as "patron-in-chief" of the two countries. Both India and Pakistan will have to arrive at a normal working relationship because "outsiders" can never act as "facilitators". – *The Pioneer, December 29, 2004*

ENTER, 'KING' GEORGE-II

The re-coronation of President George W. Bush(Jr) on January 20, 2005, very surprisingly, has been welcomed by 62 per cent of Indians in a programme on International Policy Attitudes. However, a large number of countries out of 21 that participated in the survey stated that "Bush is bad news for the world". Is this negative perception based on the previous record of the Bush Administration? The past can be a good guide for assessing the approach of any political leader because he is expected to continue with his tested and tried policies. Roger Cohen in the New York Times very aptly stated: "The first-time view of America as an unrivalled power with a single focus, uninterested in consultations, its perceived arrogance captured by the photographs at Abu Ghraib, will be hard to change."

Mr. Cohen could have been proved wrong by President Bush if he had given any new "message" after his re-election. However, the President maintained on January 13 that the war against Saddam Hussein was "absolutely" necessary. In an interview to NBC on January 18, President Bush gave an ultimatum to Iran and said, "I hope we can solve it diplomatically, but I will never take any option off the table." Is this the language of a changed and chastened Bush, who has not only destroyed Iraqi society, but also has made a complete mess of that country? He has obstinately maintained that Iraqi elections on January 30, 2005, are "not going to be perfect". Elections in Iraq will be held because President Bush wants it.

The moralistic and fanatically ideological approach of the Bush Administration is reflected clearly not only by the President himself but also by his Secretary of State, Ms. Condoleezza Rice. In her testimony before the Senate on January 19, Ms. Rice expressed her opinion like an interventionist-imperialist. Her statement on Russia, along with President Bush's aggressive approach towards Iran, clearly conveys the message that a re-elected President is an unrepentant imperialist and interventionist. She said, "The Russian Government is quite constructive in many areas," adding, "(In Russia) we see the path to democracy is uneven and its success is not assured."

It is not just Russia or Iraq or Iran – the whole world must behave according to the standards laid down by President Bush. He started his second term on January 20, 2005, with a pledge to seek "freedom in all the world" because "it is the just path to peace in an era of terrorism across the globe". Hence, anti-terrorism beginning with September 11, 2001, continues to be the guiding force of the Bush Administration's policies on the world stage. President Bush said, "In a world moving towards liberty, we are determined to show the meaning and promise of liberty." Is the world safe under such a hyper power? President Bush vowed to spread liberty and freedom "to the darkest corners of the world" with an ultimate aim of "ending tyranny in our world".

President Bush summed up his global policy by stating: "Our goal, instead, is to help others find their own voice, attain their own freedom and make their own way." The upshot of his ideological doctrine is that as in the past four years, wars will be imposed on targeted countries by the "military-industrial" complex represented by President Bush, Vice-President Dick Cheney and Defence Secretary Donald Rumsfeld.

President Bush may perhaps continue to follow the same old policies towards India and Pakistan. During her Senate confirmation hearing, Ms. Rice made two statements on India and Pakistan which are a continuation of Colin Powell's policies on India. "The US is cooperating with India on a range of economic and security issues," she said adding, "this, even as we embrace Pakistan as a vital ally in the war on terror, and a state in transition towards a more moderate and democratic future."

On the basis of the above statements of President Bush and Ms. Rice, the euphoria expressed by some Indians on the re-election of the President is totally misplaced and unwarranted. For, the world, including India, should be prepared to see wars and aggressions on countries to be decided by the US. The outcome will be, first, India will have to pay more for imported "oil supplies" because the US has decided to destabilise our allies like Iraq, Iran, et al. In an inter-dependent world, India will have to pay a heavy price for war-ravaged Iraqi society and Iran, if the US decides to implement its aggressive agenda of "teaching lessons" to any country in the name of "securing the world for freedom". India's relations with Arab countries are dependent not only on oil but also on deep economic transactions, which have been usually beneficial to both. Indians in large number were compelled to quit their jobs in Iraq because of US invasion.

Second, US will have to keep on supplying arms to Pakistan in return of that country's support to US's misadventures in the Arab world. The Pakistani establishment, especially military, has always felt comfortable and well-rewarded by serving the interests of US in Central Asia, Afghanistan, Iraq, Iran et al. The US-supported "armed machine" of Pakistani generals has made the country lose interest in settling any dispute with India including Jammu & Kashmir. American militarisation of Pakistan has acted as a great "disincentive" for Pakistani generals to restore "normalcy" with India.

Third, India has justified every excessive defence expenditure by pointing an accusing finger at Pakistan. The "nuclear lobby" in India succeeded in its misadventure by pointing out that Pakistan possessed nuclear weapons, and weapons competition between the two countries has become "unstoppable" because the US is directly involved in arming Pakistan. How can bilateralism succeed when a country has decided to grow in the protective shadow of a war-monger superpower?

Indians have always suffered, directly and indirectly, because of aggressive American policies in the region, and domestic war-mongers have taken advantage of this situation both in India and Pakistan. US policies have imposed heavy financial burden on India and destroyed the civil society of Pakistan. The confidence building measures between India and Pakistan undertaken by the Manmohan Singh-led UPA Government and President Musharraf can never succeed if the US keeps on treating Pakistan as a "frontline" state for dealing with Arab and Central Asian countries.

The re-elected US President poses a real challenge to Indian foreign and defence policy-makers. Can a multi-polar world of India, China and Russia be created? It will be possible only when countervailing forces emerge strong enough to contain a hegemonistic and aggressive America. It is in the enlightened self-interest of India, Russia and China to form a "trilateral" group and work in cooperation while dealing with American interventionist policies in Asia and the Arab world. Mr. Putin's Russia is as much threatened as Iraq or Iran because the US wants to dominate Central Asia, an area of legitimate national interest to Russia, India and China. – *The Pioneer, January 25, 2005*

SCALING DOWN THE SUMMIT

The 13th SAARC summit, which was to be held in Dhaka on February 6-7, 2005, has been postponed at India's specific request. Indian Foreign Secretary Shyam Saran said on February 2, "If you have the kind of environment... which prevails today, we genuinely believe that the desired outcomes are not possible. So we should wait until the time is propitious to have such an important and significant summit." India is solely responsible for derailing the institutional arrangement of mutual negotiations among the seven South Asian countries.

It is a lame excuse on India's part to express its inability to attend the summit because the security environment in Bangladesh is not suitable for the SAARC meeting. The dispute between India and Bangladesh, however, has emerged because of different perceptions the two countries have, especially regarding illegal Bangladeshi immigrants into India and sanctuary provided by the Bangladesh establishment to Indian insurgents and terrorist groups. A state of political deadlock exists because allegations levelled by India are rejected by Bangladesh, and there seems to be no possibility of resolving the disputes.

It is not only the Manmohan Singh-led UPA Government which is not able to break the ice, the former Vajpayee-led NDA Government too had created barriers by publicly stating that "Hindu Bangladeshis" can stay but the "Muslim Bangladeshis" will have to leave because of their "illegal status". The Vajpayee Government gave a communal colour to the issue of Bangladeshi migrants. The UPA Government too has not been able to convince the Bangladeshi Government about the genuineness of its allegations.

The postponement of the SAARC summit at India's behest has further antagonised Dhaka. It is the deep-seated distrust between India and Bangladesh on political disputes that has created barriers before a fruitful dialogue. Another factor which influenced Indian decision makers to seek postponement of the summit was the political developments in Nepal where the King has taken over the country. India reacted very strongly against King Gyanendra's arbitrary action. Mr. Saran said, "The constitutional monarchy and multi-party democracy are the two pill1ars of political stability in Nepal. This principle has been violated."

True, India-Nepal relations have been more than "special" – both at Government and people-to-people level. New Delhi cleverly linked the situation in Bangladesh and Nepal, and the Indian Foreign Secretary clearly stated on February 3, "Nobody can deny there is a serious situation prevailing in the neighbourhood. What has happened in Nepal is not an ordinary event. What has been happening in Bangladesh is not ordinary either."

Every South Asian country has faced political volatility, but opportunities to meet at political levels have always been on the agenda of the seven neighbouring states. Did our neighbours react in the manner we have on Nepal's King Gyanendra's action, when Indira Gandhi declared Emergency from 1975 to 1977? India should have used the opportunity at Dhaka to involve the Nepal King in discussions for the restoration of democracy in that country. It is absurd to suggest that India's participation along with Nepal would have provided legitimacy to the King's arbitrary action.

Bangladesh has alleged that India has violated the SAARC Charter by withdrawing from the summit. And Pakistan has expressed that the opportunity of a bilateral meeting between the Prime Ministers of India and Pakistan has been lost.

The larger issue is that relations among the SAARC states are full of problems. It is in the interest of all these countries to achieve a level of regional cooperation for the common good. South Asian countries will swim or sink together, because cooperation will bring dividends to all and conflict will lead to disaster. Regional imperative of mutual cooperation is being ignored and economic losses are being suffered by all the SAARC countries. India cannot have a gas pipeline from Iran because a mutual distrust exists between India and Pakistan. Politics of mutual conflict has become a hindrance to fruitful economic relations.

The dispute between India and Pakistan has imposed an unbearable defence expenditure which otherwise could have been fruitfully utilised for economic development. Military competition between the two countries has taken a turn for the worse because both these antagonists have declared themselves as nuclear weapons states. South Asian countries are now exposed to nuclear misadventure.

It is no one's case that India is solely responsible for antagonistic relationships with some of its neighbours, especially Pakistan and Bangladesh. The argument here is two-fold: First, India, as the largest country in the region, has a major responsibility to undertake policy initiatives for the resolution of even intractable neighbouring conflicts by making reasonable compromises with neighbours. Second, every South Asian country must accept the logic of geographical interconnections and economic mutuality based on economics of interdependence.

It deserves to be stated that the first decade of the 21st century has shown to the Third World that American imperialism can ruthlessly interfere in the domestic affairs of quarrelsome neighbours. India and Pakistan have enough experience of US involvement in their disputes. The only alternative available for SAARC countries for safeguarding their freedom is through regional integration.

The real obstacle in the way of South Asia's progress is the politics of adversarial relations. It is at the political level that disputes have to be settled. Politics has to be in a commanding position if SAARC countries must arrive at solutions to their disputes on the basis of mutual give-and-take. It is neither idealistic nor utopian to suggest that South Asians as a whole have wasted many opportunities of progress during the last 50 years because of mutual distrust and hostilities.

Incidentally, South Asian countries are following in the footsteps of their erstwhile European colonisers. They were involved in wars with one another for many centuries. The European Union is a product of wars between its member countries till the middle of last century — hard lessons have brought them, whether reluctantly or enthusiastically, on a common platform. Should South Asia repeat the historical experience of wars by European countries before settling down?

Or should it learn from their experience and follow the path of constructive negotiations?

Every effort should be made to extend the frontiers of friendship among the seven South Asian countries by recognising the fact that every one of them will reap the benefits from regional cooperation. At the same time, India has to take many more initiatives before it can expect even minimum normal relations with its neighbours. SAARC is the best forum to bring these seven countries together. – *The Pioneer, February 8, 2005*

RICE MENU NOT NICE FOR INDIA

US Secretary of State Condoleezza Rice's first visit to Asia, in her official capacity, began with her arrival in New Delhi on March 16. It was officially described thus: "It was enough for both sides to agree on the contours of an agenda post-Next Steps in Strategic Partnership (NSSP). This includes a comprehensive engagement on energy issues and a strategic dialogue that will examine the possibility of joint manufacturing of arms and other military equipment." It requires low level of intelligence to suggest that Ms. Rice has visited India just to formalise the on-going negotiations on strategic partnership with India.

Further, only defence lobbyists are celebrating Ms. Rice's visit because she has promised more defence-related supplies and agreements on "dual use technologies". They seem to forget that America is quite active in the global arms bazaar, and the arm sellers from Britain, France, Russia and the US are always looking for lucrative defence sale opportunities in India. Besides, the American Ambassador in India has already warned that his Government does not approve of India's decision to explore the possibilities of a gas pipeline for the supply of oil from Iran. Ms. Rice, therefore, does not need a personal visit to convey its anti-Iran policy.

An influential pro-American defence lobbyist in India has enthusiastically commented: "In the next two decades, there will be only three centres for defence equipment – the US, European Union and Russia. We have to start evaluating the merits of working with each of them. The latter two will not be able to keep up with the US in terms of equipment quality. Furthermore, as the dominant power in the foreseeable future, there would be greater advantage in building a security relationship that inevitably accompanies the purchase of substantial defence equipment." Since the sale and purchase of defence equipment is a lucrative business, the so-called "defence lobbyists" are projecting a rosy picture of the growing collaboration between the Bush Administration and India. Besides, they see the presence of Ms. Rice, in place of Colin Powell, as a positive development for India.

Any serious analysis of US foreign policy demands the demystification of Ms. Rice's sweet talks that wrap the real interests and strategies of the US. The Americans seem to be worried about the rising power of China. On the eve of her visit, Ms. Rice observed that the US does not have a "posture against China" but Washington is concerned about China's military modernisation. She further stated, "There are several ways to deal with it."

Perhaps the most important has been the need for the US "to create strong alliances in the region that will contain the growing aspirations of China". American policy-makers have clearly stated that the "Red sun rising" has to be managed by being active...in making certain that our alliances in the region areas strong as possible."

Thus, Ms. Rice's visit clearly conveys to its "friends" like India that America is forging alliances to "contain the emerging China". Is India ready for an alliance with US against the rising dragon? India has to come to terms with the sole super powers' global hegemonic project. In this context, India has just two options: It can either ally with the US against China, or create an axis of India, China and Russia against US hegemony.

The Vajpayee Government voted for the first option when, after Pokhran-II in May 1998, a confidential letter was sent to then US President, Bill Clinton, that said: "India's nuclear programme is directed against Pakistan and China". It justified its nuclear misadventure by pointing out to the Americans that India had threat from "Pakistan and China". Much water has flowed down the Ganges since then. The Americans have come out in the open saying China has to be "contained" and "managed", and India should join hands with the US to meet the Chinese challenge.

Is India moving in a subtle manner towards the American designs in Asia? The US has assured India that its "energy needs and defence requirements" and India-America "partnership" would be mutually beneficial. It deserves to be stated that India has not yet jumped into the bandwagon of American "alliance politics" in Asia, and attempts are being made by both India and China to overcome their hoary past. While the process of building India-China friendship is steadily moving forward, a powerful pro-America and anti-China social constituency exists in India.

A powerful section of Indians views China as a future economic competitor and a military challenge. This social constituency is able to manipulate India's anti-Pakistan sentiments by projecting China-Pakistan axis against India. It is happening at a time when political direction of goal-oriented foreign policy has been missing in India. Today, bureaucrats like Brijesh Mishra, J.N. Dixit, Natwar Singh and Yashwant Sinha are managing foreign policy. They have no vision to take the country out of such complex situations.

The Indian political class, and not the foreign policy bureaucrats, have to decide on the issue of the country's relative sovereignty because "unilateralism" and "multi-lateralism" have direct impact on its role under the new imperialist global world order. The real meaning of the Nehruvian world view was that decisions were to be taken by Indians on the basis of merits of the case. Politics played a pre-eminent role in policy-making, and civil servants were simply asked to "fill in the details" and implement policies under the direction and supervision of political leadership.

The mainstream Indian bureaucracy has always been favourable towards America. Only the strong political leadership was able to tame its pro-Americanism during the heydays of non-alignment in the Cold War era. The collapse of Soviet Union and the erstwhile East European Socialist State system in the beginning of 1990s, along with the collapse of state-led planning system in India, brought Indian pro-liberalisers and pro-Americans in the forefront of opinion-making. The Nehruvian model of relative state autonomy has become a dirty word, and a half-hour lunch meeting between the Prime Minister and the American President is termed an achievement.

Indian foreign policy is thus becoming pro-America because of the replacement of political leadership by foreign policy bureaucrats and economic liberalisers. It has to be politically decided that India, China and Russia have to come together to act as a "countervailing" force in the existing unipolar imperialist global order. In the absence of multi-polarity, the Indians will be Seven Sisters' Parliament.

BETWEEN THE LINES: JOURNEY FOR PEACE

Symbols in politics can play the role of accelerators in the process of substantive transformations. The Srinagar-Muzaffarabad bus service that started on April 7 has been hailed as "peace caravan". It is a great occasion because the bus service has turned into a people's movement. In spite of the threat of terrorists and the Hurriyat's call for a bandh, the occasion created an atmosphere of festivities and celebrations among the divided families of Kashmir. Emotions turned into tears during reunion of people from both sides after 58 years of separation.

The Congress-led UPA Government, supported by every democratic party, group and leader of the Valley, has gathered courage to start a journey for peace, dialogue and negotiations between India and Pakistan. Incidentally, threats from terrorist groups have brought the political leaders of both sides under a common platform. Both have condemned the April 6 fidayeen attack on innocent passengers. The assault, which was executed a day before the bus journey, was intended to derail the peace process. But Chief Minister Mufti Mohammad Sayeed made the Government's intention clear: "Such acts wouldn't derail the peace process."

The presence of Prime Minister Manmohan Singh, along with Congress president Sonia Gandhi and other political dignitaries, has established the fact that the country is determined to restore normalcy in Jammu & Kashmir. The people on both sides of border have expressed their joy and happiness over the resumption of broken ties between the 'divided' Kashmiris through bus service. The moment was indeed redolent and symbolic of possibilities. This has been possible essentially because the people from both sides have endorsed the idea of bus service, which was eventually acknowledged by their political leadership. India's people-centric approach to peace in Kashmir is for all to witness. In fact, the success of this bus service will spell the beginning of the end of terror in the Valley.

The bus journey can be a turning point in the history of Kashmir, as the people can see the alternative to terror. It deserves to be mentioned that during the dark phase of Punjab—the Blue Star Operation of 1984—Sikhs were completely alienated from the Government of the day. But victory against terrorism was achieved only when the same people turned against terrorists after the Operation Black Thunder. The Golden Temple in Amritsar is their holiest place, and if one military operation aroused the masses against the Government, another operation turned them against the merchant of death.

Terrorism cannot be contained militarily unless terrorists are delegitimised in the people's eyes. It is seen in Iraq where the masses see the US as an "occupier". No wonder one comes across everyday about the news of bloodshed from Baghdad. Similarly, the ongoing peace process in Nagaland with insurgent groups would not have been negotiated without the people's desire for peace in the State.

It should be remembered that the terrorism and insurgency is nurtured by the public opinion. Similarly, the act of terror can be liquidated when the people's sentiment demands so. Perhaps, the Valley is experiencing similar sentiments. The popular perception is in favour of peace.

India and Pakistan have to resolve bilateral disputes for peaceful coexistence and co-prosperity. There are powerful lobbies in both countries that believe in military solution of the Kashmir issue. The recent sale of the F-16 fighter aircraft to Pakistan legitimises Indian warmongers to purchase F-18 aircraft. This could begin a dangerous race for armament in the subcontinent.

The bus journey has attracted the media attention of both countries. Every major source of opinion-making is highlighting the people's enthusiasm for such bold steps. Indeed, this is a great asset for peace process in Kashmir. The atmospherics are electrified, and the opponents of peace have realised the immense potential of people-to-people contact. With the bus service shaping the sub-continental history by narrowing down the differences between India and Pakistan, the jihadi constituency is also expected to lose its shine.

The fidayeen attack on passengers, a day before the bus journey, was clearly an act of desperation and frustration among terrorists. Chief Minister Mufti Mohammad Sayeed aptly summed up: "It is an attack on the common people." Public policymakers have got a clear message that the peace process is unstoppable that will encourage the process of negotiations for further peace. The people on both sides of the Line of Control can now begin to reap benefits of the resumption of ties that was broken during the Partition. The bus journey definitely heralds the goal of creating "soft borders" between India and Pakistan.

– *Sunday Pioneer, April 10, 2005*

SIX TETE-A-TETES OR A DIALOGUE OF SEVEN?

The 13th summit of the South Asian Association for Regional Cooperation (SAARC) to be held at Dhaka in the first week of February was postponed at India's instance, leaving a bitter taste in the host country's mouth. It deserves to be clearly stated that the resolution of bilateral disputes is a pre-requisite for economic benefits for all countries of the region. Bilateralism is not a substitute for regionalism and an effort has to be made by every country to extend the areas of regional cooperation in South Asia.

This perspective of linking of bilateralism with the goal of strengthening SAARC seems to be missing in the February 14 policy statement of foreign secretary Shyam Saran. He said: "We must also recognise, regrettable though this may be, that the countries of South Asia, while occupying the same geographical space, do not have a shared security perception and hence a common security doctrine... In South Asia, at least some of the states perceive security threats as arising from within the region."

Further, the foreign secretary observed that "SAARC is still largely a consultative body, which has shied away from undertaking even a single collaborative project in its 20 years of existence. In fact, there is deep resistance to doing any thing that could be collaborative." While India clearly expressed its bilateral difficulties with neighbouring countries on February 14, the neighbours have also many "unfinished" problems and disputes with India and as a large country of the region, India is expected to make compromises with neighbours.

When the Vajpayee government decided to declare itself a nuclear weapon State, it sent an official confidential letter to the then US President Bill Clinton saying that India has a threat perception from its two neighbours China and Pakistan. Can India then blame its neighbours who "perceive security threats as arising within the region?"

India's nuclear adventurism was immediately responded to by Pakistan, which also declared itself an open nuclear weapon State. The foreign secretary in his statement of February 14, 2005 asked neighbours to demonstrate sensitivity to India's vital concerns. Reciprocal expectations exist in Pakistan and Bangladesh.

It is in the enlightened interest of all the seven countries of South Asia, including India, to make every effort to promote areas of economic cooperation by transcending the constraints of bilateral disputes. It can be stated unambiguously that every country will gain if South Asian cooperation gains its natural momentum.

India and Pakistan's positive decisions on February 16, 2005 on gas pipeline, the opening of bus route in divided Kashmir, and confidence-building measures (CBMs) on nuclear missiles seemed unachievable in 2004. India and Pakistan seem to be moving forward in a gradual manner to resolve bilateral differences. A reasonable solution to the Kashmir dispute will help in substantial reduction of defence expenditure in both countries.

India has great energy requirements and normal relations with Pakistan and Bangladesh can open new opportunities for the energy requirements of growing economies of India and the region.

It is a cliche to state that politics of one kind can facilitate economic cooperation and politics of another kind can obstruct it. Every South Asian country has experienced great difficulties in the way of the growth of economic interdependencies in the region as a whole because of an inclement political climate. The river dispute between India and Pakistan needed a mediator like the World Bank because of lack of mutual trust between the two.

America has always jumped into the troubled waters on Kashmir and everyone knows that America is not a neutral arbiter in any dispute in the Third World. The irony is that India and Pakistan have surrendered their sovereignty and provided an opportunity to the hyper power of the 21st century to 'interfere' in our region on the pretext of resolving our bilateral disputes.

The choice in twenty first century is either cooperate with one another or get 'dictated' by the hyper power, the US. This newspaper editorially commended (Feb 16) the foreign secretary's "new policy towards India's South Asian neighbourhood that is at once more muscular and more pragmatic than what passed for policy in the past."

This understanding is absolutely off the mark because the real meaning of the foreign secretary's statement is that India is still tied down with bilateral 'disputes' with its neighbouring countries and it has no large roadmap for the future of South Asia including its own. India is keen to become a permanent member of the United Nations Security Council by forgetting that a Security Council member cannot be effective if it has serious disputes with its own neighbours.

Why is it that the institutional mechanism of South Asian Cooperation is not moving forward? India is solely responsible for its failure to motivate the neighbouring South Asian countries to evolve common economic and trade policies by transcending their territorial and geographical boundaries. Indian policy makers have failed to reconcile bilateralism with regional multi-lateralism and the postponement of the scheduled 13th SAARC Summit at Dhaka substantiates the argument that India has not evolved a balance between bilateralism and regionalism.

The ongoing process of confidence building between India and Pakistan should be extended to Bangladesh. India should act as a "prime mover of regional cooperation". In summation it may be suggested that the latest message of Indian foreign secretary should not remain a rhetoric and India should follow in letter and spirit that "we are prepared to do more to throw open our markets to all our neighbours." Bilateral disputes should not be permitted to obstruct the growth of constructive regional cooperative enterprises and new foreign policy options have to be exercised to strengthen regionalism to face the emerging challenges of new globalism. – *The Economic Times, April 16, 2005*

FOR LOVE OF UNCLE SAM

The UPA Government has completed one year in office, and on May 22 i t released a 42-page report *A Caring Government – One Year of the UPA Government* highlighting its achievements. Its claim, however, was rebutted by the Opposition NDA on May 23 when it released a "chargesheet" titled *A Year of Non-Performance and Misgovernance*. The chargesheet has five chapters on the failures of the UPA Government, and one such chapter is on *mistakes in foreign policy*.

It states that the Government "lacked in firmness in dealing with Pakistan" and "believed more in giving than in taking" and that it "was hesitant on raising the issue of cross-border terrorism with Pakistan". Another serious criticism levelled was that "far from pursuing an independent foreign policy, as promised in the national common minimum programme, the UPA Government has agreed to subject itself to inspection by US authorities with respect to the so-called dual-use items imported even from a third country" – a demand which was earlier rejected by the Vajpayee Government.

It is expected that the foreign policy of a mature democracy like India will have "continuity" with some "changes" with "change of government", and that a broad area of "agreement" will exist between the government of the day and the opposition. It may be too much to expect an agreement on every issue by major political players, but some "stability" in foreign policy is necessary to make other countries believe they are not dealing with transient governments but a politically "predictable" country.

Neither Atal Bihari Vajpayee nor Manmohan Singh have worked on the basis of a well though out "framework of foreign policy". This is clearly reflected in India's complete acceptance of a unipolar global order led by the United States.

A few facts may be mentioned to substantiate the argument that India's basic foreign policy framework has an element of continuity, irrespective of the change of Government. First, Mr. Vajpayee and Manmohan Singh have not made any effort to create an alternative "triad" of India, Russia and China to act as a countervailing force to contain the brutal military power of the sole superpower, the US. Second, like Mr. Vajpayee, Manmohan Singh has pursued the policy of strengthening and solidifying India's bilateral relationship with the US.

Third, both have accepted the foreign policy doctrines of neo-conservative George Bush's America. Indians feel very happy to project its "great democracy" before the Americans who have decided to establish democratic regimes in West Asia and former Soviet territories. Both Mr. Vajpayee and Manmohan Singh have followed a passive foreign policy while dealing with the issue of US aggression against Iraq. The Bush Administration has completely destabilised the Iraqi society, and like the previous NDA Government, the present Government, too, has no words of condemnation on the ongoing social violence in Iraq.

Fourth, neither Mr. Vajpayee nor Manmohan Singh have ever condemned puppet regimes installed by the US – whether in Afghanistan or Iraq or in Central Asian countries like Georgia or Ukraine. India has refused to express its disapproval of US's open interventions in the internal affairs of developing countries. This is because India does not want to annoy the Americans.

The upshot of all this is that the NDA "chargesheet" is completely farcical because both Mr. Vajpayee and Manmohan Singh have sailed on the same boat of pro-Americanism. The NDA and UPA governments have always celebrated every instance of improvement in bilateral relationship between India and the US. They are both "gung-ho" globalisers, and for them America is the Mecca of support and patronage.

Moreover, the bilateral relationship between India and Pakistan is also a story of continuity, of building step-by-step bridges between these two neighbours. The best comment has come from Pakistani Foreign Minister Khurshid Mahmud Kasuri, who stated on May 27 that "we were upset when the Government of Atal Bihari Vajpayee, a courageous man, fell... We were not quite sure how the next Government would be." He continued, "But Prime Minister Manmohan Singh and President Musharraf struck an instant chemistry in New York." The Pakistani President has also transformed; in 2005 he is not the Musharraf of Kargil or Agra Summit.

For the first time in the history of Indo-Pak relations a Pakistani head of state has openly stated to "delink the Kashmir dispute from religion" in "deference to Indian secularism". He has also said that the dispute should be discussed and negotiated on the basis of regions and sub-regions of Jammu & Kashmir. It is for the Indian Prime Minister to catch the bull by the horns and seize upon this opportunity to move forward on the road to peace.

Manmohan Singh is in the habit of saying that solution should be found by looking "outside the box", and General Pervez Musharraf has provided a new model of region-based discussion on the Kashmir issue. It may be possible that his own personal experience with a section of Pakistani terrorists may have convinced him that religious fanatics only create bloodshed and do not bring solutions.

It is also possible that American "friends" of India and Pakistan are pressuring both countries to find solutions to their "historical dispute". Many American think-tanks have devoted their attention to Kashmir. It is also probable that General Musharraf has found some change in the Chinese attitude towards Pakistan and India.

Bilateral relationship between India and China is also undergoing a change for the better, and the Pakistani President may have a feeling that China's "blind" support to Pakistan against India may have been buried by the present Chinese and Indian leaderships. It is no secret that Pakistan took full advantage of the hostility between China and India.

The Kashmir issue requires "give and take" on the part of both the countries. Along with the ongoing CBMs, especially the opening of bilateral travel facilities, Kashmir must be brought to the negotiating table. The Congress has always played a historic role in following difficult and uncharted path in foreign policy under Jawaharlal Nehru, Indira Gandhi and Rajiv Gandhi.

Perhaps the Congress of the Manmohan-Sonia duo may think it necessary to pursue an out-of-the-box foreign policy? The sceptics and military hawks in India must accept that status quo in Kashmir on the LoC is not the solution. Even if General Pervez Musharraf indulges in kite flying, India must take innovative foreign policy initiatives to undo the damage of the historical baggage of partition. – *The Pioneer, May 31, 2005*

BANDUNG TO JAKARTA

Asian countries have come to be seen as emerging global powers. Unfortunately, this story of new Asia was not the guiding spirit of deliberations at the Jakarta meet.

The Bandung Conference of the newly-liberated 21 Asian and African countries was held with great fanfare on April 18, 1955. President Sukarno of Indonesia inaugurated the conference with two slogans: 'Live and let live' and 'Unity in diversity'. The 50th anniversary of this historic meet was celebrated in Jakarta on April 19, 2005 and the number of participant countries had risen to 106.

The leaders of 106 nations declared in 2005 that "the 1955 Bandung conference remains as a beacon in guiding the future progress of Asia." However, the 10-point declaration on April 25, 1955, deals with a world which just does not exist in 2005. That conference dealt with problems of world peace, colonialism and nuclear weapons and the solution offered in 1955 was Panch Sheela "for promotion of international peace and security".

Not only this. To the cold war politics of the bipolar world, Nehru responded by saying at Bandung that "for anyone to tell us that we have to become-followers of Russia or America or any country in Europe is not very creditable to our new dignity, our new independence, our new freedom, our new spirit."

The atmospherics which conditioned the conference has ceased to exist. The last decade of the 20th century has witnessed a complete break with the past and it has led to the natural demise of the Bandung spirit and its product the NAM, since bipolarity has been replaced by unipolarity. In any case, the dream of Afro-Asian solidarity was not realised even in 50 years.

The only reference to Asia and Africa made at the Jakarta conference looked completely unrealistic: Dr. Manmohan Singh while addressing the 106 Asian and African countries on April 24,

2005, told the gathering that NAM remained "a valid and effective instrument to ensure that the architecture of international institutions is democratised and made more representative." While Dr. Singh's reference to the continuing relevance of NAM is irrelevant, his plea for "democratisation of international institutions" has been advanced to demand a permanent seat in the UN Security Council (UNSC) for India.

Foreign minister Natwar Singh also raised the issue of restructuring of the UNSC at the conference. The nine-point agreement signed at Jakarta referred to the need of a new Asian-African Strategic Partnership (NAASP). The declaration has stated that "the strategic partnership provides a momentum in achieving peace, prosperity and progress."

The Jakarta conference ended without achieving anything concrete because, unlike the Bandung one, it did not grapple with the real challenges posed by the new logic of the unipolar world system. Not only this. The new reality of Asian and African countries at the beginning of 21st century was completely ignored because the 50 years from Bandung to Jakarta have witnessed not only dramatic changes from bipolarity to unipolarity, even within Asian and African countries, the old problems of the era of decolonisation are dead.

A new Asia has emerged on the global scene and countries of Asia have been described as "economic tigers" or "emerging global power," etc. In the first decade of 21st century, India and China have to be taken very seriously as global economic players. Unfortunately, this story of new Asia was not the guiding spirit of deliberations and discussions at the Jakarta conference.

The end of cold war (1945-90), has brought America on the scene in Asia with very different economic and strategic interests in this region. Asians have to reckon with the implications of US presence and involvement in the region. India, China and Japan are three major powers in the Asia of the 21st century and all these countries have to come to terms not only with one another at a bilateral level but also these three will have to decide about their collective role in the shaping of Asian destiny in a unipolar world.

The crux of the issue is that America is a competitor in Asia. For its security and global interests, Americans have to pitch the powerful Asian countries against one another. An important area of competition in Asia is for energy resources as the growing economies of China and India will need huge energy for consumption. Here, the duo will face tough competition from the EU and US. The Caspian region for its oil and gas reserves is an object of great interest for the US, Russia, China, Japan and India. Will America allow any significant space in Caspian Sea to India and China for oil resources?

President Putin of the Russian Federation has accused Americans of interfering in former Russian Republics to gain a foothold in the region. Americans are flexing their muscles in Central Asia, and along with Japan and South Korea, the US has assured alliances in East Asia. In short, Asia continues to be a favourite playground of super power competition.

Economic and strategic interests of the sole superpower in Asia cannot be safeguarded if Japan, India and China or China, Russia and India emerge as a 'trilateral bloc of countries' to act as a countervailing force in a US-led unilateral world order. But can Asians themselves unite to protect relative autonomy of their region from the interventions and diktats of the US and EU? The real issue is that unlike EU or NATO, the Asian nation-states have not been able to evolve any common agenda for the whole region.

China versus Japan or India versus Pakistan, is a reality of Asia and at the present every Asian country is busy in strengthening relations at bilateral level with the US, which cannot accept the idea of an Asian common market. It is essential for the US to accentuate competition and conflicts within Asia. Unfortunately, Asian countries do not have a common perspective on the meaning and role of US power in this region and the Jakarta conference has not taken even the first step to grapple with the logic of unipolarism. – *The Economic Times, June 18, 2005*

AMERICA'S KISS OF DEATH

A second term for President George Bush in the White House has led Indian foreign policymakers to dream of occupying a high seat in the United Nation's Security Council (UNSC). Prime Minister Manmohan Singh and his Foreign Minister Natwar Singh have made this issue the primary objective of India's foreign policy. To achieve this goal, Indians have started knocking at the door of the White House because without US support, the existing arrangements in UNSC cannot be altered.

Indian foreign policymakers have not hesitated to beg for support for a permanent seat in the UNSC from a country which has shown nothing but contempt for the UN – including the Security Council – while pursuing its imperialist agenda in Iraq. The UPA Government, like the previous NDA Government, is following a foreign policy which is completely pro-US, irrespective of its imperialist doctrine.

In this context, the visits to the US by Indian foreign and defence policymakers assume significance; they will be setting the agenda of the forthcoming July 18 summit between President Bush and Manmohan Singh in Washington. The US has committed itself to making India a "major power in the 21st century", and the Indian ruling class is ready to do anything to please the Americans. The Indian Parliament passed the Weapons of Mass Destruction Act as demanded by the Americans in return of defence deals.

The signal is clear: If India wants access to US's civil nuclear technology or if it wants the US to lift its embargo on high-tech defence supplies, Parliament will accept any 'conditionality' laid down by the superpower.

It is not incidental that a major Indian newspaper published a survey on June 23/24 that Indians were more pro-America than citizens of any other country. The message was that the US has a very powerful social constituency in India and that the Indian Government is in tune with the sentiments of pro-US feelings of the Indian elite.

Foreign Secretary Shyam Saran, in his meeting with US Under-Secretary of State for Political Affairs Nicholas Burns on June 24 and 25, cleared the "contours of Mr. Singh's upcoming visit to the US". While many bilateral agreements are under discussion, Indians want cooperation from the US in civilian use of nuclear energy. The US is asking for "additional non-proliferation commitments by India".

Indian foreign and defence policy makers are zealously pursuing their goal of establishing close relationship with the US for supplying the latest weapons system so that India can build a powerful modern war machine to establish its status as a major power in the 21st century.

British Prime Minister Tony Blair has said that Europe faces "grand strategic future" if it shies away from "urgent economic reforms" while "emerging giants like India and China power ahead". Mr. Blair added, "The USA is the world's only superpower. But China and India, in a few decades, will be the largest economies, each of them with populations three times that of the entire EU."

The Indian ruling elite is possessed by the idea of an "emerging great power of the 21st century" because US and UK are certifying our future 'greatness'. They desire 'symbols' of national power like nuclearisation, permanent UNSC membership, and a powerful war machine. These symbols can be obtained only with US support. Manmohan Singh's forthcoming visit to the US is one more attempt to seek concessions and cooperation from the global superpower.

It is clear that India is making every effort to curry favour with the superpower, but Indians seem to be pretending that the US is not seeking any special role from India to promote and defend US's national interests. Bilateral relations between India and US are not between equals, and expectations of reciprocity are also based on unequal power relations between these two countries.

The US treats Pakistan as a 'frontline state' and, in spite of frequent protestations from India, the US can never abandon Pakistan just because it is hostile to India. The US can be a facilitator between India and Pakistan in their dispute over Jammu & Kashmir, but it will never impose a decision on Pakistan because it needs it for its larger strategic interests in the oil rich Islamic countries of the Gulf and Central Asia.

The logic of bringing US-Pakistan relations into this discussion is to establish a point that if the US is helping Pakistan on the basis of 'reciprocity', Indo-US relations cannot be an exception to this general rule of foreign policy based on bilateralism of 'unequal' powers. Hence, the attempt by Indian foreign policymakers to keep under the carpet the 'conditions' under which the US is willing to help India in achieving its national goals. The foreign policy establishment is evading this important issue from public scrutiny.

US Secretary of Defence Donald Rumsfeld, during the Asian Security Conference held in Singapore on June 3 to 5, expressed his country's "threat perception from China". He elaborated that China's defence expenditure is much higher than what its official document claims. "Since no nation threatens China, why this growing investment in defence?" A pillar of US foreign and defence policy has been to identify an 'enemy' country and make alliances to confront it. Post-Cold War phase, China has emerged strong. Hence, the US is firming up 'alliances' to deal with an emerging China.

Is India a candidate for US strategies against China? This question cannot be ignored because the Vajpayee Government had identified China and Pakistan as India's enemies in an official communication to President Bill Clinton while explaining the nuclear tests conducted by India in 1998. Is the Manmohan Singh Government brushing this issue of China-US-India relations under the carpet? The Indian Parliament should seek a public statement from the Prime Minister about the quid pro quo for US generosity towards India.

The story does not end with this. The US is violating every international law while dealing with prisoners of war from Iraq and Afghanistan at Guantanamo Bay. Vice-President Dick Cheney said on June 14 that there was no plan to close the prison. The Indian Parliament should ask the Government to make its position clear on serious violations of international law by the US.

Petroleum Minister Mani Shankar Aiyar is making every effort to ensure that the Iran-Pakistan-India gas pipeline project takes shape. However, US National Security Adviser Condoleezza Rice told him on June 13 that this project could violate the Iran and Libya Sanction Act (1996) of the US. Ms. Rice's statement was reiterated by US Under-Secretary of State for Political Affairs Nicholas Burns on June 25 in Delhi. He said, "Our problem is with the Government of Iran. We believe that Iran, as a state founder of terror, has been extremely unhelpful in the Middle East."

Has India succumbed to US pressure and abandoned the project? After all, the American friends of India consider Iran "a founder of terrorism". The political framework of India's foreign policy needs to be clearly spelt out by the UPA Government. It is to be hoped that the Congress of today will follow Nehru's tradition of foreign policy and take Parliament into confidence on the concessions given to the US by the Government.

– The Pioneer, June 28, 2005

SYMBOLS OF NATIONAL POWER

The first official visit of prime minister Manmohan Singh to the United States from July 18 to 20, 2005, preceded by defence minister Pranab Mukherjee's signing of a 10-year defence agreement between India and the US on June 29, 2005, deserves to be understood and analysed in the context of changing perceptions of the ruling classes about the status of India in the 21st century.

The Indian ruling elite seems to feel that India has arrived as a 'middle power' in the international arena and now it should not play the role of just a developing country, dependent on concessions given by the super powers. Indians are not alone in their perception that their country is an 'emerging power' of the 21st century. President George Bush and Secretary of State Condoleezza Rice have made public statements testifying that India is a new 'emerging power' in Asia. The latest World Bank report issued on July 13 has also declared that India has 'arrived' by joining the 'league of the world's biggest 10 economies.'

It is a well known fact that nation-states search for new 'symbols of power' to assert their economic status among nations of the world. The world capitalist system is based on the structures of hierarchy because of the distribution of unequal economic power. Countries with great economic strength have to achieve new distinctive symbols of power with a view to differentiate themselves from the absolute majority of economically backward and disadvantaged category. Hierarchy of economic power has to be translated into hierarchy of military power among the unequal nations of the world.

The Indian ruling classes are involved in 'acquiring' national status symbols which they consider are commensurate with their new economic status of the 'league of 10 economic powers' in the world. Hans J. Morganthu in his classic had long ago stated that 'power among nations' is determined by their military and economic capacity to influence and dictate policies to other nation states. Indira Gandhi was an eminent student of Morganthu school of 'power among nations' when, in 1974, she served notice to the super powers that India is a new nuclear power. The first Pokharan nuclear explosion in 1974 was a symbol of national assertion by Indira Gandhi. This journey of nuclearisation of India was completed by the Hindu Rashtravadis in May 1998 with Pokharan II.

The Indian elite, along with Hindu chauvinists and militarists, have never forgotten that China militarily humiliated India in 1962 and this powerful lobby in politics and society has created the concept of expenditure on defence 'as a holy cow' for Indians. India asserted its military power in 1971 by helping to dismember Pakistan. Every weapon of war available in international market has witnessed buyers from the Indian state and this urge for the acquisition of latest 'defence technology' has been concretised by Pranab Mukherjee who on June 29, 2005, signed an important defence agreement with the US. Military might is a symbol of national power and India's increased purchasing power is used for strengthening its military standing among the nations.

Further, the Congress-led UPA government, following in the footsteps of Indira Gandhi's quest for 'symbols of national power' has made a permanent seat in the UN Security Council as the goal of its foreign policy. The desire of India to occupy the high table of permanent membership in UN Security Council is an agenda of the 'emergent economic power' of the 21st century.

The Union government has not fought for the restoration of the status of UNSC, which was totally ignored by the US when it launched a war against Saddam Hussein in 2003. Neither have the policy makers in India objected to the Bush declaration that 'Americans will launch a pre-emptive war against any country'. India cannot oppose US military interventions because it cannot reach the SC status without the consent of the sole super power.

The upshot of above description is that adventurist nuclearisation and militarisation of India and its struggle to become a permanent member of the UNSC and other related goals of foreign and economic policy are based on the premise that India has arrived on world stage. It must be stated that the quest of Indian ruling classes to receive international recognition as an emergent economic and military middle power depends on the patronage of Americans.

The Indian ruling and political classes represented both by the BJP and the Congress have recognised the fact that without the consent of the US, India will remain a toothless paper tiger. The Americans seems to be acceding to the wishes of the Indian state leaders for allowing them to play a global role. The US has announced its love for establishing 'democracy from above' in feudal, military and authoritarian countries in the Islamic world and Indians are projecting their democratic credential before the new Messiah of global democracy. Americans have a very hospitable climate in India because every influential class, strata, group or lobby is willing to do 'business with America'. Anti-Americanism is a thing of the past and prosperous social groups in India identify themselves with a prosperous and powerful America.

Will America respond to the desires of their friends in India? The pro-American powerful social constituencies are a necessary but not a sufficient reason to motivate the US to patronise India of the 21st century. If Indians have new dreams of grandeur of regional power status, Americans are unabashed interventionists and adept at playing one country against the other. In a 2003 report by American Council on Foreign Relations on South Asia, it has been clearly stated that the US has an opportunity to influence major regional developments and India-US should work on 'genuine partnership'. In other words, India can depend on US friendship and generosity if India supports American 'interests' in Asia; unstated but well known fact is that India versus China is the American national goal in this part of the world. So India has apparently opted for a pro-American stance since without US support India cannot play its desired role of a middle power.

– *The Economic Times, July 19, 2005*

THE US IS BEST AVOIDED

The visit of the Foreign Secretary of India to Pakistan on September 1 indicates the Manmohan Singh Government's willingness to strengthen the confidence-building measures with the neighbouring country. Besides, India has recognised the need to redefine the term 'neighbouring countries' by extending it to Afghanistan, Iran and Central Asia for meeting the country's increasing energy needs.

With this objective in mind, Prime Minister Manmohan Singh visited Afghanistan towards the end of August. Also, the Indo-Iranian officials have been quite active in finding solutions to the issue of the Iran-Pakistan-India oil pipeline. It will be too simplistic to maintain that India is exploring new avenues of cooperation with Pakistan, Afghanistan, Iran or Central Asian Republics only for augmenting its sources of supply for energy. Foreign policy is always determined by multiple factors. But the geographical factor cannot be wished away, as friendly or hostile neighbours could be either assets or liabilities for a country's security.

India must take lessons from China that has resolved its disputes with all its neighbours, including Russia and Vietnam. China is also engaged in bridging its relationship with East Asian countries. After all, Japan versus China or South Korea versus North Korea situations adversely affect Beijing's foreign and defence policy. The Sino-Taiwan dispute is frozen in history because mainland China is strong enough to deal with US-supported Taiwan. Also, this issue is manageable because both of them are living with the acceptable level of status quo. In contrast, the India-Pakistan dispute on Jammu & Kashmir is complicated, but its resolution is essential to normalise bilateral relationship.

This is the reason why the UPA Government has actively involved General Pervez Musharraf and the Hurriyat Conference. Jammu & Kashmir Chief Minister Mufti Mohammad Sayeed has welcomed the Manmohan Singh-Hurriyat Conference dialogue in Delhi, saying this would lead to a wider dialogue in which other groups of the State would also participate. Ms. Mehbooba Mufti too has appreciated the move and stated that "militants need to be convinced for a ceasefire".

According to National Conference president Omar Abdullah, "Talks will help change situation on the ground only if the Hurriyat has a clear agenda." Hurriyat leader Mirwaiz Umar Farooq has maintained, "We hope the talks will take forward the process towards the resolution of the Jammu & Kashmir issue. We will try to build trust, know each other as it is for the first time we are meeting." Incidentally, the UPA Government had allowed the Hurriyat to visit Pakistan — including Pakistan Occupied Kashmir — with a view to begin dialogue with different groups in the Valley. The upshot is that India and Pakistan have agreed to discuss and find mutually satisfactory solution to the existing disputes between them.

The Kashmir issue cannot be resolved through war between the two nuclear powers because either the logic of nuclearisation "immobilises and demobilises war machine", or it leads to total annihilation of both the warring nations. It does not mean that the continuing dispute between India and Pakistan has no negative impact on their polity, economy and society. In fact, it is because of the Indo-Pakistan dispute that the illogical arms race in the subcontinent gains justification.

A new American Congressional study for 2001-2004 has pointed out that India spent $5.7 billion on arms purchase. Is it a small amount for a country involved in perpetual fiscal crisis and budgetary deficits? Every arms seller in the West is competing in the Indian market. Arms race cannot be avoided if India and Pakistan are not at peace with one another. Peace has dividends, while wars bring human misery.

If arms race is inherent in the logic of the dispute between India and Pakistan, the US has always interfered in the affairs of these two countries on the pretext of Jammu & Kashmir. This dispute has not only led to conflicts between India and Pakistan, but also provided excuse to the US to interfere in their internal affairs. The US interference has increased manifold in the post-Cold War phase of global unipolarism. If Pakistan has been a 'frontline' state for American adventurism in the Islamic world, India too has rolled out the red carpet to the US as revealed by the Government's new Strategic and Defence Agreements with the Bush Administration.

If, during the Cold War, India reciprocated American hostility by maintaining a respectable distance from it, the post-Cold War phase has brought Washington close to both New Delhi and Islamabad. How can the US, a friend of both these countries, keep away from guiding the foreign policies of its friendly regimes? Is it far-fetched to maintain that the Narasimha Rao Government opened its doors to Israel at the US's initiative, as Mr. Musharraf has done recently?

The newly found friendship between India, Pakistan and Israel cannot be explained without evaluating the role of the real master – the US. Hence, India should convince Pakistan about the resolution of their mutual disputes in the enlightened national interests of both the neighbours; or they would be pushed around to finding a solution on the suggestions of Uncle Sam.

Indira Gandhi has been faulted for giving concessions to Zulfiqar Ali Bhutto at the Simla Conference, when India was in a strong position to dictate terms on a defeated and demoralised Pakistan. Mrs. Gandhi – like Jawaharlal Nehru – followed the policy of engaging Pakistan in a bilateral dialogue, as both of them understood that the latter would seek US patronage if India played a tough card. Pakistan should also understand that its close military collaboration with the US during the Cold War did not achieve any concrete results vis-a-vis India.

The two sub-continental neighbours should learn from their own history of the past five decades of deadlock on Jammu & Kashmir. Internationalisation of this regional dispute has not led to its resolution. And despite US support to Pakistan, the status quo has continued. The issue of Jammu & Kashmir has to be treated at the bilateral level, and any umpire will be unhelpful as witnessed during the 40 years of the US's Cold War politics in South Asia.

The US can never be a facilitator between India and Pakistan, irrespective of the post-Cold War fraternal relationship between the two neighbours. This is because India's public opinion will support its Government if it keeps the initiative for dialogue with Pakistan in its own hands. A conscious democratic public opinion in the country is supportive of bilateral relations between India and Pakistan, and such a social constituency is an asset for meaningful negotiations between these two countries.

Manmohan Singh is on the right track in dealing with Pakistan, but a warning is essential: Any temptation to involve the US needs to be resisted as it will prove counterproductive. India and Pakistan should travel by their own 'bus and trucks' to pursue foreign policy goals. After all, imperialist America only promotes its own interest at the cost of its allies — whether India or Pakistan.

– The Pioneer, August 6, 2005

AGE OF SILENT CONSENSUS

It is a sign of a healthy democracy that the foreign policy of the UPA Government has initiated a public debate in the country. Our democracy is not co-terminus with the territorial boundaries of India. Every significant international event, therefore, has relevance not only for the public policy-makers, but also for the Opposition. No wonder the Manmohan Singh Government has been compelled to justify its stand to support the US resolution at the International Atomic Energy Agency on September 24 at Vienna, asking Iran to show restraint on its actions regarding its nuclear policies.

The Vienna vote was important because India supported 22 countries that were led by the US and European Union-3 — the UK, France and Germany. Unlike Russia, China, Pakistan (who abstained from voting), India went along with the Western countries against Iran on nuclear issue.

The Government justified its pro-US stand on two grounds: One, the Iran nuclear issue should be dealt with within the IAEA; and, two, the different parties "should have gained sufficient time for negotiations". India has claimed credit for restraining the Western countries "for an immediate referral of Iran to the United Nations Security Council for allegedly violating the Nuclear Non-Proliferation Treaty", as such a "referral to the UNSC" would have intensified the conflict between Iran and the US.

The US was pleasantly surprised to find India as its supporter against Iran. The Left parties described this foreign policy shift as a 'sell out' to the American imperialists. But the Government defended it in the name of India's 'national interests'. The Communists, however, have alleged that by voting against Iran, the Government has acted against the national interest.

As the BJP is in a shambles, its opposition to the Government is full of confusion and contradictions. Also, it was the BJP-led NDA Government that had accepted US hegemony over India's foreign and security policies. It was, therefore, difficult for the party to oppose the pro-US foreign policy of the Manmohan Singh Government.

What is the explanation for India's growing alignment with the US? First, an outlandish argument has been advanced by our security establishment that nuclear Iran is not in India's interest. However, it was India's nuclearisation that was not in the interest of South Asia. In fact, the Pakistani military establishment reacted by exploding nuclear weapons in response to India's nuclearisation. The very argument of national interest is quite dicey; and it can be dangerous because India's alignment with the US can alienate Tehran from Delhi. Critics have maintained that it is in India's interest to maintain friendly relations with Iran because of its energy requirements.

Second, the Government has given a clear message that the "relations with the US for nuclear concessions given by that country" are based on a quid pro quo. After all, ties between two unequal countries on such an important issue cannot be one-way traffic. India is not only ready to pay the price for its 'strategic partnership' with the US, but also prepared to be its junior partner to pursue nuclear goals.

Last, India was ostracised for its nuclear adventurism of May 1998, and its foreign and defence policy-makers from 1998 to 2005 have been making every attempt to win over the US. The Iran vote is a public acknowledgement by India that it is a trustworthy 'strategic partner' of the imperialists. The primary explanation for the new pro-American foreign policy in the first decade of the 21st century lies in India's nuclearisation. India will have to make such compromises with the West for maintaining its status as a nuclear weapon state.

A peripheral developing capitalist country like India cannot join the nuclear club on its own terms. The Atal Bihari Vajpayee Government had written in a confidential letter to the then US President Bill Clinton that its nuclear tests of May 1998 were aimed to defend the country against Pakistan and China. It is not incidental that the US has opted for India as a counter to China, as we have admitted that our nuclear programme is directed against Pakistan and China. It is not by chance that India did not join Russia and China in Vienna. India, too, could have abstained like Russia and China, but it opted for the US. The Vienna stand is not an innocent action of the Manmohan Singh Government. It is well-thought out foreign policy to reach for the US because India is not a supporter of a multipolar world. Russia and China are seriously engaged in creating a multilateral global order, but India is not a candidate for such a project. The July 18 Manmohan Singh-George Bush joint statement has clearly put India in the US camp.

The source of derailment of India's foreign and defence policies lies in its adventurist nuclearisation. It deserves to be stated that the policy of non-alignment of Jawaharlal Nehru and Indira Gandhi was integrally linked with the Indian stand on 'disarmament and peaceful world order'. Having abandoned the project of disarmament in favour of nuclearisation, the Government is forced to abandon the whole package of non-alignment and peaceful co-existence. A nuclear India cannot follow the policy of peaceful co-existence and disarmament because it has itself become a potential nuclear threat in South Asia.

This is the logic of India's vote at the IAEA in Vienna. The Canadian Government, with the consent of the US, has opened its nuclear energy and technology to the Indians. This is the first gain after the September 24 vote, and India can expect more goodies from the US and other Western countries as a reward for its support against Iran.

It has become easy for the Government to decisively shift its foreign policy in favour of the US because the BJP, too, is committed to the nuclearisation and militarisation of the country. These two parties have consensus on the nuclear weapon-determined foreign policy; and except the Left parties, other regional parties are local frogs in a well.

Manmohan Singh can sell this foreign policy in the name of national interest, because he knows the BJP is a supporter of this doctrine. The Government could never have abandoned Iran in favour of the US if it was not sure of the BJP's support. The upshot of above argument is that India has declared its alliance with the US because both the Congress and the BJP have a common understanding on India's foreign and security policies.

– The Pioneer, October 4, 2005

NUCLEAR INDIA IMMOBILISED

The rhetoric of foreign policy cannot conceal the reality of an immobilised nuclear India, as Indo-US bilateral relations have undergone a qualitative change after the former's nuclear explosions in May 1998. While addressing the Combined Commanders Conference on October 20, Prime Minister Manmohan Singh said, "It is unrealistic to expect nations to act for altruistic reasons. We must learn to deal with this new reality and plan our long-term security based on a proper appreciation of evolving trends."

It deserves to be stated that Manmohan Singh's reference to the need for a realistic foreign policy is a logical development of the ongoing process of alignment with the US. New Delhi wants nuclear collaboration with Washington. No wonder, India voted with the US against nuclear policies of Iran at the IAEA meeting in Vienna.

India declared its policy of collaboration with the US because of a policy of quid pro quo between the two countries in the area of nuclear needs of the former. India's foreign policy has become a hostage to its nuclear power ambitions, and every shift in foreign policy seems dictated by these strategies. This journey of nuclear-determined foreign policy became clear when US Under Secretary for Political Affairs Nicholas Burns and Foreign Secretary Shyam Saran met on October 21.

The Indo-US nuclear agreements of July 18 are to be scrutinised by the American Congress, as it has either to amend or reiterate its opposition to the amendments of US laws on the transfer of nuclear technology. Yet, India's vote against Iran in Vienna was not just for establishing its credential with US Congress as a 'good boy' of the nuclear club.

Nicholas Burns made a hurried visit to India on October 2 to ask the Indians "to separate their military from peaceful nuclear facilities" to show to the American Congress that India is fulfilling its promises made on July 18. The Burns-Saran meeting ended with a statement that 'reciprocal obligations' between the US and India will be carried on to placate the American Congress, which is sceptical of changing its nuclear policy.

Mr. Burns reiterated the emergence of a 'new partnership' between the US and India. He said, "American Governments tended to have policy on South Asia that was hyphenated. We tended to hyphenate India with Pakistan. We want to dehyphenate the two." India has been reminded by the US that the separation between military and civilian nuclear facilities is a 'pre-condition' for any further action by the US in fulfilling its promises contained in the July 18 agreement.

Shyam Saran, while giving his sermon on 'Nuclear Non-Proliferation and International Security' on October 24, expressed India's concern on nuclear proliferation and clandestine transfer of nuclear technology by Pakistan to Iran. Mr. Saran seems to have forgotten that the nuclearised India has forfeited its right to speak against nuclear proliferation after declaring itself as a nuclear weapon state. After all, a nuclearised country cannot limit the sovereign rights of other countries to undertake nuclear adventurism.

Mr. Saran observed: "It is important that issues which involve the Pakistan-based AQ Khan network are satisfactorily clarified as well. We see no reason why there should be an insistence on personal interviews with Iranian scientists but exception granted to a man who has been accused of running a global nuclear War Mart." He further said, "We welcome Iran's cooperation with the IAEA in accounting for previously undeclared activities, but it is important that remaining issues which involve Pakistan-based AQ Khan network are satisfactorily clarified as well."

Why has the Government raised this dead issue about the clandestine activities of AQ Khan? Why is India requesting the Nuclear Non-Proliferation Treaty signatories to probe into the AQ Khan network?

It deserves to be stated that the Western countries, including the US, had always known about AQ Khan's nefarious activities. Also, Indian military hawks were lobbying for the nuclearisation of India, and the then Prime Minister Indira Gandhi had obliged these nuclear adventurists by exploding nuclear bomb in 1974. Then Pakistani Prime Minister Zulfiqar Ali Bhutto was also talking of Islamic bomb against India's Hindu bomb lobby. Intelligence agencies around the world knew about the ongoing competition between Islamic nuclearists of Pakistan and India's nuclear rabble-rousers. How can India talk about 'new global consensus on non-proliferation' after declaring itself as a nuclear weapon state?

India had not signed the NPT or the Comprehensive Test Ban Treaty (CTBT), as it was tilted in favour of five nuclear power states. This anti-NPT and anti-CTBT foreign policy is lying in dust in the post-Pokhran-II phase. India is not a candidate for nuclear non-proliferation, as it itself is a nuclear proliferator. New Delhi's nuclear policy is guiding its foreign policy, as shown by its vote against Tehran in Vienna and the Foreign Secretary's statement on October 24.

The purpose of the above narration is to highlight a fact that both the NDA and UPA Governments have subordinated the country's foreign policy to pursue the goal of nuclear weapon state status. A new arrogance is observable among the foreign policy-makers of a nuclearised India, as revealed by its desire to sit in the club of powerful members of the UN Security Council. This is further confirmed by its desire to interfere, with the help of its American friends, in the internal affairs of other countries.

Has India become a strong global player after Pokhran-II? The answer is a big 'no'. India has not achieved the position occupied by five nuclear powers. India explained its nuclear adventurism of May 1998 to the then US President Bill Clinton by identifying Pakistan and China as a 'security threat'. Ironically, President Clinton made public this confidential letter of the Vajpayee Government. Has India become more secure after May 1998? The Kargil conflict disproved this logic.

Former US Secretary of State Colin Powell publicly observed that India and Pakistan were restrained by the US, when India put its Army on alert on Pakistan's border. The American 'umpire' played the role of making India and Pakistan 'disengage' their armies, as both countries might have been involved in the hazardous nuclear war. The US has got complete foothold in India after May 1998, and the Indians are currying every favour from the Americans to pursue its nuclear national goals — both military and civilian.

The upshot of the above description is that, in the post-July 18 scenario, India's foreign policy-makers will be tied to the American apron strings with the goal of achieving nuclear benefits from the super policeman of the world. India is immobilised and its nuclear weapon status has constrained its foreign policy options. And, it will continue to appeal the US for favours, including punishment, if any, to AQ Khan.

The crux of the matter is that India, in pursuit of nuclear power status, has become dependent on the US support for further developments in the nuclear field. One wonders whether it is a foreign policy worth emulating. – *The Pioneer, November 1, 2005*

IRAQ, AMERICA AND NATWAR

A section of the Opposition has jumped into the fray after the Paul Volcker Committee report mentioned, in an obscure appendix, that Natwar Singh/Congress party were 'non-contractual beneficiaries' of 'illegal surcharge payments' to the then Iraqi President Saddam Hussein for Oil-for-Food programme. On October 30, section of Opposition leaders, who have been marginalised in politics, got an artificial life-support system when media splashed the Volcker report.

In an extremely corrupt politico-bureaucratic regime, it is amusing to see the political class becoming so vocal on the issue of corruption. In fact, every political party — national, regional or even an individual-based – needs money for every political activity. If a party has enough financial resources to fight elections twice within a period of six months in Bihar, the cancer of corruption must have spread deep into the body-politic.

The Indian political class has no intention of cleansing public life. Its frequent noises against alleged corruption cases are just a political rhetoric to score brownie points. This phoney battle against corruption in Oil-for-Food programme is only to keep the BJP busy in public life when it is not only in a shambles, but also its own internal problems seem unresolvable by its leadership.

The UPA Government has appointed former UN Under-Secretary General Virendra Dayal "to liaise with the UN to get access to records of the Volcker report on Oil-for-Food programme", and former Chief Justice R.S. Pathak "to lead judicial probe into Volcker's allegations". In any democratic country, the political class would have waited patiently for the findings of such a high-powered inquiry into the issues brought into notice by the Volcker report.

The sole exception to this rule is the Indian democracy, as such issues are never allowed to die by the Opposition. The drama around the Volcker Committee report is likely to continue till some other scandal emerges. It is also surprising that 125 Indian companies, named by Mr. Volcker, have not attracted much attention. It seems Indians are not concerned about the cancer of corruption in public life – they are only interested in settling political scores. On November 8, Tata International Limited maintained that the Iraqi Government and the UN Committee "monitoring the Oil-for-Food programme were aware of the inland transportation fees and the after sales services fees that they had to pay on all contracts".

Why is this statement of Tata International not being highlighted by the anti-corruption champions in India? The Volcker Committee report seems to have turned into a game of one-upmanship, where the Opposition has emerged as the champion of 'clean' public life. In the process, the real culprit has been ignored.

The genesis of events in India – from October 30 to November 7 – lies in US foreign policy of the destruction of Iraq. Saddam Hussein's Iraq was put under severe 'sanctions' and its impact was felt on more than a million people who died of starvation. It is a well-known fact that a country under 'sanctions' adopts all sorts of methods and techniques to get rid of the rigours of this cruel situation. Cuba, too, has witnessed American aggression, and

President Fidel Castro has struggled hard to save his people from the cruel consequences of the US-imposed sanctions.

The erstwhile Soviet Union was a big support to Mr. Castro during the period of 'sanctions', till the USSR collapsed in 1991. The US celebrated the decline of the USSR and predicted the overthrow of the Castro regime by the dissatisfied people of Cuba. This, however, did not happen. As far as Iraq is concerned, Saddam Hussein was provided with a concession to make his people survive under the UN-supervised Oil-for-Food programme.

Tata International had no reason to believe there was anything illegal in such payments imposed by Iraqi authorities regarding inland transportation fees and after sales services fees on all contracts. If shady business practices were indulged by individuals or 125 companies that violated the law of the land, then Enforcement Directorate of India has all the powers to investigate. How do Natwar Singh and Congress come into the picture when they did not sign any document with the Iraqi regime for such business dealings? Is it not the right of a sovereign country to impose its own conditions for trade, including Oil-for-Food programme?

The US is hell-bent on proving that Saddam Hussein was guilty and its war against Iraq was justified. The warmongers in the US had alleged that Iraq possessed weapons of mass destruction, and it justified the war against that country in 2003. But the allegation could not hold ground for long, as the imperialists could not find such weapons. The emperor was found without clothes, and the 'justification' for aggressive war against Iraq proved baseless.

The brutalities of American soldiers against imprisoned Iraqis further shocked the world. It is established that neither the presence of weapons of mass destruction was correct, nor the post-war tyrannies committed by occupation armies had any justification. So, the US turned the table and brought charges of illegality and immorality against Saddam Hussein on Oil-for-Food programme. It is an attempt to prove that Saddam is a pastmaster of scandals and worse.

The boot is on the other side. The decision to impose UN sanctions against Iraq was, in reality, America's; and the Volcker report is an attempt to paint Saddam as the villain of the piece. The other part of the Volcker report is a sideshow, as the American multinationals are doing lucrative business in post-Saddam Iraq. The crux of the issue is that every event relating to Iraq is a by-product of US aggression in Iraq. It is unfortunate that we have focussed on the Volcker report without linking it with America's role in Iraq between 1991 and 2005.

A country under 'sanctions' needs support and sympathy, not condemnation by all and sundry. It is worth emphasising that a simple issue of illegal dealings by the middlemen of India during business transactions with Iraq in the Oil-for-Food programme has not been left to be investigated by the law enforcement agencies of India. If Natwar Singh/Congress are 'non-contractual beneficiaries', documentary evidence should be found to prove it.

The real issue has been ignored in the country's public discourse. The UN had used the word 'humanitarian' for Oil-for-Food programme. Should Indians not be discussing the rationale behind the word 'humanitarian' used by the UN, while sanctioning a programme for Oil-for-Food? Saddam Hussein might have made illegal gains from this programme, but the larger issue is the acute suffering of the Iraqi people because of American aggression. A distinction has to be maintained between the misdemeanour of the Saddam regime and the deprivations suffered by the Iraqi society as a result of American aggression.

Natwar Singh and the Congress party should be targeted only after it is proved by sound documentary evidence that "political influence was exercised to gain monetary advantages". Indians, however, cannot allow the US to get away with its criminal activities in Iraq, which necessitated the launching of such 'humanitarian' programme in the first place. The discussion on the Volcker report should not ignore the American angle.

– *The Pioneer, November 15, 2005*

PROBE RAM NAIK'S "BUSINESS" DELEGATION TOO

The Volcker Commission of Inquiry was instituted by UN Secretary General Kofi Annan to investigate into the irregularities, if any, during the implementation of the UN "Oil-for-Food" programme in Iraq. It deserves to be stated that the impact of 15-years of sanctions on Iraq led to starvation deaths of millions of men, women and children. In order to deal with this tragic situation, the UN undertook the responsibility of managing the humanitarian Oil-for-Food programme. In its appendix, the Volcker report observed that Natwar Singh and the Congress party were non-contractual beneficiaries, who were allotted oil quotas that could be sold at a handsome commission.

When the news became public in India, the Opposition demanded that the "guilty" Natwar Singh and the Congress party should be punished immediately. The Congress-led UPA government reacted immediately to these allegations and the PMO was asked to "investigate" into the matter. The government appointed a "special envoy", Virendra Dayal, who was sent to the UN to "get" the Volcker papers so that a proper inquiry could be conducted by R.S. Pathak, the former Chief Justice of India.

How could any Inquiry be conducted without documents of the Volcker report? Soon, Natwar Singh was stripped of his External Affairs Ministry and asked to continue as a minister without portfolio so that Justice Pathak could investigate properly. Besides, the Enforcement Directorate of India started investigating 125 private companies and individuals mentioned in the Volcker report.

The essential pillar of parliamentary democracy is that a government is "accountable" for its acts of omission and commission. It is expected of any democratic government that proper "investigations" are launched against any alleged irregularities committed by any pubic functionary. The Manmohan Singh government has followed this norm while dealing with the Volcker controversy. A former civil servant, a former Chief Justice of India and an official agency dealing with such cases (the ED) are all involved in the investigation.

It is a basic principle of jurisprudence that says that everyone should be regarded "innocent till proved guilty". The BJP-led Opposition, however, wants to "hang" Natwar Singh and the Congress party without any inquiry. It deserves to be stated that the NDA is not at all interested in cleansing the political system of the cancer of corruption. In fact, the record of BJP-in-power in dealing with allegations of corruption against then party president Bangaru Laxman, George Fernandes and Dilip Singh Judeo, to say the least, was quite pathetic. Besides, Tarun Tejpal of Tehelka, who performed a yeoman job by exposing corruption in the corridors of power, was hounded out by the party-in-government.

It is not only on matters of corruption in public life, but even on the issue of criminalisation of politics that the BJP has practised double standards. BJP leader Shatrughan Sinha refused to campaign for his party candidates in the recent Bihar Assembly elections because his own party had allotted tickets to some well-known criminals. Every political party, including the BJP, has taken a public stand that even the worst of criminals is innocent till proved guilty. The reference to the BJP is only to substantiate the argument that the party is acting irresponsibly by paralysing Parliament, as Manmohan Singh is only following the well-known practice of going to the bottom of the truth in the Oil-for-Food scandal.

The crux of the issue is: What kind of rules do the political parties want to practice in public life? Another important issue is the role of 125 businessman who have been identified by Volcker in his report on the Oil-for-Food programme in Iraq. Incidentally, the Congress sent a delegation of its own party members like Natwar Singh, Shiv Shankar, Antulay; but so had the BJP. Former petroleum minister Ram Naik led a delegation of "businessmen" to Iraq for making deals with the Saddam Hussein regime in 2001. In fact, the Oil-for-Food programme leading to illegalities had been patronised by businessman promoted by the BJP. Is a party delegation trustworthy, or a minister leading "businessmen" for specific Oil-for-Food programme? The BJP has to make up its mind because it did not send "innocent" businessmen to the regime of Saddam Hussein. How can such an issue be ignored while investigating the dubious role of Indian businessmen who were air lifted by Ram Naik to Iraq?

The moral of the story is that the Volcker report has provided one more opportunity to the political class to break the nexus between politicians and businessmen in India. The Manmohan Singh government is on the right track by probing into the role of alleged businessmen. Besides, the government should turn this crisis into opportunity by unearthing the unholy nexus between politicians and criminals. Let us hope that some good result emerges from this sordid affair of an unscrupulous business class exploiting its links with political class. – *The Pioneer, December 10, 2005*

LETTING AMERICA CALL THE SHOTS

Our foreign policy makers are actively engaged in defining the country's role and aspirations in the US-dominated 'unipolar global system'. The UPA Government has, through the process of trial and error, arrived at some definite negative formulations on India's foreign policy. The first pillar of the Manmohan Singh Government's foreign policy is that the US is a military superpower and India should come to terms with it. New Delhi's acceptance of Washington's global primacy is a defining feature of the first decade of the 21st century. It seems India has come to terms with 'unipolarity', as it has decided to become a 'strategic partner' of the United States.

Prime Minister Manmohan Singh and US President George Bush agreed on July 18 that the two countries would be 'partners' in India's 'nuclear energy enterprise'. The July 18 agreement is a watershed, as it is for the first time after Independence that our foreign policy has been conditioned and determined on the basis of US-led unipolar global system.

Soon, Manmohan Singh and Pranab Mukherjee started proclaiming the significance of 'cooperation and friendship' between the two great democracies of the world. On October 22, Foreign Secretary Shyam Saran and US Under Secretary for Political Affairs R Nicholas Burns stated that the new nuclear energy agreement is a "truly comprehensive across-the-board agreement" between the two countries, and this nuclear energy cooperation dialogue is a 'new partnership'. The US Congress is actively engaged in investigating the implications of this nuclear partnership between India and the US.

It would be "grossly irresponsible" of the "Congress as a whole to act with unnecessary haste regarding a subject which can bear no false steps", observed Henry Hyde, the Chairman of the US House International relations Committee, on October 27. Dan Burton, who led a seven-member congressional delegation to India, stated in New Delhi on November 28: "I am leaning towards a nuclear agreement. But we want a definite separation between civilian and military components of India's nuclear programme. If that is assured, I am quite sure, it will be addressed."

India has voluntarily subjected itself to international scrutiny and investigation by assuring the US of its willingness to separate military and civilian nuclear energy programme. Norwegian Prime Minister Johannes Stoltenberg said on December 8 in New Delhi, "India will have to sign Nuclear Non-proliferation Treaty (NPT) before joining the Nuclear Suppliers group." Mr. Stoltenberg unambiguously stated on behalf of the 44-member Nuclear Suppliers Group: "Under its rules, you can join the NSG only if you sign the NPT."

Our foreign policy makers are obfuscating the reality because the US cannot sell its idea of making an 'exception' to India without the NSG approval to the Indo-US nuclear deal. And, such an approval is dependent on India's signing of the NPT. Parliament should find out the reality of the July 18 deal, as the US cannot make an 'exception' in the case of India without Indians having informally agreed to abide by the provisions of the NPT. Has India assured the US on its willingness to informally follow the NPT? Foreign Policy cannot be taken at the face value of statements of diplomats. After all, the latter are experts in concealing facts from public, press, and Parliament.

The Government should not be allowed to get away with its public statements on the Indo-US nuclear deals, as the American Congress is not alone to find the real truth behind the July 18 agreement. Indian Parliament, which seems to have abdicated its role of acting as a watchdog of foreign policy, should learn from its American counterpart. The UPA Government, like the earlier BJP-led NDA regime, is leading the country into the American camp on the basis of a flimsy argument that the global reality of the 21st century demands India to come to terms with the sole superpower. Shyam Saran spelt out such pro-American tilt while addressing the Confederation of Indian Industry and World Economic Forum Summit in New Delhi on November 28. He announced the goal of India-US partnership in the light of the ongoing changes in 'balance of power' in Asia.

The Government is tying itself to the apron strings of America on the plea that a 'new international security paradigm', which has changed the balance of power in Asia, has necessitated India to establish a partnership with the US. Mr. Saran observed that China was emerging as "a global economic power with significant military capabilities", which "will have, whether we like it or not, an impact on the regional situation". He further added: "In this context of Asia, there is no doubt that a major realignment of forces is taking place." Our foreign policy makers have, in a subtle manner, tried to justify pro-American tilt by talking about the emergence of China. Does India want to play an activist role in Asia under the protective umbrella of America?

It is worth remembering how then Prime Minister Atal Bihari Vajpayee justified India's nuclear adventurism in Pokhran in 1998, in a confidential letter to the then US President Bill Clinton, by mentioning the presence of two nuclear neighbouring countries – China and Pakistan. It was not due to the absentmindedness of the then NDA Government to mention the threats from Beijing in justification of its nuclear explosions, as this line of argument was expected to pacify American policy makers on India's nuclear programme. Is hostility towards China pushing India towards America, or is America inciting India to join its own agenda of containing China?

In India, a powerful anti-China and pro-US lobby has been operating for long. The anti-Beijing forces are represented by anti-Communists and pro-nuclearisation lobby. The social constituency of globalisation is also pro-America, and it does not hesitate in exploiting anti-China sentiment to curry favour with the US.

Foreign policy does not hang in air and powerful domestic social constituencies determine the direction of important decisions of the country. Our foreign policy makers are using an alibi of changing power equations in Asia because of the emergence of China. They are projecting an imaginary Chinese ghost to seek American patronage. It is, however, far-fetched to think that India versus China of 1962 can be repeated in 2005. To think that China can be a real threat to India is nothing but to be foolhardy.

India has not even opted for a trilateral world order in place of a dangerous US-dominated unipolar world. On December 6, Manmohan Singh and Russian President Vladimir Putin observed in Moscow: "As a strategic partner, we will actively work to ensure India is able to cope with all its difficulties and issues regarding the peaceful use of nuclear technology." Is the Russian assurance on nuclear energy not enough for India to act independently in world affairs?

Mr. Putin also reiterated his 'doctrine of trilateralism' between India, Russia and China. Do the Indian foreign policy makers really desire a 'trilateral world' to counterbalance the imperialist 'unipolar world'?

The Russian President is showing a path to Indians by repeatedly emphasising the need for Russia-India-China cooperation and friendship. In fact, President Putin has provided a key to call the bluff of Indian foreign policy makers who do not see any alternative to 'unipolarism' today.

– The Pioneer, December 13, 2005

A NATION DIVIDED ON FOREIGN POLICY

Prime Minister Manmohan Singh's formal statement on foreign policy in Parliament on February 17, 2006, has not helped the Government to convince its own 'outside supporters' – the Left parties–either on India's vote at the IAEA in Geneva on Iran's nuclear issue or even on the Government's "pro-American foreign policy" as clearly reflected in the Joint Statement of President

George W Bush and Prime Minister Singh on July 18, 2006. It is extremely embarrassing for the anti-BJP 'secular' alliance Government at the Centre that the Left is vehemently opposed to Manmohan Singh's foreign policy.

On the contrary, the BJP, considered the 'enemy number one' of the Government, has openly supported UPA Government's vote against Iran's nuclear postures at Geneva on February 4, 2006. The Congress-led UPA Government is under attack, and the Prime Minister, in his defence, has made it amply clear that his Government is following a policy in pursuit of "enlightened national interest".

Over the years, the supporters and opponents of India's foreign policy have always projected themselves as defenders of national interest. It is precisely this reason that the argument in favour of national interest has become quite dubious in the history of international relations. Wars have been fought and the so-called peace treaties have been concluded by nation-states in the name of national interest.

In his address to Parliament on February 16, 2006, President A.P.J. Abdul Kalam echoed the Government stand stating that the foreign policy is guided by "enlightened national interest", and added, that "the Government expects the country may gain access to international cooperation of our civilian nuclear energy sector" by making agreements with the US.

On his part, the Prime Minister told Parliament on February 17: "On the specific issue of Iran's nuclear programme, as a signatory to the NPT, Iran has the legal right to develop peaceful uses of nuclear energy consistent with its international commitments and obligations." However, Mr. Singh warned, "The objectives of upholding Iran's rights and obligations and our security concerns arising from proliferation activities in our extended neighbourhood have shaped our position."

In spite of the BJP's support of the UPA Government on its vote on the Iran nuclear issue, the differences between the Congress and the Left have not come to an end. Incidentally, casteist and regionalist chiefs like Mulayam Singh Yadav of the Samajwadi Party or Chandrababu Naidu of the Telugu Desam Party have jumped into the foreign policy debate with a view to cater to their narrow interests. It is not without reason that the NDA Government led by Atal Bihari Vajpayee from 1998 to 2004 had smooth sailing in foreign policy issues because its regional allies had hardly any interest in global affairs.

The BJP pursued its own foreign policy of nuclearisation of India and its pro-America and pro-Israel policy for six years because the regionalist allies confined themselves to local issues, while foreign and defence policy remained in the domain of the BJP. The Congress party is facing serious difficulties not only on issues concerning vote on Iran's nuclear issue or India's agreement with the US on nuclear programme for the country, but also on the whole gamut of foreign policy issues concerning New Delhi's growing linkages with Washington because the Left has a definitive foreign policy perspective of their own.

The clash on foreign policy between the Congress and the Left has arisen because of their fundamental differences on foreign policy perspectives, especially on India's growing relationship with the US. The Left has alleged that the Congress, like the BJP-led Government, is following a pro-American foreign policy, and the Government's vote at the IAEA on Iran or its agreement with US on "separation of nuclear programme between the peaceful and military purposes" is a surrender to the whims of the Americans. The Left has received support from a section of nuclear experts who also suspect that India's attempt to separate its nuclear programme between "peaceful and military compartments" amounts to exposing India's nuclear programme to American scrutiny.

The Left has accused the Manmohan Singh Government of abandoning the time-tested foreign policy of non-alignment and India's national sovereignty is threatened by growing asymmetrical relationship with US. The cleavage between the Congress and Communists seems to be growing, and the forthcoming visit of US President George W Bush on March 2-4, 2006, may witness a public confrontation between the Government and the Communists.

It is not without reason that the Communists are worried about growing dependence of India on the US because President Bush's foreign policy doctrines are quite dangerous for Asian and Arab countries.

Can it be forgotten that the US under President Bush had launched a full-scale war against Saddam Hussein in March 2003? Is the US above suspicion of its anti-Iran nuclear issue? The US's track record under President Bush is a clear indication of a country having gone berserk in dealing with developing countries which do not accept American hegemony. Can Indians ignore President Bush's foreign policy doctrine of waging "pre-emptive war" against countries suspected of harming US national interests? The reference here is not only to the uni-polar international system but also to the policy of "unilateralism" followed by the US while dealing with any Asian or Arab country not acceptable to the Americans.

If Manmohan Singh claims to follow a foreign policy based on "enlightened national interests", the Communists too are looking at foreign policy from a national perspective. The Government cannot be the sole custodian of an interpretation of national interests. It is a sign of health of Indian democracy that foreign policy has become a part of public discourse and controversies especially during a phase of politics when India is not involved in any war-like situation. The bandwagon of patriotism can be used by Governments-in-power if a country is involved in war as it happened during the Kargil war or on the adventurist policy of Mr. Vajpayee on nuclearisation of India in 1998. Any public controversy on foreign policy during 'abnormal situations' is always put under the carpet because of people's sentiments but India is not facing any extraordinary situation of hostility from any other nation-state.

During the 1962 Sino-India border dispute, Jawaharlal Nehru was cornered by the Opposition parties on his China policy. Nehru was accused of not preparing the country against hostile China. Krishna Menon, the then Defence Minister, had to quit because the Opposition wanted someone who could be held guilty of pursuing a faulty foreign and defence policy in relation to China. Lal Bahadur Shastri gained an unearned reputation because during his brief and unremarkable regime from 1964 to 1966 Pakistan's misadventure against India in 1965 was repulsed and "Tashkent Agreement" was signed between Shastri and Ayub Khan of Pakistan.

Indira Gandhi was hailed by Atal Bihari Vajpayee as Durga for her so-called victory over Pakistan and the creation of Bangladesh in 1971. Further, her decision to explode nuclear device at Pokhran in 1974 and her nuclear adventurism in foreign policy brought bouquets; but after that, her critics and opponents in politics saw nothing good in her. The upshot of the above description is that Manmohan Singh is facing music on the foreign policy front because critics cannot be described as anti-national since India is at peace with other countries and public debate cannot be artificially stopped by raising the bogey of patriotism and nationalism.

The Indian political class is sharply divided on foreign policy because of clash of perspectives between the Congress's world view and the way of looking at global situation by the Communists. The only other relevant player in foreign policy is the BJP. It has no complaints to make against the Manmohan Singh Government. The Communists with their 65 MPs have a formidable presence in the Lok Sabha. They are in no mood to make any compromise with the Government, which, according to them, is subservient to US foreign policy goals in our region.

However, the crux of the issue is that Manmohan Singh is pursuing interconnected economic, foreign and security policies, and the critics of his foreign policy are also opposed to the economic policy of globalisation. – *The Pioneer, February 31, 2006*

A SURRENDER OF SOVEREIGNTY

The Nuclear agreement reached between the US President George Bush has evoked mixed responses and reactions from different sections of Indian society. The Indian political class is completely divided on the new directions of foreign and security policies followed by the Manmohan Singh government and serious doubts have arisen among important sections of Indian society about the meaning of emerging 'strategic partnership' between India and the United States.

George Bush and many powerful groups in the United States are extremely excited abut the new and growing linkages of friendship of their country with India, but such an enthusiasm is not fully shared by many sections of Indian society. Bush, while addressing Asia Society in Washington on February 22, 2006 stated about India that "West share a common interest in promoting open economies. The United States and India are working together to support democracy around the world", and this, according to him, makes these two countries "natural partners".

An important section of business class and defence strategists in India have actively supported the efforts of the Manmohan Singh Government for winning over the Bush Administration especially in the field of nuclear technology cooperation. The bone of contention has been the Nuclear deal between India and the US. The opponents of the Indian government have alleged that the agreement to separate the so-called nuclear plants for peaceful purposes from nuclear weapon projects is a trick played by the Americans because such an exercise is going to open a pandora's box and indigenous nuclear programme of India will be subjected to American scrutiny. A powerful section of nuclear scientists have openly criticized India's Nuclear deal with US by alleging that it is a compromise with country's national sovereignty. The mass media, both print and audio-visual, have highlighted such a polarisation of opinion among the Indian Nuclear strategists and an important section of the retired foreign service officials have also issued a statement against the government's new nuclear engagement with the US by alleging that such an agreement will bring Nuclear Non-Proliferation Treaty from the backdoor.

Incidentally. India had never signed NPT because it was considered 'discriminatory' and it blocked Indian efforts to pursue an independent nuclear programme for national purposes. India had been ostracized by the five nuclear super-powers for exploding nuclear device at Pokharan in 1974, and in spite of sanctions imposed against India by the Nuclear Power, Indians continued to develop, with their own efforts, nuclear technology and also exploded, nuclear bomb at Pokharan in 1998. This argument is advanced by nuclear nationalists who are openly campaigning against the Indian government and their demand has been against signing a nuclear agreement with President Bush. Manmohan Singh in a suo motto statement in Parliament on February 27,2006 stated that "the civil nuclear deal with the US would not affect India's nuclear weapon programme" and he went out of the way to assert that fast breeder reactor programme shall remain out of safeguards lists. The dust has not settled down and sharp differences between the supporters and opponents of 'nuclear separation deal' cannot be cemented and the Indian government's efforts to glamourise the visit of President Bush cannot succeed because controversy on Nuclear Deal cannot be easily put under the carpet and just wished away by Manmohan Shingh.

Indians are divided not only on the Nuclear deal between India and the US, the communist parties and others are opposed to President Bush's policies on Iran and Iraq and on March 2, 2006, the CPI, CPT (M), RSP, AIFB, CPI (M-L) along with JD(S) and SP decided to organise Bush's visit to Delhi. Incidentally, Indian political class is sharply divided on India's vote against Iran on its 'nuclear issue' at the International Atomic Energy Agency meeting at Geneva and a feeling exists that India's vote against Iran is at the behest of Americans. The US has threatened Iran to either comply with the conditions imposed by the IAEA on its Nuclear Programme or face 'sanctions and punishment' at the hands of United National Security Council. The critics of Indian vote against Iran's Nuclear Programme at the IAEA consider it as a betrayal of at rusted friend like Arabs by the Manmohan government which is bringing India under US umbrella. The Prime Minister defended his government in Parliament by asserting that foreign policy is based on "enlightened national interest" but unfortunately, this assertion of national interest-based foreign policy has not carried conviction with the major opposition parties in India.

It deserves to be clearly stated that the United States in general and President Bush in 'particular' seem to be following policies of aggression against many friendly countries of India like Iraq and Iran. A section of Indian society perceives that the United States and President Bush are hostile to Muslim countries and the continuing destructive and violent civil war in Iraq has frequently brought angry Indians on the streets and they consider him a real villain of the piece. It is not only in Delhi or Srinagar that a section of society have organised protests against the policies of President Bush and his perceived Indian friends in the Manmohan Singh government, a 'Coalition' of 40 groups have formed the 'Forum against' the Visit of Warmonger George Bush.

The above narrative clearly reveals that the Manmohan Singh Government is perceived as over friendly to the US and it does not seem to be in tune will the anti-Bush sentiments of the Indian public opinion. Once President Eisenhower had received tumultuous welcome during his visit to India. This not only has become an old story, but India and the US also have drifted away from each other despite strenuous efforts by the two governments to bridge the gap. The real explanation about government of India on the one hand and section of political class on the other lies in a perception that Americans cannot be trusted as equal friends of any sovereign country. The nuclear deal between with US is perceived as surrender of sovereignty by India.

– Shara Time, 11th March, 2006

BUSH HAS 'LEFT' US IN A TIZZY

US President George Bush's visit to India has been compared with the historic trip of Richard Nixon to China in the early 1970s. These two visits are, after all, seen as turning points in the relationship between the US and India and China respectively. Unfortunately, it is ignored that China abandoned Communism after Nixon's "historic" visit. Thereafter, the Chinese society witnessed a U-turn by its leaders, who opted for market-oriented Capitalism in place of equality-oriented Communism. Will history repeat itself in the case of India after the visit of President Bush?

As the euphoria created by President Bush's visit has died down, it is essential to prepare a balance sheet of the gains and losses for the two countries, especially in the field of nuclear energy. After all, the nuclear "deal" has been heralded as "historic" in the history of Indo-US relations.

The entire focus of discussion between President Bush and Prime Minster Manmohan Singh was on the "separation of nuclear programme for peaceful purposes from India's nuclear weapon system projects". On March 1, President Bush observed: "We are trying to come to a civilian nuclear power agreement. It is in the interest of the US and in the interest of the countries around the world that India develops a nuclear power industry."

Why has the US decided to assist India in the development of its civilian nuclear power industry? On March 2, Mr. Bush and Manmohan Singh announced that the agreement had been signed on terms and conditions announced by the latter in Parliament on February 27. The media, actively supported by the propagandists of the UPA Government, projected the Indo-US nuclear deal as an occasion that deserved celebration.

On March 3, President George Bush proclaimed from the historic Purana Qila that India and the US were "natural partners" not only in their struggle against terrorism, but also for the cause of "democracy and freedom" in the world. Is India going to be America's comrade-in-arm in its "ideology-based" foreign policy of forcibly shaping the world in its own image of democracy, freedom and anti-terrorism? Is India a partner in the American war against West Asian dictators?

Can two unequal countries pursue common goals in foreign policy? It is time the reality of the American state system was highlighted to understand the implications of Indo-US relations after March 3. President Dwight Eisenhower had aptly stated that the US was "ruled by a military-Industrial complex". Eminent sociologist C. Wright Mill, while analysing American democracy, wrote the country "has, in reality, a Ruling Elite while masquerading as a democracy".

The end of the Cold War after the collapse of the Soviet Union in the early 1990s created an environment for the "normalcy" between India and the US. Despite smooth bilateral relations between the two countries, especially after the Cold War, the nuclear weapon war-mongers insisted that the Government should make special efforts to curry favour with the sole superpower.

It should not be forgotten that the euphoria over the nuclear deal has adversely affected India's relationship with Pakistan and China. It is in India's interest to maintain normal, friendly and good neighbourly relationship with China and Pakistan.

Ironically, President Bush's visit to India does not seem to have affected America's relationship with Pakistan, which continues to remain its "special" ally. The US has a lot of clout over Pakistan, especially its military establishment, and this is the reason why it is not worried about the latter's reaction over Mr. Bush's visit to India. India, however, should be concerned about Pakistan's new military build-up as a consequence of growing Indo-US relations. It will be foolhardy on the part of India to ignore Pakistan's sensitivities after the Bush visit.

Is India getting involved in arms race with Pakistan after achieving a "special" military relationship with the US? The Chinese, too, have reacted adversely to Mr. Bush's efforts to legitimise India's nuclear weapons status. While it is not in India's interest to deepen the seeds of suspicions in the minds of the Chinese, it is not imaginary to state that the US will like China to be counter-balanced by India. America has a policy of making alliances with countries that view China with suspicion. Where does India stand in the American game in Asia?

The Chinese media, including The People's Daily, has warned that the Indo-US nuclear deal might lead to global nuclear proliferation. Indians have always been complaining that China is involved in actively improving Pakistan's military strength. It is plausible that Beijing may further strengthen Islamabad's military capabilities if it gets the message that Washington is preparing Delhi to checkmate it. Indians will have no one else to blame but themselves if China increases its military support to Pakistan after Mr. Bush's visit to India.

India has been involved in improving bilateral relations with Pakistan and China. March 2006, however, may prove to be a turning point, as the suspicion level of the two countries—China and Pakistan—towards India can provide impetus to a fresh arms race in South Asia. The American defence industry will be the sole beneficiary of the growing "estrangement" between India and its two neighbours. It is possible that contentious issues may become more intractable.

The entire controversy has been around the nuclear deal, but several other dimensions of the growing Indo-US relationship cannot be brushed under the carpet. President Bush admitted that he would have to convince the US Congress about the nuclear deal. More important, however, is the repercussions of the Bush visit in India's immediate neighbourhood. Moreover, President Bush's war against terrorism is perceived as "anti-Islamic". In contrast, India's anti-terror stand is just Pakistan-specific. Can India align itself with America's global war against terrorism?

Indian Muslims are not involved in anti-American terrorist activities. At the same time, our approach towards terrorism has to be different from that of the US. The US is carrying an ideology-driven foreign policy. It is expected that Indian policy-makers will not join the bandwagon of American self-righteous imperialists. One needs to understand that the nuclear deal with the US is the beginning of serious problems for India's foreign Policy makers.

– The Pioneer, March 7, 2006

IMPERIALIST TRUTHS

Ambassador David C. Mulford has truly behaved as a czar of the American empire by making a public statement that India has to tow the line of the imperialists on 'nuclear issues concerning Iran' at the February 2 IAEA meeting in Vienna. The claim of 'strategic partnership' made by the Government is completely exposed and Mulford has performed a yeoman's job by reminding Indians that American hegemony looms above.

The emperor has been found without clothes, as the claims to enlightened national self-interest made by the Government after signing a nuclear agreement with President George Bush on July 18, 2005-have been found completely hollow. The Ambassador has confirmed that the so-called strategic partnership between the US and India is based on the principle of complete 'inequality' and not on the basis of equality as claimed by Manmohan Singh.

The Indian political brigade reacted very strongly against Mulford because the self-appointed patriots saw his statement as interference in the internal affairs of an independent sovereign republic of India. The patriots are not ready to face the reality of growing subservience of India in its relations with the US.

Ambassadors are expected to act as lobbyists for their country and, like all other lobbyists, Mulford is also expected to wear a big veil of secrecy and confidentiality by sweet-talking in public and stating bitter truths in private. On the contrary, he has been undiplomatic by not following the footsteps of other ambassadors who are appointed to sell their country's interests in the dark corridors of power.

The policy of separation between 'civilian nuclear power facilities' and 'military nuclear facilities' has been projected by the Government as the greatest achievement of their agreement with President Bush, but Mulford has stated the truth that India has to pay a heavy price for getting any foreign benefits form his country. Shouldn't he be recalled for speaking in such a distasteful and imperialist manner?

Further, Mulford did not stop interfering in India's domestic affairs even after getting a rebuff for his statement on Iran's nuclear issue. He again came out with a statement in favour of Foreign Direct Investment in retail business in India.

What is the explanation for the public statements of a wily US Ambassador on domestic and foreign policies? It is simplistic to state that Mulford is not fully equipped to act as a good Ambassador because he lacks the basic quality of speaking falsehood in public and truth in private. Politics cannot be explained on the basis of weakness of personality traits of ambassadors.

The real explanation for the commanding heights occupied by Mulford is that he represents a country, which treats India as a client state. An ambassador draws his real strength from his own country and it was observable during Nehru-Indira Gandhi phase of politics that Indian ambassadors walked with their heads erect while dealing with the heads of State and Governments of the mightiest countries of the world. Nehru and Indira Gandhi pursued foreign and domestic policies of self-reliance that was the foundational stone of relative autonomy of the Indian State both in our internal and external matters.

It is not for the first time that the Americans have tried to bully the Indian policy makers but Nehru-Indira Gandhi could not be cowed down or pushed around by the so-called super powers of the cold war phase of international relations. Indians made their own decisions and exercised their own policy options from

Kashmir to Bangladesh during the Nehru-Indira Gandhi phase of politics and bullies like Richard Nixon and Henry Kissinger were shown their proper place while dealing with India. Nehru suffered greatest discomfiture during Sino-Indian border dispute of 1962, and Indira's greatest challenge was in 1971 while dealing with Pakistan on East Bengal, but even during extremely adverse circumstances, Nehru-Indira Gandhi could stand up against US's attempts to pressure and dictate the Indians.

The Golden Age of Indian foreign policy has come to an end and the new economic liberalisers and globalisers have bid goodbye to the idea of national sovereignty and equality among nation-states. Indians have forgotten the language of equality at the international level and Atal Bihari Vajpayee and Manmohan Singh have willingly surrendered Indian sovereignty to the Americans.

Ambassador Mulford has shown that he is not dealing with a sovereign country. His statements and comments substantiate the argument that India has accepted to act as a junior partner of the US. The status of an Indian nuclear weapon state is spurious and phoney and Mulford has illuminated this.

– The Pioneer, February 5, 2006

INDIA AND THE UNITED STATES

The United States of America is in the driver's seat and every country and regions has to come to reality; international balance of power based on checks and balances among nation-states has been replaced by the emergence of a sole superpower is the harsh reality and nation-states have to negotiate with the US. India cannot be an exception to this rule. India has been always an important and active player in international affairs and its policy makers have always responded to every new development at the global level.

After the 1998 Pokharan tests the established nuclear powers led by the US imposed 'sanctions' against India. Since then, the Indian security and foreign policy establishments have been negotiating with the US since the sanctions were hurting national interest. It is only on July 18, 2005 than America and India decided to become not only 'strategic partners' but also' partners' in the development of programmes for nuclear energy for peaceful purposes. The Indian decision to separate military and civilian nuclear reactors and to place the civilian ones under IAEA safeguards has sharply divided political and technocratic classes.

it has been alleged that the July 18, 2005 nuclear deal is a sell out by India to the Americans. It deserves to be clearly started that India has always refused to sign the nuclear non-proliferation treaty. The deal is perceived by its critics as an attempt by the US to push the NPT through the backdoor.

The controversies between supporters and opponents of the nuclear deal between India and the US have not been resolved as yet and a sharp division has emerged between the Manmohan Singh Government and its Communist supporters who have expressed their complete opposition to the government's vote at the IAEA in Geneva on February 2, 2006 on nuclear issue concerning Iran. The left supporters of the UPA government in a coordination committee meeting on February 13, 2006 decided to serve notice to the government that if it repeats its action of voting on March 6, 2006 at the IAEA meeting at Geneva, the Communists will have to reconsider their 'outside support' to the government which has abandoned its policy of 'non-alignment'.

The UPA government has repeatedly emphasised that its foreign policy is guided by "enlightened national interest". But the Left has accused that the government is following a completely pro-American policy whether on domestic nuclear programme or on Iran's nuclear dispute at the international level for a political divide on government's vote at the IAEA on Iran has become quite sharp and parliamentary discussion in this session will witness the government defending its actions on the basis of "national interest" and the Communists, Socialist Party, Telugu Desam et al. attacking its as Pro-American and a deviation form the policy of non-alignment.

The critics are alleging that the Indian foreign policy makers have surrendered 'national autonomy' to secure American patronage and goodwill. But the fact remains that the Indian foreign policy makers, whether of the Vajpayee government from 1998 to 2004 or the Manmohan Singh Government, are also guided by the China factor in the 21st century. It is not a state secret that China was very disturbed when India declared itself a nuclear weapon state in 1998. Further, public statements and actions of the government of India and China conceal more than they reveal because of the history of mutual suspicion and distrust about one another.

India's fixations with Pakistan has always complicated India approach towards China because Pakistan has received many a weapon system form China. The Vajpayee government in a confidential letter to President Bill Clinton in 1998 had explained that 'India's decision to nuclearise is linked with China and Pakistan because both these neighbouring countries are nuclear weapon states'. Has this policy and strategic perception of India changed in 2005? Is India looking positively towards America because of the China and Pakistan factor?

The Americans have a 'dual policy' towards China. On the one hand, US and China are important economic partners; on the other hand, the US is quite concerned about the growing military might of China. Americans are following an active policy of alliances with Japan, South Korea and a few other countries in Asia for the 'Containment' of a militarily powerful China. American foreign policy towards China is quite unambiguous and based on 'friendship' and 'containment' of a competitor, even rival, in Asia.

India cannot ignore emergence of a powerful China. It can follow either the policy of 'friendship based on suspicion' or healthy 'bilateralism' and friendship. India has very limited foreign policy options because it is suffering from ambiguities on its dealings with China. If Indian foreign and security establishment has 'low level of trust' of emerging China, it will have to strengthen its 'strategic partnership' with the US on the basis of a quid pro quo between two 'unequal powers'.

The essential pillar of foreign policy in the new context of the 21st century is 'negotiations and bargaining' or 'surrender of national autonomy' before the sole super power in return for benefits. India cannot pursue its foreign policy of non-alignment or national autonomy if it carries a list of neighbouring enemy countries. India will become a 'Junior partner' of the US, if it is not able to reach a balanced relationship with China and Pakistan. Indians have to make a clear choice of friendship with neighbours and equality of relationship with America or forget labour national autonomy while dealing with the Americans.

In other words, India's relationship with the US is dictated by regional considerations and expanding nuclearisation of Asia has created a very tough situation for Indian foreign policy makers Will India be able to balance its interests with 'national honour'?

– *The Economic Times, February 23, 2006*

MORTGAGING INDIA'S SOVEREIGNTY

Prime Minister Manmohan Singh made a statement in the Rajya Sabha on March 14 that India would not surrender the autonomy of its decision-making process regarding "nuclear deal" with the US. He observed: "Any notion that the new deal we have with the US amounts to surrender is totally misplaced." Indeed, brave words from the Prime Minister, who is an architect of the erosion of India's sovereignty on the basis of disingenuous plea of the adaptation of Indian polices to the requirements of a "changing" world order. The pillar of this new world order, according to Manmohan Singh, is that the US is "a superpower" and a "prominent market economy".

The nuclear deal with the US has been necessitated because India is forced to look towards countries that could "export capital and new technology". The basis of the UPA Government's foreign policy is that India requires the American support not only for "nuclear energy for civilian purposes", but also "capital" and "technology" for economic development. India's "enlightened national interest" can be pursued by aligning with the sole superpower of the 21st century. The UPA think tank believes such an alignment is beneficial to the country, though there seems no alternative available for the country either.

President George Bush has introduced the Indo-US Civilian Nuclear Bill in the US Congress. He has to seek the sanction of the Congress for treating India as an "exception", since the latter is not a signatory of the Nuclear Non-Proliferation Treaty. Manmohan Singh's claim that India had not surrendered its "autonomy" was exposed when the US State Department expressed its "disapproval" of Russian fuel supplies for the Tarapur reactors.

The Bush Administration argued that the timing of the Russian announcement was inappropriate, as the US Congress was engaged with the details of the Indo-US nuclear deal. Russian Prime Minister Mikhail Fradkov, during his visit to India on March 16, announced that the Tarapur reactors would be supplied fuel. Manmohan Singh had justified the nuclear deal with the US on the basis that the nuclear energy was required for India's economic growth. But the Russian offer seems to have upset the Americans because, for them, the Russians have jumped the queue in India. While President Bush could negotiate on the issue of nuclear cooperation, it seems Mr. Fradkov is not "autonomous" to strike any nuclear energy deal with India. Manmohan Singh's phoney claim of India's "autonomy" has been exposed by America's mild "veto" to the Indo-Russian agreement on Tarapur. It seems India is expected not to negotiate with any friendly supplier of nuclear reactor and fuel, till the US Congress gives green signal to the Indo-US nuclear deal. It is just the beginning of the so-called autonomous relationship between the two unequal allies. The phoney claim of India's autonomy cannot be accepted on its face value without identifying the reasons behind America's decision to provide a "special and exceptional status" to India. What is the compulsion for President Bush to provide exceptional nuclear status to India, and not to Pakistan? After all, Pakistan has been a tried-and-tested ally of the US. Former President Bill Clinton had described Pakistan as an ally in the war against terrorism, which is a common goal of Washington and Islamabad. What has happened between the presidency of Mr. Clinton and Mr. Bush that made the US abandon Pakistan in favour of India?

President Pervez Musharraf and the people of Pakistan are feeling let down by the special nuclear status accorded to India. It will be enlightening to understand the security interests and goals of the US vis-a-vis India in the 21st century. It does not require a prophet to predict that the US must be expecting a pound of flesh for extending concessions to India. Also, the nuclear deal has put the American seal of approval on India's nuclear weapon state status. Why has the US abandoned its anti-nuclear proliferation regime for India?

The cat is out of bag and the US National Security Strategy Document of March 17 mentions: "India now is poised to shoulder global obligations in cooperation with the United States in a way befitting a major power." On page 49, President Bush describes India as a "major power that shares our commitment to freedom, democracy and rule of law". Mr. Bush further observes: "India is a great democracy, and our shared values are the foundations of our good relations." He has referred specifically to the nuclear agreement as "a roadmap to realise the meaningful cooperation that had eluded our two nations for decades".

The document clearly shows that the US has patronised India as a part of its global strategic goals of the 21st century. In the document, President Bush lauds India and expresses concern over the Middle Kingdom's (China) "continuing military expansion in a non-transparent way". He expects that China "must act as a responsible stakeholder that fulfils its obligations". Do we get any message from the American Security Strategy Document? The message is loud and clear that the Americans are in the business of forming alliances in Asia to contain the emerging China.

Pakistan has been left high and dry because the US is not sure about the future direction of the relationship between Islamabad and Beijing. The Bush Administration cannot trust Pakistan as far as China is concerned, but it has high expectations from the powerful anti-China social forces in India. Therefore, India can be a credible ally of the US against China along with Japan and South Korea.

It is easy for us to celebrate our nuclear weapon state status, but difficult to preserve national sovereignty, as India's growing economic dependence on "capital exporting countries" will turn it into a camp follower of imperialism. Meanwhile, China and Pakistan will adapt their strategic and security goals in the light of the Indo-US alliance. Therein lies our problems. Unlike the Cold War era, India has opted to align with the US. At the same time, it needs to be stated that the foreign policy of country is closely integrated with its economic path.

The Jawaharlal Nehru-Indira Gandhi phase of politics has come to an end. The Congress, fully backed by the BJP and India's military-industrial establishment, has buried the country's autonomous national political development. In the early 1990s, India witnessed a complete break with the past by taking the path of economic liberalisation, which led to its integration with global capitalism. The economic policy of global integration was further pursued by the BJP along with its Pokhran misadventure in 1998. Thereafter, India began its fullscale search for foreign capital and technology, along with the desire to pursue nuclear aspirations. Both these goals have brought India under the American shadow.

The upshot of the above description is that the convergence of India's economic and foreign policies has led to a situation where both the Congress and the BJP are not worried about its autonomy in international relations. Where is the social constituency for the defence of nation-to-nation autonomous relationship in international relations? The UPA Government has fully consented to mortgage India's sovereignty. – *The Pioneer, March 28, 2006*

INDIA-US STRATEGIC RELATIONS

The public discourse on the significance of the 'strategic partnership' between India and the United States has been trivialized by its supporters who have characterised it as the 'building partnerships for the development of India-US civil nuclear cooperation,' emphasizing the agreement as going a long way in helping India meet its energy requirements for economic development. One the other hand, the military-industrial-nuclear weapon lobbies represented by Atal Bihari Vajpayee have criticized the US-India nuclear deal", quoting the US Assistant Secretary for South Asia, Richard Boucher, that 'India would be urged to further define its minimum credible deterrent to facilitated amendment of the US Atomic Energy Act' according a 'special waiver' to India. The Hindu Rashtravadi, Vajpayee, representing the sentiments of India's nuclear bomb lobby, issued a stern warning that, 'The nation shall pay a heavy price in future by closing its options on the size of its credible minimum nuclear deterrent. Our nuclear armed neighbours shall face no such constraints...India should retain the right to conduct nuclear tests if any other country, such as China or Pakistan, were to do so.'

It needs to be clearly stated that the public discourse on the India-US nuclear deal should be liberated from the narrow and limited interpretations of the defenders of nuclear energy resources or the champions of the nuclear bomb. The real significance of the new economic, foreign and strategic policies pursued by India can be appreciated and analysed only by linking the so called 'India-US Partnership' with the 'New National Model of Development' followed by India from the beginning of the 1990s, wherein India willingly and voluntarily decided to 'integrate and link itself' with global imperial centres of capitalism led by the sole military super power of the 21st century.

Immanuel Wallerstein in his After Developmentalism and Globalisation, What? (2004) has indulged in wishful thinking that "...the triadic struggle between the United States, Western Europe and Japan/East Asia is the principal locus of capital accumulation in the capitalist world economy...', as if the so-called triad are roughly equal contestants in the attempt to reorganize the global production and financial systems. Wallerstein appears to have missed the reality of American-led NATO military bloc, which has made America a pre-eminent power for the whole of the European Union even as American military alliances with Japan, South Korea and other East Asian capitalist economies have brought these countries under the shadow of American hegemony. Is Japanese military involvement in Afghanistan and Iraq at the command of the Americans as accident? Similarly, American and Europe are working together in dealing with Iran's nuclear problem, substantiating the argument that the 'triad' of capitalism is not engaged in any meaningful inter-capitalist struggles or conflicts. No wonder the Indian ruling classes are agreed that the pre-eminent global status of America should be recognized for it will be beneficial and desirable for India to become an 'ally' of the sole global superpower.

The military-industrial complex which rules America has described India and China as two powerful emerging economies and is convinced that a militarily strong China is a 'competitor' to American hegemony, especially in Asia. Evidently, this situation is not acceptable to imperialist America. Both Strobe Talbott and Robert J. Einhorn stated that 'The US by acknowledging India as a major power and a strategic partner, has finally given India the recognition it has wanted for so long. The onus is now on India to live up to the trust that the Americans have placed in them and show the world that it is a responsible nuclear nation.' The only amendment which should be made to the Talbott-Einhorn formulation is that America's new and special emerging relationship with India is not merely confined to the nuclear deal but is a comprehensive and all-embracing 'alliance' between a real superpower and a country which wants to establish 'regional pre-eminence' with the support of America. Hence the question: what does America expect from India.

Condoleezza Rice, in her testimony before the Senate Foreign Relations Committee on 5 April 2006, stated the nuclear deal is a 'strategic achievement for both countries' and that India has agreed to the Missile Technology Control Regime and safeguards under International Atomic Energy Agency. She continued, 'We believe this initiative will unlock the progress of our expanding relationship in other areas and lead to expanding business opportunities for both countries.' The cat was out of the bag when Rice said that 'India was the only non-aligned country to vote for the referral to the UNSC on the Iran nuclear issue.' The three pillars of foreign policy issues as represented by George Bush are (a) export of democracy; (b) unilateralism, and (c) pre-emptive military action to safeguard American national interests. India has accepted to be a partner in the US project of the 'export of democracy' by contributing to Kofi Annan's Democracy Fund. Nor has India launched a campaign against America for misleading the entire world on Iraq, even when no weapons of mass destruction were found. India has remained a mute spectator to American military adventurism and unilateralism in the name of restoring or projecting democracy in Iraq and Central Asia. This clearly indicates that India as a 'junior alliance partner' of the US has not only abandoned the Nehru-Indira model of relative autonomy of the state in relation to other states, including the super powers, but has fully accepted American hegemony in global affairs.

Is there a social explanation for the complete break with its own past in the Indian national model of deployment? It does not require a genius to see that India is suffering from a deep crisis of capital accumulation because of the narrow social base of its market. The new economic policies of imposed fiscal structural adjustment along with a package of liberalization, privatization and deregulation of capital markets were not only a response to the balance of payment crisis. Even after a decade and half of the new economic policy regime, the Indians can only claim the 250 million new middle class as their social constituency for market and if this structurally 'limiting' factor has to be overcome to help accumulation, the only option is to integrate India with other centres of global imperial capitalism. The political and bureaucratic class along with the big industrial groups and the surplus generating rural and urban petite bourgeoisie seem to have arrived at an agreement to integrate India with global capitalism led by the United States. America is a 'giver' and India is a 'taker' and a quid pro quo among unequals is always in favour of the 'donor' or 'giver'. This is the reality of India's relationship with the US and it is a misnomer, even misrepresentation of facts, so characterize such a relationship as 'Building Partnerships' (*Seminar* 560, April 2006).

The emerging US-India alliance has to be seen in the broader political economy of global-imperial capitalism and the politics and economics of a developing capital is country like India. Hence the issue is not only 'nuclear energy for civilian purposes', but India's place in the world capitalist system led by American hegemonic power. India is also concerned with China's rising economic and military power and given the history to Sino-Indian mutual mistrust, it is plausible to argue that India would like to counterbalance China with the support of the United States. Moreover, since the United States has open targeted China, India as China's competitor can be a reliable ally even though it is negotiating with China at a bilateral level. India's ambition as a nuclear weapon state cannot be limited to just decorative and protective goals. India versus China is a plausible game plan of the Indian nuclearists and India cannot meaningfully compete with China without the protective umbrella of America. In effect, India's ambition to play the role of a South Asian policeman while containing Chinese power has brought it under the umbrella of the real super power. It is this emerging 'alliance' between a real super power and an ambitious regional power that lies at the heart of the matter. Other issues are peripheral.–*Seminar, May 2006*

8

India, Pakistan and Kashmir

ENGAGE PAKISTAN SERIOUSLY

India and Pakistan have to continuously involve themselves in meaningful dialogue to promote mutual national interests in a very dangerous "unipolar" 21st century. The logic of the emergence of "hyper power" imperialist America is that either regional or sub-regional disputes are resolved by the involved nation states or the sole "global policeman" will interfere and dictate solutions to countries involved in bilateral disputes. India and Pakistan are high on the agenda of American interventionists.

India and Pakistan do not need any new knowledge of Western intervention in their affairs. The latest evidence has come from US Secretary of State Colin Powell, who, in an interview with USA Today on October 20, stated: "As far as India and Pakistan are concerned, our diplomatic efforts have paid off and things have changed in very, very important ways over the last three-and-a-half years." Jaswant Singh's protestations against Mr. Powell's statement do not carry any conviction because it is evident that India and Pakistan will have to negotiate either on their own or on the basis of pressures exercised by the US.

Another compelling reason to engage themselves in bilateral negotiations, in spite of their history of wars and hostilities, is that the enlightened self-interests of both these countries demand that the mischief done by Partition is to some extent "undone". Partition has not resolved any issue between India and Pakistan and the British scheme of drawing of boundaries of these two countries has left a legacy of only disputes and conflicts. We in India know it well. Pakistan Prime Minister Shaukat Aziz observed on October 25, "The best of CBM for Pakistan is to engage India in two things – dialogue on Kashmir and progress on the gas pipeline. I really believe in it. When you create a mutual dependency, you open many doors."

India's approach towards Pakistan should follow the logic of October 20, when India and China stated that they would follow a "two-track approach" to resolve "their long-standing border dispute" leading to a "comprehensive boundary settlement". And India correctly made no reference to Parliament's resolution while discussing bilateral issues with China's State Councillor, Tang Jiaxum. India has adopted the correct approach towards China and this positive thinking was also reflected on October 21 at the third trilateral meeting between the foreign ministers of India, China and Russia at Almaty. The significance of this meeting was to evolve a common approach to "common regional and international concerns". The three countries stated, "We will work together to strengthen the fight against terrorism, which is the scourge of mankind." This spirit of mutual negotiations as expressed at Almaty should be extended to India and Pakistan for the resolution of mutual disputes including the historically inherited Kashmir issue.

Nuclearisation of India and Pakistan has changed the rules of the security games, and the status quo cannot be altered with wars by any of these two countries. The real impact of nuclearisation has been felt by war mongers who had prospered on the insecurities of new states since the 1950s down to the '90s because these self-appointed security and defence experts cannot sell their pet theories of danger from India or Pakistan. They had an upper hand and exploited the anxieties and the feelings of insecurity within these countries and armed race became the order of the day.

Militarisation and modernisation of security apparatus was legitimised on the basis of threat perceptions by leaking the so-called intelligence reports to the media. Defence and security experts, irrespective of their pretensions, have become unemployed and irrelevant because the failed stand-off between Indian and Pakistani armies in Kashmir has given a clear message that nuclearisation of the two neighbours has made "conventional war" redundant. The believers of military solution of disputes were very powerful as they played on the emotions of citizens. The Kargil War was the last adventure when conventional war option was closed. Today, bureaucratic and military elites in both the countries must work on confidence building measures and keep the logic of nuclear weapons state status uppermost in their minds.

The Cold War not only led to hostilities between the two states; even common citizens developed hostile attitudes on the basis of filtered and controlled information provided by the media in the name of patriotism and nationalism. The gullible were led to believe that the two neighbouring countries were always in a state of military preparedness to settle their disputes. The Vajpayee Government and its Defence Minister George Fernandes wrote in a confidential letter, which was made public by the Americans, that the nuclear tests in May 1998 were legitimate because India felt threatened by China and Pakistan.

Defence is a "holy cow", and if, as late as in 1998, the Government policy was to describe China and Pakistan as hostile countries, it is natural that both these countries would have similar opinion about India. The 21st century has opened a new chapter in bilateral relationship by emphasising people-to-people contact as a pillar of CBMs. India and Pakistan are gradually moving toward normalisation of their relationship, and in this context public rhetoric on both sides is bound to convey some new messages, and this is the meaning of President Musharraf's latest proposals for the demilitarisation of zones in Kashmir.

A step-by-step approach is always rewarding if fundamentalist positions on Kashmir by both the countries are not parroted everyday. If there was any significance of Manmohan Singh-Pervez Musharraf meeting in New York on the eve of UNGA session of September 2004, it was that new "atmospherics" have to be created for tackling bilateral issues including Kashmir.

Pakistan's sole spokesman is President Musharraf and it is his job to create consensus in his own country. National consensus is easy to achieve in a military regime, but Indian democracy has its own logic and a lot of effort has to be made at the political level to arrive at a minimum agreement on the consensual approach towards Pakistan. Politics has to be in command while resolving difficult Indo-Pak disputes. But at present it is tired and retired bureaucrats and out-of-date defence security experts who seems to be at the helm. All former prime ministers and leaders of national parties should be organised under a National Foreign Policy Council led by the tall political leadership of the Congress.

Bureaucrats, both civilian and military, have a lot of pretensions, but ultimately it is the much-maligned political class which understands the pulse of the people. If on the one hand India and Pakistan are settling down for long and difficult negotiations, on the other political leadership in India has mortgaged political responsibility to bureaucrats who cannot be considered fit for such an onerous responsibility.

– *The Pioneer, November 3, 2004*

TAKE MUSHARRAF SERIOUSLY

In a televised address on July 21, Pakistan President Pervez Musharraf firmly conveyed the message that Pakistan and the Islamic ummah is receiving global notoriety because of the activities of misguided Islamist militant groups. It is suggested that the public expression of views by General Musharraf against Islamist terrorism was in response to July 7 and July 21 bomb explosions in London. After all, most of the perpetrators of these attacks were found to be of Pakistani origin.

It can be argued that Mr. Musharraf wanted to explain the rationale behind the arrest of several suspected militants and the raids on madarsas. Besides, he might be seen as conveying a message to Pakistan's critics in the West that Islamist jihadis do not enjoy state protection. It can also be seen as a statement to educate the people of Pakistan who are likely to be misguided by the Opposition's protests against the arrest of suspected militants.

Regardless of the reasons that motivated the General to address the nation, his pronouncements deserve to be noted with seriousness. After all, every development in Pakistan has its repercussion in India. Further, India maintains that it is the Pakistan-trained terrorists who indulge in violence in Jammu & Kashmir. Pakistan is accused of exporting terrorism in the Valley as a part of its strategy of waging low-intensity war against India.

The Indian leadership has used every international forum to indict Pakistan as a promoter of terrorism. It keeps reminding the US that terrorism as a part of public life does not begin with September 11, 2001, and that the US policy-makers should not distinguish between terrorist violence in their country and terrorist violence in other countries, especially India.

If terrorism is a global phenomenon and Pakistan appears to be the hub of terrorists, every statement of Mr. Musharraf deserves to be analysed thoroughly, especially by Indians. Particularly, his July 21 observations deserve to be highlighted. First, Mr. Musharraf stated, "I urge you, my nation, to stand up and wage a jihad (holy war) against extremism and to stand up against those who spread hatred and chaos in the society."

Second, the General specifically identified two extremist organisations, Hizbul-ut-Tahrir (Liberation Party) and Al Muhajiroun (The Migrants), and stated, "They had the audacity of passing an edict against my life and yet they operate with full impunity. They also give sermons of hate and anger and violence." Third, he took note of the 'allegation' that "madarsas and seminaries were being used as training grounds for militants and extremists", and ordered for their registration. Raids were being conducted against some of these training centres of militancy.

Last, Mr. Musharraf went into the history of the origin of militancy in Pakistan and stated that the 'Kalashnikov culture' had crept into Pakistani society in the last 26 years. The Al Qaeda has spread to "cities and mountains" and mujahideen were "openly indulging in recruitment, training, collecting donations and publishing and circulating jihadi literature". He further stated, "But these people are against it. They say they want to pursue the path of jihad. They want to wage jihad in the world, everywhere."

Mr. Musharraf condemned the jihadis for bringing a bad name to Pakistan and the Islamic ummah. He rightly said that instead of "casting aspersions on Pakistan... a lot (has) to be done by Pakistan internally. And I may suggest there is a lot be done in England as well". Prime Minister Manmohan Singh correctly expressed his concern on terrorism during his official visit to the US and President Musharraf too stated in his July 21 statement that "militant Islamist groups are trying to stall peace process with India".

The million dollar question is: How does one respond to Mr. Musharraf's pronouncements and his anti-militant activities in Pakistan? An anti-Pakistan section of our policy-makers may discard them as a clever move of a wily dictator who is worried about saving his own constituency in the West after the London blasts. It is a valid argument that the Pakistani Army has actively created and supported militant Islamist groups to launch their anti-India low-intensity war.

General Zia-ul Haq, the father of obscurantist Islamist terrorist groups, deftly used US assistance to mujahideens to fight the Soviet Union in Afghanistan. General Zia and the Pakistani Army benefited from the US-Soviet conflict in Afghanistan and did not protest against the entry of millions of refugees from the war-ravaged Afghanistan. Pakistan, along with Afghanistan, became the centre of jihadi ideology, and being a frontline state for the American war, Pakistan got military equipment.

The Pakistani Army along with local mullahs and theologians encouraged the ideological indoctrination of young jihadis who carried on violence against their targets of hate. It has also been suggested that President Musharraf, like Zia-ul Haq, is also currying favour with militant Islamist parties and organisations to sustain himself in power and the state patronage is available to them under his regime. If it is accepted that General Musharraf is the patron-in-chief of Islamist terrorists, his statement of July 21 becomes irrelevant for India. Then it is solely addressed to provide comfort to the British nationals who have become the latest victims of terrorism in the West.

Does it mean that Mr. Musharraf is just playing a game of public denouncement of Islamist militancy and providing them with full state patronage? A section of rabid anti-Pakistan elite in India seems to have already dismissed his public condemnation and disowning of militant Islamist groups in his country.

Indian democracy has always thrived on heterogeneity of views on all important issues, including Pakistan. While rejecting the opinion of anti-Pakistan fundamentalists in the country, it can be unambiguously stated that the bull should be caught by the horns and India should trust Mr. Musharraf as a well meaning anti-fundamentalist leader. It should not be forgotten that terrorist groups have made several assassination attempts on his life. Further, Pakistan is operating in a changed global context in 2005. It is fighting against global terrorism, which has become a political and intellectual agenda in every country — from America to Russia, and from China to India.

Can Pakistan really ignore fundamentalism and still operate its pro-terrorism policies there? The upshot of above argument is that Pakistan is facing a great challenge from extremist elements. Even if it desires, it cannot go back to the old way of using religious fanaticism as an instrument of state policy vis-a-vis other states, including India. While democratic Pakistan is a better bet to contain the menace of religion-based public life, President Musharraf is the current dictator of Pakistan and India must do business with him.

A large number of sectarian, militant and religious fundamentalist groups in Pakistan are involved in fratricidal conflict against one another. The Pakistani society itself has fallen victim to such sectarian and religious violence. Pakistan is unable to control its several well-armed militant groups which have grown in strength because of the weaponry given to them during the Afghan war. Only a democratic Pakistan can restore social normalcy within the country because the struggle for democratic rights is also linked with the fight against jihadis, who are also the enemies of democracy in Pakistan.

Mr. Musharraf is caught in this Hobbesian state of war of "all against all" in Pakistan. If he is admitting that he happens to be leading a very troubled and violent Pakistan, Indians should continue to negotiate with the dictator and wait for democracy to bring normalcy there. Only a normal, democratic Pakistan is in the interest of a democratic India. – *The Pioneer, July 26, 2005*

SHEDDING KASHMIR FIXATION

The September 5 meeting of Kashmir's Hurriyat leaders with the Prime Minister should be looked in the broader context of the changing character of Indian foreign policy towards Pakistan and Kashmir under Manmohan Singh. A deeper understanding of the contentious issues involved in the Kashmir dispute can be reached if this conclave is viewed against India's foreign policy.

The visit of Indian foreign secretary to Pakistan on September 1-2, 2005 is an important indication of the Manmohan Singh government's serious intentions to strengthen the Confidence-Building Measures between India and Pakistan with a view to move forward with Composite Dialogue on contentious issues between these two neighbouring countries.

Indians have also recognised that the definition of neighbouring countries has been revised and extended to Afghanistan, Iran and Central Asia for meeting the increasing energy needs of the fast growing economy of India. Manmohan Singh himself visited Afghanistan at the end of August 2005, and Iranian and Indian Ministers have been quite active in finding solutions to the issue of Iran-Pakistan-India oil pipeline. It will be very simplistic to maintain that India is exploring new avenues of cooperation with Pakistan or Afghanistan or Iran or Central Asian Republics only for augmenting its sources of supply for energy. Foreign policy is always determined by multiple factors but geographical factor cannot be wished away because friendly or hostile neighbours can be either assets or liabilities for the security and prosperity of any country.

Indians have to learn a lesson from the Chinese foreign policy makers who have resolved important disputes with all its neighbours including Russia and Vietnam. China is also engaged in bridging its close relationships with East Asian countries because Japan versus China or South Korea versus North Korea situations adversely affect the foreign and defence policy of China. Taiwan dispute is frozen in history because the Mainland China is strong enough to deal with American supported Taiwan. China-Taiwan dispute is manageable because both of them are living with acceptable levels of status quo unlike the Indo-Pak tussle over Kashmir that the two neighbours cannot wish away and its resolution is essential to normalise relationship between India and Pakistan. This is mainly the reason for Manmohan Singh's foreign policy makers' active involvement with President Pervez Musharraf and the Kashmiri political groups like the Hurriyat which have for long been considered persona non-grata by the Government of India.

Chief Minister Mufti Mohammad Sayeed has welcomed PM-Hurriyat dialogue expressing hope that this will lead to wider dialogue in which other J&K groups take part. Mirwaiz Umar Farooq maintained that 'We hope the talks will take forward the process towards a Kashmir resolution. In our talks, we will try to build trust, know each other as it is for the first time we are meeting.' Incidentally, the Manmohan Singh government had allowed the Hurriyat leaders to visit Pakistan including Pakistan Occupied Kashmir with a view to open dialogue with groups in our Kashmir. The upshot of this description is that India and Pakistan have agreed to discuss and sort out the Kashmir dispute.

It cannot be resolved through war between two nuclearised countries because either the logic of nuclearisation 'immobilises and demobilises war machine' or it leads to total annihilation of both the contenders who opt for territorial victories through nuclear war. It does not mean that the continuing Kashmir dispute between these two neighbours does not have serious negative impact on their polity, economy and society. The continuing arms race between India and Pakistan does get justified because of Kashmir dispute. A new American Congressional study for 2001-2004 has pointed out that India has spent US$ 5.7 billion on arms purchase. Is it a small amount for a country involved in perpetual fiscal crisis and budgetary deficits? Every arms seller of western countries is competing in Indian market for the sale of arms. Arms race cannot be avoided if India and Pakistan are not at peace with one another. Peace has dividends and wars bring human miseries.

If arms race is inherent in the logic of Kashmir dispute between India and Pakistan, America has always interfered in the affairs of these two countries on the pretext of Kashmir dispute. Kashmir dispute has not only led to conflicts between India and Pakistan, it has also provided excuses to American interventivists in the affairs of these two countries. America's involvement in Pakistan and India has increased in the post-cold war phase of global unipolarism. If Pakistan has been a 'frontline' state for American adventurism in the Islamic World, Indians have also accorded a red carpet treatment to the Americans as clearly revealed by the Manmohan Singh government's new Strategic and Defence Agreements with the Americans. If during the cold war period, Indians reciprocated American hostility by maintaining a respectable distance from that country, the post-cold war phase has brought America close to both India and Pakistan. How can America, a friend of both these countries, keep away from guiding the foreign policies of its friendly regimes? Is it far fetched to maintain that the Narasimha Rao government opened its doors to Israel on American initiative as Pervez Musharraf has done in 2005? The newfound friendship between India-Pakistan and Israel cannot be explained without pointing a finger towards the real American masters.

Hence, the Indians have a clear choice to take initiatives on their own and convince Pakistan about resolution of the Kashmir Dispute in the enlightened national interests of both the neighbours or both the countries would be pushed around to find a solution on the suggestions of the American Big Brother. Ms. Indira Gandhi has been faulted for giving concessions to Zulfiqar Ali Bhutto at Simla Conference when India was in a stronger position to dictate terms on defeated and demoralised Pakistan. India and Pakistan can learn from their own history of the last more than five decades of stalemate and deadlocks on Kashmir dispute and any internationalisation of this regional dispute has not led to its resolution. Kashmir dispute has to be treated at bilateral level and any umpire or referee will be quite unhelpful as witnessed during the forty years of cold war politics of the Americans in South Asia.

– *Sahara Time, September 17, 2005*

VALLEY OF CONTRADICTIONS

If India is serious about resolving the Kashmir issues, it must involve all possible players, including Pakistan, in the dialogue process.

History was made in Jammu & Kashmir on April 24, 2006 when more than 61 per cent electorates voted in a free and fair election, despite the call of various terrorist outfits to boycott it. Can people's participation in electoral politics be interpreted as a referendum against terrorism?

The Chief Electoral Officer observed that the participation of voters in Jammu & Kashmir was an "all-time high". In fact, the voters' turnout in the constituency of Ghulam Nabi Azad was about 76 per cent. The message, therefore, was clear that multi-party electoral politics and come to stay in Kashmir and the voters prefer politics of ballot, if given an opportunity as opposed to the politics of bullet.

Congress president Sonia Gandhi, the real centre of power in the UPA regime, had shown great political foresight by forming the Congress-PDP coalition Government in Jammu & Kashmir and, later, by ensuring a smooth transfer of power from PDP leader Multi Mohammad Sayeed to Ghulam Nabi Azad.

Prime Minister Manmohan Singh, too, has launched a "two-track approach" in finding a solution to the Kashmir issue - "(a) negotiations with Kashmiri political groups of India; and (b) negotiations with Pakistan on Jammu & Kashmir".

Manmohan Singh and the Hurriyat leaders held a round of discussions in 2005, and the second round of talks is proposed to be held in Delhi on May 3. The New Delhi meeting between the Prime Minister and the Hurriyat leaders may convince their latter to participation in the second round table conference on Kashmir in Srinagar on May 25. This is important because the Hurriyat had boycotted the first round table conference.

It deserves to be understood that every political group, irrespective of its political viewpoint, should be involved in finding the solution to the Kashmir issue. Thus Manmohan Singh's strategy to persuade Hurriyat chairperson Mirwaiz Umer Farooq to participate in the ongoing process of discussions on Jammu & Kashmir deserves to be welcomed.

The Hurriyat leaders boycotted the first round table meting because they were "unhappy with the slow pace of the dialogue", besides the unwieldy number of participants who could not arrive at any "meaningful" decision. The Prime Minister has been holding "talks" with political groups of the State, but should be understood that such "talks' with Kashmiris not enough to arrive at any worthwhile solution without the involvement of Pakistan in the negotiation process.

India and Pakistan have taken several "measures of mutual confidence building" for creating proper atmospherics for hard decisions on Kashmir. The Government of India has enough political and constitutional resources to satisfy some important demands of the Kashmiris.

In fact the politics of accommodation is needed for satisfying the aspirations of multiple social groups within the country. The ongoing "ceasefire" with the NSCN (I-M), along with negotiations, is the best way to deal with domestic groups, which have grievances of being "neglected" by the Centre.

General Pervez Musharraf is not the only hard nut to crack. There are several extremist lobbies in India that are not ready to concede even an inch of autonomy to Jammu & Kashmir. These lobbies see the Ste as a Muslim problem and, hence, they do not see any merit and demands. These extremist groups in India and Pakistan have always held their respective governments, to ransom and every step for normalization of bilateral relations between the two countries has been blocked by raising the bogey of surrender and capitulation.

India has a clear option in the 21st century of either accepting the hegemony of the US or seeking solutions, on contentious issues with Pakistan and China. India cannot maintain its "autonomous state status" without getting rid of the historical baggage of Jammu & Kashmir. The US has been treating India and Pakistan as "equal allies". Hence it is futile for us to expect that the Americans will facilitate in finding any viable solution on the Kashmir dispute by sacrificing the interests of Pakistan. India and Pakistan will have to resolve the issue on their own.

Manmohan Singh's proposed visit to Pakistan in mid-2006 is quite significant. The ground work is being done by the Government of India, which has been holding discussions and only with the Kashmiri groups but also the Government of Pakistan on confidence building measures regarding nuclear weapons and Saichen. While Gen Musharraf has offered certain proposals to India on Jammu & Kashmir, Manmohan Singh seems to be leaving no stone unturned to find a way out.

If terrorism is a reality of the Valley, the functioning democracy too is a fact that cannot be wished away. The upshot of above description is that finding an acceptable solution to the Kashmir issue is in the enlightened self-interest of the parties concerned. India, too will achieve an "autonomous status" in the international sphere, if it is able to resolve this issue successfully.

–Pioneer, May 3, 2006

Index